KU-202-712

Psychology in Progress

General editor: Peter Herriot

Thinking in Perspective

Psychology in Progress

Already available
Aspects of Memory
edited by Michael M. Gruneberg and Peter Morris

Forthcoming
Issues in Childhood Social Development
edited by Harry McGurk

Philosophical Problems in Psychology
edited by Neil Bolton

The School Years: A Social Psychological Perspective
edited by John Coleman

Brain, Behaviour and Evolution
edited by David Oakley and Henry Plotkin

Thinking
in
Perspective

Critical essays in the
study of thought processes

edited by
ANDREW BURTON
and
JOHN RADFORD

METHUEN

First published in 1978 by
Methuen & Co Ltd
11 New Fetter Lane London EC4P 4EE

This collection © Andrew Burton and John Radford 1978
Individual chapters © the respective authors 1978

Typeset by C C C and printed and bound
at William Clowes and Sons Limited,
London and Beccles

ISBN 0 416 85830 9 *(hardback)*
ISBN 0 416 85840 6 *(paperback)*

Contents

Foreword

I had the interesting experience of reading through this rich collection of essays all in a gulp, at one continuous sitting as it were. Indeed, it is an astonishing experience, and for several good reasons.

In the first place, the sheer range of studies that qualify for inclusion under the general label 'thinking', is staggering not only in its diversity of content (chimpanzees attempting to get out-of-reach bananas at one end, to an undergraduate solving syllogisms at the other) but in the method and presuppositions that underlie the choice of materials and tasks (where the range is so dauntingly multidimensional as to defy description). Husserlian phenomenology fills the pages of one chapter close by another that examines computer simulations of semantic memory or 'cannibal-and-missionaries' problems. Indeed, if one imagines the study of thinking as a street of many mansions, one would wonder whether the street is a neighbourhood, for it is doubtful (perusing the bibliographies attached to each chapter) whether the occupants of the houses have ever met – save perhaps in a negative way. Often they take some particular neighbour as a presiding villain from whom they would wish to save the street. Gestalt psychologists wished to save us from the simple additive theorem of associationism; Piaget battles against the trap of associationism and the methodology of Carnapian positivism: behaviourists

deplore the private experience of the introspectionists and phenomenologists, and so on.

How then did all of them land on this street? How could the rubric
'thinking' be applied to them all? The answer, I think, is not hard to
find. Each of the protagonists genuinely directs himself to the universal
question of how, in the face of insufficient 'surface' information or
'means' a human being (or, better, an organism) manages somehow to
reach an answer or an end. How does one complete a syllogism given
only the premisses, how does one apply a rule to a novel instance, how
does one assemble the junk on the experimenter's table to manage to
build a coat rack? Somehow, one manages to 'go beyond the
information given', and the problem for the psychologist is to
formulate a general theory of such behaviour and then, with its aid,
to tease out the constituent processes that lead to problem solution or a
valid answer or even a constant error. The reader will find in the
chapters that follow a rich diversity of theories, stemming from
different philosophical traditions, each of them requiring for investigation a somewhat different type of task and a different method for
analysing what it is that their subjects do to make the leap to solution.
Some will argue that the leap is in no sense unique to thinking: that
even the simplest perceptual tasks require an inferential step, or that
'productive' thinking deserves its inverted commas as nothing more
than the *re*production of priorly acquired responses distributed across
a 'simple' generalization gradient.

But there is something interestingly common about each of the
chapters, a kind of *leit motif* that runs through the book, sometimes
dirge-like, sometimes *allegro vivace*. Almost without exception, there is
a refrain about artificiality: that the experiments or observations of
this school or that are 'artificial', unrepresentative of the way in
which thinking occurs in real life. (Indeed, some of my own past work
is severely and justifiably taken to task for just such unrepresentativeness
in several of the chapters!) When the theme is rendered *allegro* it is to
celebrate the conviction that things are 'getting better' – more
'natural' tasks are being used or more cross-cultural or cross-situational
comparisons in thinking are being made. Gloomier expressions of the
theme are prompted by the difficulty of delineating what in fact
constitutes 'natural' or ecologically representative thinking. Is there a
'natural logic' that one taps in one's subjects, as Mary Henle claimed
in a celebrated paper? Can one think of the natural logic in much the
same way as one thinks of an innately determined syntax in all

language which manifests itself through locally determined realization rules for particular languages? If there are no universals about the process of thinking, then the results of each experiment or observation are wholly dependent on the task and the situation on which it is based and it would be as truly the case that nature imitates science as Oscar Wilde once argued that life imitates art. I take it as a sign of vigour that problems of this order are being faced and elucidated, and the reader will find rich discussions of this and related questions spread throughout the chapters of this book.

The general reader and the specialist alike will owe a debt of gratitude to the authors and editors of this volume for their brave efforts to put the study of thinking into perspective.

Wolfson College,
Oxford.
February, 1978   JEROME BRUNER

Notes on the contributors

Neil Bolton is Professor of Education at the University of Sheffield and was formerly Senior Lecturer in Psychology at the University of Durham. His publications include papers on intellectual functioning in the elderly, concept formation and divergent thinking. Books include *The Psychology of Thinking* (Methuen, 1972), *Intellectual Functioning in the Aged*, with R. D. Savage et al. (Methuen, 1974) and *Concept Formation* (Pergamon, 1977). His current research interests are the development of mathematical concepts in childhood and phenomenological psychology. He is editing a book on philosophical problems in psychology, to be published by Methuen in the 'Psychology in Progress' series.

Andrew Burton is Senior Lecturer in Psychology at the North East London Polytechnic and co-author of *Thinking: Its Nature and Development* (Wiley, 1974). His research interests are in the experimental analysis of altered psychological function in brain damage and sleep disorders.

Esme Burton is Senior Lecturer in Psychology at the North East London Polytechnic. Her current research is concerned with perception, particularly pattern recognition.

George Butterworth lectures in developmental psychology at the University of Southampton. He was a British Council Visiting Fellow at the Centre d'Epistemologie Genetique, University of Geneva (1974) and Visiting Assistant Professor at the Institute of Child Development, University of Minnesota (1976–7). His research interests are in cognitive development in infancy and early childhood.

J. B. Deręgowski lectures in psychology at the University of Aberdeen, but spends much of his time in Africa conducting research into cross-cultural aspects of perception. His publications include 'Pictorial perception and culture' *Scientific American*, 1972; 'Illusion and culture' in R. L. Gregory and E. H. Gombrich (eds) *Illusion in Nature and Art* (Duckworth, 1973) and 'Perception' in H. C. Triandis (ed.) *Handbook of Cross-cultural Psychology* (Allyn and Bacon, 1977).

J. St B. T. Evans is Senior Lecturer in Psychology at Plymouth Polytechnic. He has published a number of experimental and theoretical articles, primarily on the psychology of deductive reasoning. His current research interests in this field include psycholinguistic approaches, the use of mathematical models and, in collaboration with P. C. Wason, further investigation of the 'dual process' theory of thinking.

W. E. C. Gillham is tutor to the MA course in child and educational psychology at the University of Nottingham. His main publications are: *Teaching a Child to Read* (University of London Press, 1974); *Psychology Today* (ed., Teach Yourself Books, 1975); *The Visual World of the Child* (trans., Allen and Unwin, 1976); *Reconstructing Educational Psychology* (ed., Croom-Helm, 1978); and *The First Hundred Words: A Basic Language Programme for Mentally Handicapped Children* (Allen and Unwin, 1978). His research is concerned with developing forms of assessment referenced to remediation and with the development of language in mentally handicapped children at the one-word stage (this latter project is funded by the Nuffield Foundation).

John Radford is Dean of the Faculty of Human Sciences at North East London Polytechnic, where he has built up one of the largest departments of psychology in the UK. He has published (jointly with Andrew Burton) *Thinking: Its Nature and Development* (Wiley, 1974) and two volumes in Methuen's 'Essential Psychology' series (jointly with Richard Kirby): *The Person in Psychology* (1975) and *Individual Differences* (1976). John Radford has been largely responsible for the introduction of psychology as a GCE 'A' level subject. He is currently chairman of the Association for the Teaching of Psychology and of the standing advisory committee of the British Psychological Society on 'Education in Psychology'.

Elizabeth Valentine lectures in psychology at Bedford College, University of London. She has published papers on topics ranging from activity in rodents to reasoning in adults, and has held teaching posts at North East London Polytechnic and the City of London Polytechnic. Her main interests are in theoretical and cognitive psychology.

N. E. Wetherick is Senior Lecturer in Psychology at the University of Aberdeen. His main research interests are in the development and decline of inductive thinking capacity, the philosophical foundations of psychology, and the semantic aspects of short-term memory.

John Wilding lectures in psychology at Bedford College, University of London, where he teaches cognitive psychology. His main research interests are in the area of attention, memory and stimulus identification, on which topics he has published in several journals. He is currently joint editor of the Bulletin of the British Psychological Society.

Acknowledgements

An important feature of the prenatal history of this book was a series of seminars devoted to each of the chapter topics held at Bedford College during 1976 and 1977. These were not only thoroughly enjoyable in themselves but also of immense value in clarifying the underlying issues and themes. We should like to thank all involved especially those who came in spite of obvious geographical difficulties. We should particularly like to thank Liz Valentine who arranged and patiently rearranged her own commitments in order to accommodate the constantly shifting timetable for these and who also provided valuable criticisms on some of the manuscripts. We have also had useful discussions and correspondence with Harry Fisher of North East London Polytechnic, Peter Herriot of City University, London, and Professor Jerome Bruner who wrote the Foreword.

A. BURTON

London, September 1977   J. RADFORD

Editors' introduction

Experimental studies of thinking tend to cluster around particular problem areas such as concept formation, creative thinking, imagery, and so on. However, it is important to remember that these investigations are carried out from a number of separate theoretical viewpoints. This has a number of important implications. To begin with, every theory has its range of convenience in terms of the problems it seeks to tackle. Also, from the sort of approach taken stem differences at the methodological level. Since it is easy for this close relationship between theory, method and data to be overlooked, when the material is organized within conventional problem areas, the main task of this book is to consider the psychology of thinking specifically in relation to approaches and methods. We believe that each of the approaches we have identified makes a distinctive and worthwhile contribution to the study of thought processes. Each chapter both stands on its own and complements the others.

It will be helpful to distinguish between *methods, theoretical positions* and *approaches* since the focus of each chapter is usually on one of these in particular. Chapter 1 on introspection, for example, covers a range of related *methods* for studying mental events and raises a number of fundamental methodological issues. In other chapters (e.g. those on Gestalt psychology, behaviourism, Piaget, computer simulation and psychoanalysis) the starting point is a clearly identifiable psychological *theory* – in the chapter on phenomenology the origin is philosophical rather than psychological. Yet other chapters (e.g. those on psychometrics, cross-cultural studies and logic) embody somewhat broader overall *approaches*, within which a variety of methods and theories may be identified. However, while there are these broad differences in emphasis, each chapter is concerned to some extent with all three aspects and therefore with issues at a number of different levels. Introspection for example is clearly a method, or a set of methods; it reflects a number of very complex interwoven assumptions about the nature of mental events and, particularly as it was used in early psychological studies, about what the ultimate task of psychology should be; and introspective data have been, and still are, used to corroborate particular theories of cognitive function. The discussion of Piaget's theory also illustrates the three aspects. There is the theory itself; its broad philosophical framework; and finally, the particular methods of inquiry which have grown up with the theory. To this extent therefore, all the chapters are concerned with a number of common issues as well as having a special focus of interest.

What sort of view of thinking emerges from this book? We might begin by looking at the aims of each chapter. It was generally agreed that, while there would be no rigid format, it would be useful for each chapter, as far as possible, to include some discussion of a number of specific points. These are:

1 In what context and for what reason did the perspective arise?
2 What, if any, were the explicit aims of the originators? What did they hope to achieve?
3 What major theoretical and/or methodological concepts characterize the perspective?
4 Is there anything in the methods of investigation that is peculiar to the perspective, or that is of particular importance?
5 What research or other work is now directly influenced by the perspective? Does the perspective have any wider implications?
6 What is the present status of the perspective? What has it achieved – specifically in our understanding of thinking? Does it promise anything for the future?

Because the amount of attention required by each of these issues tends to vary with the perspective under discussion, and because we did not adopt a standard framework, these points are not necessarily raised explicitly in each chapter. However, these various themes do provide the reader with a common basis for making comparisons amongst the different perspectives.

Next, what can be said about the wider question of the current status of the psychology of thinking as portrayed in this book? To consider this it will be useful to discuss very briefly the present state of cognitive psychology more generally. Although it is widely accepted that the 'cognitive approach' has acted as an enormously effective driving force over the past ten or fifteen years, there is also a growing feeling that, somehow, not much overall progress has been made. Neisser (1976) argues that while conceptual boundaries have been swept aside, and while psychologists are now in a position to make use of a range of powerful experimental paradigms and to perform experiments of great technological ingenuity, we still lack a theory which may be applied to 'what people do in real, culturally significant situations'. Neisser believes that at least two factors are responsible. These are in fact logically separate but, in practice, have tended to become two interwoven themes. The first is that we have devoted too much attention to hypothetical mechanisms by which the individual processes information from the environment in order to 'construct' a model of reality. In doing so, Neisser argues, we have underestimated the need for cognition to be reality based – that is, the need for people to discover what is actually 'out there' (as e.g. Gibson's theory, 1969, proposes) in contrast to responding to some internal representation of the world (as proposed by e.g. Gregory, 1970; for a thorough discussion see Gregory, 1974). The second point is that experimental studies of cognitive processes are not sufficiently concerned about the *ecological validity* of the phenomena under investigation. There is a danger that experimental effects may apply only to the psychological laboratory. This latter criticism has also been voiced by others; Baddeley (1976), for example, feels 'a little uneasy' about current research into human memory and emphasizes the need for experimental results to be checked against reality. A similar concern has also been expressed about the validity of certain models and techniques used in psycholinguistics research (e.g. Miller and Johnson-Laird, 1976; Tannenhaus et al., 1976).

Such sentiments are to some extent echoed in this book. For example, Evans concludes that 'any honest appraisal of research into human reasoning must acknowledge one very penetrating criticism, namely that experiments to date have been very artificial'. Wetherick criticizes some of the basic assumptions of work on concept formation and concludes that the accepted view of 'scanning' and 'focussing' strategies (Bruner, Goodnow and Austin, 1956) may be incorrect. He suggests that there has been a breakdown in the correspondence between the experimenter's model and what is found in the real world. Other examples of the loss of contact with reality might well include psychometrics, discussed by Gillham, although here the causes are slightly different in that they arise mainly from problems of statistical inference and related difficulties; and computer simulation, discussed by Wilding, whose overall assessment is actually favourable, but who comments nevertheless that 'the main weakness of simulation studies is the restriction of the possibilities to a limited set of situations'.

However, the complaint that laboratory investigations are unrepresentative (or 'irrelevant' to use the contemporary slogan of contempt) is scarcely novel. Also it is difficult to see how we can make any progress in the long run without systematically validated theories. The more telling of Neisser's points therefore is the first argument, namely that in order to succeed, psychological theories will have to give a more thoroughgoing account of the part played by the environment in cognition – in Neisser's own words: '. . . the details of the real world in which perceivers and thinkers live, and the fine structure of information which that world makes available to them'. As far as thinking is concerned, it could be argued that in Piaget's theory (see Chapter 4) psychology already has a theory which largely meets Neisser's criteria. It is a theory which through its concepts of *assimilation* and *accommodation* explicitly relates the activity of the individual to the demands of his environment and, in doing so, as Bolton (1972) suggests, steers a course between the two horns of a dilemma – that of acknowledging that the organism does not bend passively to the demands of the environment while at the same time recognizing that it does not have complete freedom to construe environmental events in whatever way it chooses. However, at the risk of misrepresenting the theory by oversimplifying it, and at the risk too of putting forward a counsel of perfection, it could be said that Piaget's theory does not describe other than in general terms what it is in the *environment* which actually produces changes in the organism during its development. It is the structure of the organism rather than the details of the environment which receives most attention. Roughly speaking, Piaget tells us how the beast digests but little of the sort of diet it needs.

Neisser (1976) suggests that cognition is best viewed as a skill. In some ways Piaget's model of thinking comes quite close to this conception. The analogy with skills captures several aspects of perception which, as we have seen, Neisser considers to be important, in particular the continuous interaction of the subject with the environment. Therefore, applying this approach to thinking, a more systematic analysis of thinking as a skill might be achieved through a re-examination of the approach of, for example, F. C. Bartlett (1958) who espoused exactly this position. Interestingly, the need for a reappraisal of Bartlett's approach to human performance has recently been stated by Broadbent (1977) in a critical analysis of the concept of 'levels' of information processing. According to Broadbent, Bartlett held views about levels of performance which were much less limited than contemporary uses of the term in psychology. In particular, Bartlett proposed that different processing levels are organized in a hierarchical fashion, higher levels actively controlling the operation of lower ones. Broadbent also presents fresh experimental evidence to support Bartlett's analysis. Some of the experimental studies discussed in Chapters 1 and 5 might be said to support the concept of separate levels and therefore to reinforce Broadbent's argument.

Whether or not psychology succeeds in developing an adequate theory of thinking, research will of course continue to be guided by each of the perspectives this book presents. Our belief is that the attempt made here to evaluate the different approaches and to examine their merits and weaknesses should bring us closer to a perspective through which we may give consideration both to the activities of the thinker and the complexities of his environment.

ANDREW BURTON
JOHN RADFORD

References

Baddeley, A. D. (1976) *The Psychology of Memory*. New York: Harper and Row.
Bartlett, F. C. (1958) *Thinking: An Experimental and Social Study*. London: Allen and Unwin.
Bolton, N. (1972) *The Psychology of Thinking*. London: Methuen.
Broadbent, D. E. (1977) *Quarterly Journal of Experimental Psychology 29*: 181–201.
Bruner, J. S., Goodnow, J. L. and Austin, G. A. (1956) *A Study of Thinking*. New York: Wiley.

Gibson, E. J. (1969) *Principles of Perceptual Learning and Development.* New York: Appleton-Century-Crofts.

Gregory, R. L. (1970) *The Intelligent Eye.* New York: McGraw-Hill.

Gregory, R. L. (1974) *Concepts and Mechanisms of Perception.* London: Duckworth.

Miller, G. A. and Johnson-Laird, P. N. (1976) *Language and Perception.* London: Cambridge University Press.

Neisser, U. (1976) *Cognition and Reality.* San Francisco: W. H. Freeman.

Tannenhaus, M. K., Carroll, J. M. and Bever, T. G. (1976) *Psychological Review 83* (4): 310–17.

1 Perchings and flights: Introspection

Elizabeth Valentine

Introduction

'The word introspection need hardly be defined – it means, of course, the looking into our minds and reporting what we there discover.' So wrote William James (1890). Not everyone has accepted this formulation. A more cautious claim might be that it was an activity which put one in a position to make statements which purport to describe one's own mental processes. In the history of psychology it has been used in a variety of ways and has suffered changing fortunes. Radford and Burton (1974) distinguish three groups of activities: (i) self-observation, in which the individual aims to observe his experiences (we might call this introspection proper); (ii) self-reports, in which the individual relates experiences, perhaps of an unusual kind, without trying to be particularly objective; and (iii) thinking aloud, in which the subject attempts to provide a running commentary on some mental activity as it proceeds. McKellar (1962) draws attention to a number of respects in which introspective studies may vary: the degree of training of the experimenter and the subject, the general circumstances and particular stimulus conditions in which the report is obtained, the degree of systematization of the procedure and the intended recipient of the report. In summary, introspective reports can be obtained in a whole range of conditions, from free association as practised by psychoanalysts at one end to classical introspection as practised by the structuralists at the other, which vary according to the nature and degree of the constraints imposed.

History

Structuralists

The history of introspection in psychology has been well documented by Boring (1953). The first experimental psychologists, the structuralists of the late nineteenth and early twentieth centuries, accepted the empiricist view that all knowledge is derived from sensory impressions and ideas (a doctrine Humphrey, 1951, labels 'presentationalism'). Thus, they considered that the subject matter of psychology was immediate experience and its primary aim 'to analyse the structure of the mind; to ravel out the elemental processes from the tangle of consciousness' (Titchener, 1898). For this purpose the prime method was to be introspection. Wundt recommended 'Selbstbeobachtung' (self-observation), for which highly trained subjects and strictly controlled conditions were required, so that the determining conditions of mental experiences could be clearly specified and results from different observers cross-checked. Titchener's tirade against the 'stimulus-error' gives one indication of what the training involved. Committing this crime involved relying on previous knowledge and reporting meaningful properties of the stimulus object rather than restricting oneself to a description of 'pure' experience, e.g. describing a stimulus as a table rather than as a trapezoidal, brown patch. Few would now consider such a programme possible but one can see what the structuralists were aiming at. Their approach rests on a number of assumptions, most of which have subsequently been seriously called into question: the possibility of dissecting experience into sensory elements, the availability of these to introspection and the usefulness of such an exercise.

Würzburg psychologists

Wundt considered that higher mental processes such as thinking were so socially conditioned that they could not be investigated by experimental methods. Thus the first experimental attack on thought processes was left to Külpe and his followers, working at Würzburg in the first decade of this century, who attempted to extend systematic introspection to the areas of association and judgement. These experiments have been well reviewed by Titchener (1909) and in Humphrey's (1951) authoritative treatment. Essentially they consisted in presenting the subject with a task such as comparative judgement, free or partially constrained association, or evaluation of statements, and then instructing him 'to report immediately after uttering the response word all that he experienced from the moment of hearing the stimulus word until his response. Whenever necessary, the experimenter tried to complete the subject's statement by questioning him. However, he did this only rarely in order not to influence the subject' (Messer, 1906)[1]. The following is an example from Bühler (1907) of an introspective report to the question 'Can our thought apprehend the nature of thought?': 'The question struck me comically at first; I thought it must be a trick question. Then Hegel's objection to Kant suddenly occurred to me, and then I said, decidedly: Yes. The thought of Hegel's objection was fairly full; I knew at the moment precisely what the whole thing was about; there were no words in it, though, and there were no ideas either. Only the word 'Hegel' came up afterwards, in auditory-motor form.' Watt (1905) developed a fractionation method in which the subject was asked to concentrate on one of four stages of the task, in the hope of narrowing down the nature of the thought process. Altogether these methods constituted a much freer use of introspection and success depended much on the skill of experimenter and subject. There was not the stress on training subjects, who were often few and highly selected, and procedures were frequently unstandardized.

Nevertheless, their work led to two main conclusions, which had important implications. Firstly, the shattering discovery of imageless thought. Subjects were frequently unable to give a coherent reply to their experimenters' enquiries; they were unable to report that their consciousnesses contained sensations or images. This discovery threatened to endanger not only the theory of presentationalism but also the method of introspection. What use was it if it failed to produce any goods? Secondly, they concluded that thinking was not just a matter of reproductive, associative tendencies but that the response obtained depended also on dynamic, motivational factors, which they called 'determining tendencies'. The 'Aufgabe' (task or instructions) produced an 'Einstellung' (set): presented with 2 and 4, whether the response produced is 6 or 8 will depend on whether the subject was set to add or multiply. These sets were likewise not available to introspection.

There was a further problem. Titchener (1909) refused to accept the Würzburg results, criticized their methods and argued that thinking always contained sensory components of some kind even if these were only kinaesthetic. Opponents claimed that introspection was unreliable because it led to disagreements which could not easily be resolved. With hindsight it seems likely that the disagreements were in large part due to differences in procedure. Introspection fell into disuse for three reasons: the artificiality of the theoretical framework in which it had been carried out, difficulties in resolving disagreements and lack of fruitfulness.

Behaviourists
There was, however, one worse fate to befall it: the legacy of logical positivism. Positivists aimed for a unified science in which all knowledge was based on public, objective observation. Watson (1913), like most psychologists, obsessed with methodological respectability, ruled out introspection as a possible method in psychology on the grounds of subjectivity: 'Psychology as the behaviourist views it is a purely objective, experimental branch of natural science. Its theoretical goal is the prediction and control of behaviour. Introspection forms no essential part of its methods, nor is the scientific value of its data dependent upon the readiness with which they lend themselves to interpretation in terms of consciousness.' Thus behaviour replaced experience as the subject matter of psychology, 'objective' observation replaced introspection as a method and behaviourist explanations replaced mentalistic ones. Experimenters were still allowed to listen to what their subjects said provided that they did not take their utterances at face value but treated them in the same way as other responses, i.e. as verbal reports.

Act psychology, phenomenology and Gestalt psychology
Introspection of a more naturalistic kind was being carried out by other groups of people before the turn of the century. Brentano (1874), the leader of the act school of psychology, held the view that psychical phenomena are essentially acts which necessarily 'intend' objects, e.g. if one is seeing, one must be seeing something. He believed our inward perception of such objects was infallible, as distinct from our knowledge of the external world, which depended on fallible perception. Brentano might be considered a representative of the continental tradition of phenomenology, founded by Husserl

(1901). For these phenomenologists, the primary data for our knowledge of the external world and for all sciences were phenomena, appearances in immediate experience, which are to be viewed in a naïve, meaningful way devoid of presuppositions as far as possible. This approach was extended from perception to thinking by the Gestalt psychologists (see Chapter 2), who began a tradition of work on problem solving, in which restructuring was seen as the crucial factor.

Psychopathology
The other main area in which introspection has been used is psychopathology. Psychoanalysts take an essentially behaviourist line about what their patients say: utterances have to be interpreted; in fact they are more likely to be taken at face value if subsequently denied by the patient. Non-psychoanalytic therapists have been more inclined to take what their patients say at face value, e.g. Kelly (1955), who claims that the patient is the best authority on himself, and Rogers (1965), who regards unconditional acceptance and empathy on the part of the therapist as necessary conditions for successful therapy.

Thus introspection has been with us in one guise or another all along. However, there has been something of a paradigm shift in its favour during the last couple of decades. Psychology has witnessed a renewed interest in conscious experience as part of the subject matter of psychology, together with a re-examination of introspection as a method (see e.g. Burt, 1962; Holt, 1964; Joynson, 1972; Radford, 1974; and Zener, 1958).

Theoretical problems

The nature of introspection
Considerable energy has been devoted to the question of how introspective reports should be characterized. Good discussions are to be found in Ayer (1959), Natsoulas (1967, 1970) and Ryle (1949). There are two extreme positions: the mentalist view, according to which the subject observes events in an inner cinema, to which he has direct, privileged access, which determine and are referred to in his report; and the behaviourist view, according to which the experimenter observes the verbal reports given by the subject, which are expressions of, and provide inferential evidence for, their determining psychological

processes. Over the last fifty years favour has shifted from the former to the latter view, and 'introspections' have tended to become 'verbal reports' or 'protocols' accordingly. Both views can be misleading: the mentalist one if it implies that introspective reports are infallible or that one can introspect at the same time as engaging in mental activity and without interference between these activities; the behaviourist one if it implies that people never have knowledge of their mental states and if it fails to distinguish between introspective reports and ejaculations. It is clear that there is a tangle of issues here.

Exponents of the view that introspection is impossible have largely rested their case on the argument that one cannot do two things at once, at least with the same apparatus. It was probably first stated clearly by Comte (1842): 'As for observing in the same way intellectual phenomena at the time of their actual presence, that is a manifest impossibility. The thinker cannot divide himself in two, of whom one reasons whilst the other observes him reason. The organ observed and the organ observing being, in this case, identical, how could observation take place? This pretended psychological method is then radically null and void.' But as John Mill (1882) replied: 'It might have occurred to M. Comte that a fact may be studied through the medium of memory, not at the very moment of our perceiving it, but the moment after: and this is really the mode in which our best knowledge of our intellectual states is generally acquired.' Messer (1906) empirically confirms this point: 'None of the subjects' reports contradict the fact that introspection is retrospective observation. No subject stated that the two events occurred in parallel, i.e. the response as such . . . on the one hand, and the simultaneous observation of this response on the other hand.'

Privacy

It has frequently been alleged that introspection differs from other forms of acquiring knowledge by virtue of being private and that this subjectivity rules it out of the scientific court. As Ayer (1959) points out, privacy may mean a number of things. Firstly, it could mean that the subject is the only person who has access of any kind to this information. This is just possible but rather unlikely. It may be more likely to be true for pains than for motives. It is generally the case that there are other behavioural and/or physiological observations that can be made that are relevant to the truth of an introspective report. Indeed, since Wittgenstein (1953), it has commonly been held that descriptions of private events are derivative from public descriptions. Moreover, an introspective observation is usually publicly communicable.

A second interpretation of privacy might be that the subject is the only person who has access of this particular kind to the information in question. This seems to be a contingent truth of our present situation but it seems logically possible that at some future date someone might be able to have knowledge of another's mental state in the same way as he does.

A third question is whether the subject is the final authority on his introspected state, and in particular whether his report is infallible. People *are* in a privileged position about their own mental states but their authority is neither exclusive nor final. Harré and Secord (1972) recommend an 'open souls doctrine' which accepts people's 'commentaries upon their actions as authentic, though revisable, reports of phenomena, subject to empirical criticism. . . . In cases of dispute, if we wish to maintain the outside observer's point of view over against that of the person himself and his avowals, then a special case has to be made out.' Freud forced the view that people can be mistaken about their mental life 'but because one sometimes makes mistakes . . . it does not follow that one always makes them or even that one makes them frequently' (Kelvin, 1956).

Finally, there is the question of whether introspection is disqualified as a scientific method on the grounds of subjectivity. We have seen that its privacy is only a matter of degree. As Schrödinger (1958) pointed out of physics: 'All this information goes back ultimately to the sense perceptions of some living person or persons, however many ingenious devices may have been used to facilitate the labour . . . The most careful record, when not inspected, tells us nothing.' Observations are always private and particular; scientific statements are always public, general and inferred (see Perkins's, 1953, distinction between statements of fact and statements of law). The difference between perception and introspection is simply that in the former case we find it easier to reach inter-subjective agreement. The apparent unreliability of introspective reports in the early studies was largely due to differences in method and various kinds of artifact, such as experimenter effect and demand characteristics. A more recent experiment which demonstrates the greater susceptibility of introspection to these sources of bias is one by Sheehan and Neisser (1969), in which subjects were asked to report on their experience of imagery in a pattern reconstruction task. It was found that the variables which affected imagery vividness ratings were (i) the experimenter and (ii) whether ratings were given before or after an introspective enquiry which focussed attention on imagery.

No correlation was found between reported vividness of imagery and performance on the pattern reconstruction task. Other experiments, however, have obtained correlations between introspective reports and behavioural measures, e.g. Cooper & Shepard (1973) found that latencies for judgements as to whether a rotated test figure was the same as or different from a standard figure were consistent with subjects' reports that they performed the task by mentally rotating an image of the stimulus. Inferences from introspective reports can be improved in exactly the same way as inferences from other data: by extending the theoretical and empirical network. In this connection, it is intriguing to note that two of the techniques proposed by Orne (1962) to deal with the problem of demand characteristics are pre- and post-experimental enquiry.

Practical problems

Inaccessibility
More serious than any of these arguments about subjectivity was the discovery that large portions of the psychological arena were unavailable to conscious introspection. In general, what James (1890) called the 'perchings', the substantive aspects of thinking containing sensory images, tend to be available to consciousness, whereas the 'flights', the transitive aspects containing fringe ideas and relations in the margins of attention, tend not to be. If we liken the thought process to a calculation, it is the running totals of which we are aware rather than the operations. Indeed, Hayes's (1973) interesting work on the function of imagery in mental arithmetic, in which subjects report using images to store partial results of a solution process, provides empirical confirmation of this idea. It would also be consistent with the view that consciousness is a function of the perceptual apparatus, as in Freud (1895): 'Consciousness is the subjective side of a *part* of the physical processes in the neuronic system – namely, of the *perceptual* processes (ω-processes); and its absence would *not* leave physical events unchanged but would imply the absence of any contribution from the W (ω)-system.'

Inaccessibility was one of the most important conclusions of the Würzburg work. Similar results were obtained by others. The following is a protocol from Woodworth (1906) whose subject had answered 'Diamonds' to the question 'What substances are more costly than gold?':

> I had no visual image of the diamond: the thought of diamonds was there before the sound of the word. You don't think of the words before you are going to say them . . . the words come so quickly that you don't have a chance to think of them before you say them.

Binet (1903) examined his young daughters' reactions to words. Armande gave the following responses:

> With these words that I write almost unconsciously, the image comes only after the word is written; it comes, and, if it comes at all, is very vague and it is often effaced by the search for the next word.

> The thinking is something I know at once without having sought it by means of words; it appears to me as some sort of feeling. I don't know what to say.

And on 'negation': 'this quite vague feeling, but which I am sure of, is a thought without words.'[2]

A more recent selection from Grove (1973), who taxed subjects after a semantic memory task, verges on the absurd: 'I read first the left word and then the right'; 'Easy – I read the two lines, then there was a delay before I said "yes"'; 'Where the statement was true I answered "yes" . . . then where I judged it to be false I answered "no"'.

At best this means that protocols will be incomplete. De Groot (1965), who gives extensive discussion to the problem, comments: 'With some subjects gaps and pauses in reporting are frequent and of such a long duration that they cannot be assumed to result from actual pauses in thinking. He may just temporarily forget his second task (to think aloud), or he may not be able to verbalize adequately what he is or has been doing mentally.' The central issue of how these thoughts may be translated into words is thoroughly discussed by Natsoulas (1967).

A further problem is that 'quite often thoughts move so quickly that the spoken word cannot keep up with them. The subject is then forced to skip steps or to deliberately slow down his thinking (if possible) which thereby disturbs the thought process' (De Groot, op. cit.).

A problem that must be familiar to anyone who has included protocols amongst his data is that they are frequently unintelligible. In fact Skinner's (1953) rejection of introspection has been not on the grounds of a positivist methodology but on account of the difficulty of disambiguating reports of private events. Some individuals are better at introspecting than others. This raises problems of interpretation and selection. De Groot suggests that tape recordings are checked over with the subject after the experiment but this procedure is not free from the danger of bias either. Experimenters are sometimes tempted to select 'typical' illustrative protocols. This may be all right for hypothesis formation but it is not acceptable for hypothesis testing. De Groot employs a minimum frequency criterion which must be met for a protocol to be considered typical.

Distortion

The fact of limited processing capacity, as we have already noted, means that introspection must become retrospection. This introduces the possibility of mnemonic distortion. In some cases it may take a considerable time to complete an introspective report. De Groot discusses the way in which the likelihood of errors from this source must be weighed against that of errors due to mutual interference between introspection and thinking, which occurs when there is close alternation between the two processes, as in 'thinking aloud'. The structuralists were not unaware of these problems, but they were perhaps more sanguine about them than subsequent psychologists have been. To quote from De Groot (op. cit.) once more: 'Verbalizing one's thoughts unequivocally adds *an extra burden* to the subject's task. On the one hand, the added instruction to think aloud, necessarily influences the thought process to some degree; on the other, concentrated thinking on the problem itself must somewhat hamper its reporting.' His subjects reported two effects: (i) a slowing down of the thinking itself, and (ii) the obligation to think more explicitly than normal. The degree to which the instruction to think aloud was felt as a disturbance varied considerably among subjects, being most troublesome to thinkers of the intuitive type.

Deception may be intentional or unintentional. De Groot instances cases where subjects deliberately suppressed proposals of which they were ashamed. Another charge to be taken seriously is the claim, made famous by Freud, that introspections are rationalizations[3]. A recent experiment by Evans and Wason (1976) in which subjects justified, with a high degree of confidence, common erroneous solutions to a problem, which purported to be correct, certainly supports this idea. In a previous paper (Wason and Evans, 1975) they postulated the existence of two processes: a type I process which underlies behaviour and is generally unavailable to consciousness, and a type II process which underlies protocols and is available to consciousness. (The relation between these two processes is one of the most interesting and least investigated problems in psychology.) In a study of the selection task, which involves making inferences from conditional statements (see Chapter 5 for a detailed discussion), they claim to have demonstrated a discrepancy between the two processes. Protocols (reasons given for the choice made) appear to show the logically appropriate strategy in the condition where the consequent is negative (the majority of subjects mention falsification) but an inappropriate strategy in the condition where the consequent is affirmative (only a minority of subjects mention falsification). Behavioural responses (selecting which cards need to be turned over to evaluate the rule) also appear correct in the former condition but incorrect in the latter. However, on the basis of other data (Evans and Lynch, 1973) it is plausibly argued that in both conditions they reflect 'matching bias', i.e. they are determined by the items mentioned in the rule regardless of their logical operators.

This experiment illustrates the way in which conclusions based on one type of evidence from a limited situation can be misleading. The relative fruitfulness and validity of introspective reports and performance measures as bases for inference can only be established by extensive, empirical investigation. Part of the reason for psychologists' tendency to assume the inferiority of introspection is their previous misplaced belief in its superiority.

In conclusion, introspection is subject to the same problems as other methods but in some cases to a greater extent. Can anything be done to improve the reliability and validity of such reports? Natsoulas (1967) suggests four procedures: (i) positioning reports in a theoretical network; (ii) securing supplementary reports concerning report behaviour; (iii) employment of a public criterion as a check; and (iv) the statistical and experimental elimination of alternative hypotheses, e.g. by the use of converging operations (defined by Garner et al., 1956, as 'any set of experimental operations which eliminate alternative hypotheses and which can lead to a concept which is not uniquely identified with any one of the original operations, but which is defined by the results of all operations performed').

Empirical studies

Representation

The aim here is not to provide an exhaustive survey but rather a selection of representative examples, which illustrate the ways in which introspection has been used in the study of thinking. The division into 'representation' and 'process' is for the purposes of convenience; ultimately no hard and fast distinction can be maintained.

Classical introspection went out of favour partly because of the analysis of content that was proposed. However, many people have made the point that the failure of one use of introspection does not preclude all other possible uses. Introspective reports of the content of experience might be employed either because phenomenal experience *per se* is of interest, or in order to use it to make inferences about a behavioural process. In the former case it is likely to be the primary method, in the latter case a secondary or complementary method. Most of the early studies, such as Binet's, used introspection in a quasi-clinical manner, as one of a number of methods, in an attempt to get an overall picture. Luria's (1968) outstanding study of the mnemonist, Shereshevskii, also falls into this category.

Introspection is accepted without question in the areas of perception and psychophysics. The first area that might reasonably be considered to fall within the domain of thinking is imagery. It is difficult although not impossible (see e.g. Brooks, 1967) to see how this can be studied without the use of introspection. The early studies by Fechner (1860) and Galton's (1883) questionnaire relied on people's reports of their experiences of imagery. Both drew attention to marked individual differences in its possession and the results of Galton's study are well known. He found the occurrence of imagery to be more frequent and vivid amongst children, housewives and 'common labourers' than in eminent men of science.

A topic of particular interest within this general area has been the phenomenon of eidetic imagery, a particularly vivid form, characterized by a high degree of accuracy. Early studies by Jaensch (1930) claimed an incidence rate of 60 per cent in children and 7 per cent in adults. However, these figures have since been queried. One of the best attempts to tighten up controls has been a study by Haber and Haber (1964) which specified four criteria for images to be considered eidetic; these were that they must (i) be positively coloured; (ii) persist for at least 40 seconds; (iii) pass an accuracy score of at least 6/9 details correctly reported; and (iv) be scannable. Measured against these standards, only 8 per cent of a sample of 151 children aged between 7 and 12 years qualified as eidetikers. The first two measures rely entirely on subjects' verbal reports, the third can be objectively checked and the last can be confirmed by observing eye movements. Not only were the eidetikers a discrete population as measured on these scores but their verbal reports also were qualitatively different, confidently referring to vivid, complete images 'out-there', and unqualified with the 'I think . . .' or past tenses associated with the verbal reports of the non-eidetikers.

An ingenious method of checking the validity of reports of eidetic images, by making the possibility of getting the answer right by chance extremely remote, was demonstrated by Stromeyer and Psotka (1970). Their material consisted of two random dot stereograms (each containing 2,000 elements) identical except for a figure (in one case a square) which was shifted laterally a few elements. One stereogram was presented to one eye and the subject instructed to form an eidetic image of it. The other stereogram was presented to the other eye after an interval (sometimes as long as several days). Successful superimposition of the eidetic image onto the presented pattern enabled one eidetic subject to see the figure in depth and to point correctly to the corners of the square.

Another topic of persistent interest has been the role of imagery in chess thinking. Binet's (1894) studies, based on the introspective reports of blindfold chess players, revealed marked individual differences in the degree of abstraction of imagery. It became clear that even the most vivid imagers did not see exact copies of the board but that their images were selective and more likely to represent the strategic importance of a position. These are some examples:

> *Sittenfeld:* Accurately to describe my thinking, I ought, whenever it is a question of visual memory, to say not 'chess-board' but 'position' for that is all I really see . . . I recognize a given piece not by its special shape but by its possibilities for movement, that is to say its action.

14   Thinking in perspective

> *Goetz:* I see only the range, the action of the pieces. . . . Thus a
> bishop for my internal eye is not a piece carved in a
> more or less baroque fashion, it is an oblique force.
> *Tarrasch:* I don't see the squares as distinctly black and white but
> only light and dark. As for the colour of the pieces, the
> difference is even less marked. They look to me more as
> enemies or allies. The shapes of the pieces appear only
> distinctly: I consider principally their capacity for
> action.

That the ability to recognize familiar patterns is what distinguishes chess masters has been shown, using short term memory tasks, by De Groot (1966) and Chase and Simon (1973).

Other studies have sought to assess the relative contributions of imaginal and verbal modes of representation in thinking. Much of the Würzburg work can be construed in this light. Binet's interest lay in investigating individual differences in this matter. One study (1894) compared two prodigious calculators: Inaudi, who depended largely on auditory imagery, and Diamondi, who depended largely on the use of visual diagram forms. His conclusions were based partly on introspective reports and partly on measures of performance as a function of mode of presentation and mode of interference.

With the rise of behaviourism, meaning came to be treated largely as a matter of verbal mediation. One of the main proponents of the reintroduction of imagery as a hypothetical construct has been Paivio (1971). This approach has been the subject of attack by Pylyshyn (1973) who argues that cognitive representation is essentially abstract and propositional. If the history of psychology were more carefully studied, perhaps this kind of controversy might be avoided. Armande's response to 'tomorrow' in the study quoted above (Binet, 1903) was:

> *Armande:* I had a very vague image of the dining room. These were
> mainly thoughts.
> *Binet:* Say what you mean by a thought.
> *Armande:* That which is translated by words and feelings, it is
> vague, it's too difficult.
> *Binet:* Come on, courage, try to explain again.
> *Armande:* That which presents itself in several ways. Sometimes
> suddenly, without my expecting it. At other times following
> upon other thoughts.

The modern argument for the defence has been put by Kosslyn and Pomerantz (1977) who point out that it does not follow from the fact that a particular mode of representation is adequate that it is the only possible one, and that the efficiency of a representation depends in part on the purposes to which it is put.

Process

A study which might be thought of as a sequel to Binet's work on calculators is Hunter's (1962) cross examination of the mathematician, Aitken. This showed Aitken's ability to be partly the result of a large repertoire of facts about numbers (e.g. he knew the factors of all the numbers up to 1500) and partly the result of a large repertoire of calculative plans: his choice of strategies was guided by the storage and processing limitations of working memory and aimed at minimizing the number and difficulty of the steps involved.

A classic case of the application of introspective techniques to the study of problems which require heuristic strategies is Duncker's (1945) monograph on problem solving. His subjects ranged from infants not 'yet able to handle a spoon when eating' to mathematicians, and his problems accordingly from practical ones involving a variety of everyday objects, including selecting suitable objects for unusual uses, to mathematical ones. The best known is the problem of how to destroy an inoperable stomach tumour by radiation without damaging the surrounding tissue. Typically, subjects were instructed to think aloud. This he distinguished from introspection (where attention is directed on the subject himself) by virtue of the fact that attention is directed on the problem, the subject, so to speak, allowing his thought to become verbal. In fact, the subject was encouraged to speak aloud even the most fleeting and foolish idea. He was allowed to ask the experimenter questions and the experimenter might ask the subject for clarification. In this way Duncker hoped to reveal the process of problem solution. For the tumour problem he constructed a family tree of possible solutions. He concluded that the functional value of tentative solutions served as productive reformulations of the problem, which became increasingly more specific. 'We can describe a process of solution either as development of the solution or as development of the problem', he wrote. Many of his ideas were developed by De Groot and Newell et al., whose work is discussed below.

Probably the most extensive introspective study of thought processes has been De Groot's (1965) work over the past thirty years on thought and choice in chess. It also contains an extremely good discussion of the introspective method. His main interest has focussed on the choice of move problem, in which subjects (chess players ranging from amateurs to grand masters) are presented with a position and asked to make one move, thinking their deliberations out loud. His stated aims are to provide a systematic description and interpretative analysis of the resulting protocols, with a view to forming hypotheses about the macroscopic structure and operational dynamics of this goal-directed, productive thinking. Three main stages are suggested: (i) orientation, in which broad plans are cast; (ii) exploration and investigation, in which problems are formulated, goals set up, operations carried out and evaluations made; and (iii) proof, in which final checks are made. Active phases, in which plans are tried out, alternate with passive, transitive phases, containing pauses during which past findings are integrated. De Groot took as his point of departure Selz's (1922) notion of thinking as a hierarchically organized, linear series of operations. He takes recurrences of typical sequences in the data, which he interprets as reflecting the application of subsidiary methods in order of priority (as in a pop up, push down list), as evidence for hierarchical organization. Shallice (1972) has argued that, despite the limitations of method, 'his findings provide some of the best support for the primarily serial-processing nature of complex thought'.

A famous attempt to tighten up and provide the detail so frequently lacking in this type of study is that of Newell and Simon (1961), who hail cybernetics as providing a resolution of the mentalist, problem-oriented psychology favoured by Gestaltists and the mechanistic, technique-oriented psychology favoured by behaviourists. Their approach is through computer simulation, although the original source for, and ultimate test of, their theory has been thinking aloud protocols. The 'General Problem Solver' programs that they have developed contain methods of setting up goals, such as the transformation of one expression into another, and of attaining them, e.g. by the application of appropriate operations. Originally applied to the solution of symbolic logic problems, they have been extended to various fields, including chess playing. During problem solution, subjects are asked to state the operations they wish to carry out and to talk aloud about what they are thinking about. The aim is then to construct a program which will generate the same behaviour as the subject which, if the fit is good enough, will be considered a theory of problem solving within certain domains. As a result of the 'striking correlations'

obtained, Newell and Simon (1972) claim to have a good approximation
to such an information-processing theory, large proportions of the
subjects' protocols being accountable for in terms of the types of goal
and methods outlined in the theory. The match, however, is not perfect:
gaps, order differences and subject differences in the protocols remain
to be explained. (For a full discussion of this work, see Chapter 8.)

The introspective analysis of creative thinking has a long tradition.
One collection appears under the editorship of Ghiselin (1952). With
regard to the structure of creative thinking, most reports have testified
to the apparently spontaneous occurrence of inspiration, often while
on a journey, e.g. Mozart (quoted in Holmes, 1878): 'When I am, as
it were, completely by myself, entirely alone, and of good cheer – say,
travelling in a carriage or walking after a good meal, or during the
night when I cannot sleep; it is on such occasions that my ideas flow
best and most abundantly. *Whence* and *how* they come, I know not;
nor can I force them.'

There has also been general confirmation of Wallas's (1926) proposed
four phases: preparation, incubation, inspiration and verification.
Poincaré (1924) writes:

> Most striking at first is this appearance of sudden illumination, a
> manifest sign of long, unconscious prior work. The role of this
> unconscious work in mathematical invention appears to me
> incontestable, and traces of it would be found in other cases where
> it is less evident ... There is another remark to be made about the
> conditions of this unconscious work: it is possible, and of a certainty
> it is only fruitful, if it is on the one hand preceded and on the other
> hand followed by a period of conscious work.

The interaction between conscious and unconscious processes was also
one of the main findings of exploratory conversations with dramatists
undertaken by Binet and Passy (1895). One of their subjects, du
Curel, described the process of *dédoublement*:

> When *dédoublement* occurs, there is without doubt alternation. For
> ten or fifteen minutes – perhaps even half an hour – my characters
> hold the stage and my own person fades out, then for the next two
> or five minutes the latter reappears while my characters retreat
> into the background, and so on ... Thus a character's speech could
> be riddled with my corrections and yet come as a surprise when I
> read it over ten minutes later ... My characters and I therefore

take it in turns to be conscious and unconscious, without ever meeting at a conscious level.

Their study also brought to light considerable individual differences in the mode of working. The following are two attempts to define the process in more detail:

Poincaré (op. cit.): Ideas rose in clouds; I felt them collide until pairs interlocked, so to speak, making a stable combination. By the next morning I had established the existence of a class of Fuchsian functions, those which come from the hypogeometric series; I had only to write out the results, which took but a few hours.

And Einstein, in answer to Hadamard's (1945) enquiries:

The psychical entities which seem to serve as elements in thought are certain signs and more or less clear images which can be 'voluntarily' reproduced and combined ... It is also clear that the desire to arrive finally at logically connected concepts is the emotional basis of this rather vague play with the above mentioned elements. But taken from a psychological viewpoint, this combinatory play seems to be the essential feature in productive thought ... According to what has been said, the play with the mentioned elements is aimed to be analogous to certain logical connections one is searching for.

A recent, imaginative study of absent mindedness by Reason (1976) indicates that the method of introspection is not dead. Thirty-five volunteers kept diaries of 'non-planned' actions for a fortnight. These lapses were then classified into four main categories according to the function presumed mainly responsible: (i) storage failures, in which part of the plan or a preceding action is forgotten; (ii) test failures, where a subroutine is exited too early or too late, presumably because a feedback loop is missing; (iii) discrimination failures, where a stimulus is incorrectly identified, usually because it is very similar to an expected one; and (iv) selection failures, in which an inappropriate, usually well-practised, action is substituted for the intended one. Reason has gone on to provide a flow chart analysis, in which he tries to specify points susceptible to absent mindedness. His diaries also provide hypotheses about *when* these lapses are likely to occur, viz. during the performance of a well-earned habit in low arousal conditions, when preoccupied with something else, trying to do two things at once or when suffering some kind of general stress. He shows that the same analysis can be applied to cases where the consequences are considerably more serious, viz. aircraft disasters.

Summary and conclusions

Historically, introspection was first overestimated and then underestimated. It is subject to a number of problems, in particular inaccessibility and distortion, but these problems are not different in kind from those that beset other scientific methods, all of which depend on inference. They can all be improved in the same ways, by extending the empirical and theoretical networks, and are ultimately judged by the same criteria of plausibility and consistency.

With regard to the content of thinking, introspection provides the primary method for data about the experience of thinking, which may be of interest in itself or as a means for making inferences about the process of thinking. In this latter regard, introspective reports may be of little relevance, although theories which predict these as well as performance measures are to be preferred. The process of thinking is for the most part unavailable to consciousness but introspection can enable a macroscopic description of the structure to be inferred and can suggest hypotheses about the underlying operations. Introspection frequently plays an important role in hypothesis formation and together with other behavioural measures and simulation, which are necessary to provide tightening up and to fill in the details, it can play a complementary role in hypothesis testing.

Notes

1 I am grateful to Astrid Weld for providing me with translations of relevant passages from Messer's monograph. The other translations are from Titchener (1909).
2 The translations from Binet are taken from Reeves's (1965) excellent treatment of his work.
3 This question is extensively discussed in a paper which appeared just after this chapter was written, see below Nisbett and Wilson (1977).

References

Ayer, A. J. (1959) Privacy. *Proceedings of the British Academy* 45: 43–65.
Binet, A. (1894) *Psychologie des grands calculateurs et joueurs d'echecs.* Paris: Hachette.

Binet, A. (1903) *L'Etude Experimentale de l'Intelligence.* Paris: Schleicher Frères.
Binet, A. and Passy, J. (1895) Etudes de psychologie sur les auteurs dramatiques. *L'Année Psychologique 1* (1): 60–118.
Boring, E. G. (1953) A history of introspection. *Psychological Bulletin 50* (3): 169–89.
Brentano, F. (1874) *Psychologie vom empirischen Standpunkt.* Leipzig: Duncker and Humblot.
Brooks, L. R. (1967) The suppression of visualization by reading. *Quarterly Journal of Experimental Psychology 19* (4): 289–99.
Buhler, K. (1907) Tatsachen und Probleme zu einer Psychologie der Denkvorgänge, i. Über Gedanken. *Archiv für die gesamte Psychologie 9* (4): 297–365.
Burt, C. (1962) The concept of consciousness. *British Journal of Psychology 53* (3): 229–42.
Chase, W. G. and Simon, H. A. (1973) The mind's eye in chess. In W. G. Chase (ed.) *Visual information processing.* London: Academic Press.
Comte, A. (1842) *Cours de philosophie positive.* Paris: Bachelier.
Cooper, L. A. and Shepard, R. N. (1973) Chronometric studies of the rotation of mental images. In W. G. Chase (ed.) *Visual information processing.* London: Academic Press.
De Groot, A. D. (1965) *Thought and choice in chess.* The Hague: Mouton. (First published in Dutch in 1946.)
De Groot, A. D. (1966) Perception and memory versus thought: some old ideas and recent findings. In B. Kleinmuntz (ed.) *Problem solving.* New York: Wiley.
Duncker, K. (1945) On problem solving. *Psychological Monographs 58* (5) Whole No. 270: 1–113.
Evans, J. St B. T. and Lynch, J. S. (1973) Matching bias in the selection task. *British Journal of Psychology 64* (3): 391–7.
Evans, J. St B. T. and Wason, P. C. (1976) Rationalization in a reasoning task. *British Journal of Psychology 67* (4): 479–86.
Fechner, G. T. (1860) *Elements of Psychophysics.* New York: Holt.
Freud, S. (1895) *The Origins of Psychoanalysis: Letters of Wilhelm Fliess, Drafts and Notes.* London: Imago (1954).
Galton, F. (1883) *Inquiries into Human Faculty.* London: Dent (1905).
Garner, W. R., Hake, H. W. and Eriksen, C. W. (1956) Operationism and the concept of perception. *Psychological Review 63* (3): 149–59.
Ghiselin, B. (ed.) (1952) *The Creative Process.* Berkeley: University of California Press.
Grove, C. (1973) Retrieval time and the organization of memory. Unpublished Ph.D. thesis, North East London Polytechnic.
Haber, R. N. and Haber, R. B. (1964) Eidetic imagery: I. Frequency. *Perceptual and Motor Skills 19* (1): 131–8.
Hadamard, J. (1945) *The Psychology of Invention in the Mathematical Field.* Princeton: Princeton University Press.
Harré, R. and Secord, P. F. (1972) *The Explanation of Social Behaviour.* Oxford: Blackwell.

Hayes, J. R. (1973) On the function of visual imagery in elementary mathematics. In W. G. Chase (ed.) *Visual Information Processing.* London: Academic Press.

Holmes, E. (1878) *The Life of Mozart including his Correspondence.* London: Chapman and Hall.

Holt, R. R. (1964) Imagery: the return of the ostracized. *American Psychologist* *19* (4): 254–64.

Humphrey, G. (1951) *Thinking: An Introduction to its Experimental Psychology.* London: Methuen.

Hunter, I. M. L. (1962) An exceptional talent for calculative thinking. *British Journal of Psychology 53* (3): 243–58.

Husserl, E. G. (1901) *Logische Untersuchungen: Untersuchungen zur Phänomenologie und Theorie der Erkenntnis.* Halle: Niemeyer. (Translation of volume 1 by J. N. Findlay, *Logical Investigations.* New York: Humanities Press, 1970.)

Jaensch, E. R. (1930) *Eidetic Imagery and Typological Methods of Investigation.* New York: Harcourt Brace.

James, W. (1890) *Principles of Psychology.* New York: Dover (1950)

Joynson, R. B. (1972) The return of mind. *Bulletin of the British Psychological Society 25* (86): 1–10.

Kelly, G. A. (1955) *The Psychology of Personal Constructs.* New York: Norton.

Kelvin, R. P. (1956) Thinking: psychologists and physiology. *Acta Psychologica 12* (2): 136–51.

Kosslyn, S. M. and Pomerantz, J. R. (1977) Imagery, propositions and the form of internal representations. *Cognitive Psychology 9* (1): 52–76.

Luria, A. R. (1968) *The Mind of a Mnemonist.* New York: Basic Books.

McKellar, P. (1962) The method of introspection. In J. Scher (ed.) *Theories of the Mind.* New York: Free Press of Glencoe.

Messer, A. (1906) Experimentell-psychologische Unterschungen über das Denken. *Archiv für die gesamte Psychologie 8* (1): 1–224.

Mill, J. S. (1882) *Auguste Comte and Positivism.* London: Trübner. 3rd edition.

Natsoulas, T. (1967) What are perceptual reports about? *Psychological Bulletin 67* (4): 249–72.

Natsoulas, T. (1970) Concerning introspective 'knowledge'. *Psychological Bulletin 73* (2): 89–111.

Newell, A. and Simon, H. A. (1961) Computer simulation of human thinking. *Science 134:* 2011–17.

Newell, A. and Simon, H. A. (1972) *Human Problem Solving.* Englewood Cliffs: Prentice-Hall.

Nisbett, R. E. and Wilson, T. De C. (1977) Telling more than we can know: verbal reports on mental processes. *Psychological Review 84* (3): 231–59.

Orne, M. T. (1962) On the social psychology of the psychological experiment: with particular reference to demand characteristics and their implications. *American Psychologist 17* (10): 776–83.

Paivio, A. (1971) *Imagery and verbal processes.* New York: Holt.

Perkins, M. (1953) Intersubjectivity and Gestalt psychology. *Philosophy and Phenomenological Research 13* (4): 437–51.

Poincaré, H. (1924) *The Foundations of Science.* New York: Science Press. (First published Paris: Flammarion, 1908.)

Pylyshyn, Z. W. (1973) What the mind's eye tells the mind's brain. *Psychological Bulletin 80* (1): 1–24.

Radford, J. (1974) Reflections on introspection. *American Psychologist 29* (4): 245–50.

Radford, J. and Burton, A. (1974) *Thinking: Its Nature and Development.* London: Wiley.

Reason, J. (1976) Absent minds. *New Society 38* (735): 244–5.

Reeves, J. W. (1965) *Thinking about Thinking.* London: Secker and Warburg.

Rogers, C. R. (1965) *Client-centred Therapy.* New York: Houghton Mifflin.

Ryle, G. (1949) *The Concept of Mind.* London: Hutchinson.

Schrödinger, E. (1958) *Mind and Matter.* Cambridge University Press.

Selz, O. (1922) *Zur Psychologie des produktiven Denkens und des Irrtums.* Bonn: Friedrich Cohen.

Shallice, T. (1972) Dual functions of consciousness. *Psychological review 79* (5): 383–93.

Sheehan, P. W. and Neisser, U. (1969) Some variables affecting the vividness of imagery in recall. *British Journal of Psychology 60* (1): 71–80.

Skinner, B. F. (1953) *Science and Human Behaviour.* New York: Macmillan.

Stromeyer, C. F. and Psotka, J. (1970) The detailed texture of eidetic images. *Nature 225*: 346–9.

Titchener, E. B. (1898) The postulates of a structural psychology. *Philosophical Review 7* (5): 449–65.

Titchener, E. R. (1909) *Lectures on the Experimental Study of the Thought Processes.* New York: Macmillan.

Wallas, G. (1926) *The Art of Thought.* London: Jonathan Cape.

Wason, P. C. and Evans, J. St B. T. (1975) Dual processes in reasoning. *Cognition 3* (2): 141–54.

Watson, J. B. (1913) Psychology as the behaviourist views it. *Psychological Review 20* (2): 158–77.

Watt, H. J. (1905) Experimentelle Beiträge zu einer Theorie des Denkens. *Archiv für die gesamte Psychologie 4* (3): 289–436.

Wittgenstein, L. (1953) *Philosophical Investigations.* Oxford: Blackwell.

Woodworth, R. S. (1906) Imageless thought. *Journal of Philosophy, Psychology and Scientific Methods 3* (26): 701–8.

Zener, K. (1958) The significance of experience of the individual for the science of psychology. In H. Feigl, M. Scriven and G. Maxwell (eds) *Minnesota Studies in the Philosophy of Science II:* 354–69. Minneapolis: University of Minnesota Press.

2 The whole idea: Gestalt psychology

Esme Burton
and **Andrew Burton**

Introduction

It is difficult to assess the Gestalt school's contribution to thinking for
two reasons; firstly, one is presenting the viewpoint from 'outside' the
privileged circle, and the Gestaltists did tend to present themselves as
an evangelizing force fighting the twin oppressors (S–R psychology
and rigid experimentation) of true human nature; secondly, the
Gestalt school is not, either in research methods or subject matter, a
cohesive one. Rather it embodies a collection of views about the
orientation to human behaviour psychologists should adopt, the sorts
of things they should be studying and the level of explanation they
should seek. There was little of the 'systematic' approach about the
Gestaltists, in the sense of developing or deriving a large number of
testable hypotheses from a limited set of postulates and assembling a
body of experimental data. In many ways, Gestalt psychology did not
develop in a linear fashion; rather their research resembles a series of
forays from a central core of tenets to which they constantly returned,
and which remained little altered over the years.

To those accustomed to the psychology of the 1970s and especially to
the British tradition of psychology, it may be hard to appreciate the
relevance of some of the Gestaltists' cherished views, or the vigour with

which they were proposed. To begin with, therefore, a brief outline of the historical context in which the movement developed is appropriate (for a more detailed exposition the reader is referred to Boring, 1950). The Gestaltists were Europeans and had received their training in the sophisticated intellectual atmosphere of the late nineteenth century, with an emphasis on theoretical and philosophical arguments as much as on experimental data; and, in psychology at least, on 'mental' contents and processes (such as experiences and feelings – Wundt defined psychology as the science of immediate experience) and the introspective analytic method. By the beginning of the twentieth century the analytic approach, holding that all sensations are compounds formed initially from unrelated and inert elements that come to be associated by mere contiguity, was already facing problems and undergoing revision. For example, novelty is difficult to explain by simple contiguity. Wundt had earlier recognized this and had introduced a principle of 'creative synthesis'. Another issue was that many aspects of human perception have features that cannot be explained by contiguity of discrete mental atoms: a melody remains the same even when all the individual notes are altered by transposing the key; a circle is circular whatever its size or colour. This had been recognized by both Mach (1886) and Von Ehrenfels (1890). The quality that remains the same however much the elements within the pattern change was called 'Gestaltqualität' by Von Ehrenfels. An attempt was made to incorporate such 'form-qualities' into existing theories by adding (as Mach did) such notions as 'circleness' to the list of elementary sensations, or by postulating a higher-order set of elements formed by combination (Von Ehrenfels's suggestion). However, the continuing difficulty of explaining the structured nature of experience led to alternative approaches developing both in Europe and the United States.

   In the United States the change was one of subject matter rather than method: the analytic approach was retained but applied to different aspects of behaviour, notably learning and *overt* responses: i.e. actions rather than experience. Wertheimer (1880–1943), Koffka (1886–1941) and Köhler (1887–1967), the founder members and main exponents of Gestalt psychology were to remain Europeans until the 1930s, although visits were made to America in the 1920s, and their alternative took a radically different line. They were still concerned to develop an understanding of what they thought were the most intrinsic aspects of human behaviour, namely mental events or experiences. But, they said, if it is impossible to explain the complex essentially structured nature of these by combinations of elementary sensations, why not turn the problem on its head and assume that *structure* itself is fundamental to experience, and that the elements, rather than determining, are themselves determined by the whole, or *Gestalt*?

This was the basis of the Gestalt approach to human behaviour: to take as fundamental, familiar psychological phenomena, and to work to discover functional relationships *between* them, rather than analyse the phenomena themselves. They did not reject analysis but demanded that the level of analysis should be appropriate to the problem. The emphasis is thus on 'phenomenal experience' (phenomenon: that of which a sense or the mind directly takes note). There are links here with the phenomenology of Husserl (1859–1938) which included the belief that consciousness is directed towards something and that all the features or aspects of objects are united into an experience called the 'noema' (the *Gestalt?*). (Cf. chapter 10 for a discussion of the contribution of phenomenology to the study of thinking.) As Köhler (1942) said, 'We want to know not merely *what* happens in mental life, but also *how* and *why* it happens.' The Gestaltists felt that psychology had adopted the scientific model too rigidly and had become obsessed with investigating facts rather than relationships between facts; Köhler again: 'One of the main tasks which Psychology has to solve consists in the discovery of those *functional relations* which are responsible for the occurrence and the characteristics of our experiences' (1942, italics inserted). The Gestaltists thus were advocating a new starting point – looking at the wood instead of the trees – yet not imposing a simplistic model on behaviour where such simplicity may not exist. To quote Köhler again:

There was a great wave of relief – as though we were escaping from a prison. The prison was psychology as taught at the universities when we were still students. At the time, we had been shocked by the thesis that all psychological facts (not only those in perception) consist of unrelated inert atoms and almost the only factors which combine these atoms and thus introduce action are associations formed under the influence of mere contiguity. What had disturbed us was the utter senselessness of this picture, and the implication that human life, apparently so colourful and so intensely dynamic, is actually a frightful bore (Köhler, 1959).

Gestalt principles of behaviour

So far we have said nothing directly about thinking, and this is not really surprising since the Gestalt psychologists were not developing a theory of thinking, but a set of philosophical, theoretical and methodological principles for understanding human experience, a grandiose re-orientation for psychology, of which the thought process was only a part. The properties of mind were held to be common to all psychological processes. Wertheimer was to contribute prominently to the school's approach to thinking but his first writings in 1912 – those often associated with the start of the Gestalt movement – concerned a perceptual phenomenon, the *phi-phenomenon* or apparent movement. Indeed, much of the Gestalt writing concerns perception, mainly because it illustrates general principles most clearly and compellingly.

What are these general principles? First, and perhaps the most essential, that an intuitive grasp of the overall significance of behaviour is more desirable than a precise but mechanistic explanation; second, that we should try to understand relationships between events, not just the events themselves; third, that no event occurs in isolation, but only in a context, and that one can only understand the event by considering the context (or field). One might mention again here that although the Gestaltists have been labelled 'anti-analytic' they were not absolutely against the analysis of behaviour – but they insisted that the level of analysis should be appropriate.

From this general orientation developed some more specific principles. Köhler pointed out that 'functional relationships' are often not available to direct experience. He writes (1942): 'Thus the rules in which we formulate these relationships imply the occurrence of certain functions in a realm that is surely not the phenomenal realm. As psychologists we cannot say more about this world of hidden existence and hidden functional dependence than is contained in those rules. Therefore the rules themselves tend to sound disappointingly formal and abstract.' He also believed, however, that psychological events and brain events (i.e. physiological processes) have a formal relationship, a relationship embodied in the principle of 'isomorphism'. Since brain events are – or, he hoped, would be at some point – observable, we *do* have a way in which to support psychological suppositions: i.e. by seeking biological correlates. If one has found that psychological event B follows A consistently, one is tempted to infer a functional relationship between the two events. The relationship remains merely an inference as it cannot be experienced directly. However, if one can find brain events corresponding not only to A and B but also to a *third* intervening event, one has support for assuming the validity of the functional relationship. The whole argument derives from the assumption of isomorphism. Köhler did make this assumption and believed that physics, chemistry and biology would yield useful evidence for the psychologist.

This assumption of isomorphism helped foster another Gestalt principle: that of the *field*. A 'field' to the physicist is, roughly speaking, a network of forces working on an object and determining its behaviour. A magnetic field will control the behaviour of iron filings within it. Köhler had had extensive training in the physical sciences; this, together with a belief in isomorphism, led him to the assertion (1942) that '. . . the field concept had to be put in the very centre of the theory of perception' (and thus in the theory of all behaviour). A psychological field embodies all the forces acting upon a mental phenomenon and determining its nature. These forces include motivation, belief, memory, and organizational tendencies combining elements (e.g. closure, similarity and proximity). The field is thus in a sense the 'context' in which behaviour occurs. But 'context' is a passive term, whereas the Gestaltists stressed the active, dynamic nature of mental processes (hence 'forces'). The field is also a *determining* factor, whereas a context may not play any active role. The guiding principle in this psychological field was the Law of Prägnanz – a simplicity principle governing behaviour – whereby we organize mental events into the 'best' whole or *Gestalt*, best seeming to be synonymous with simplest, balanced, least effortful, and most elegant: almost an aesthetic principle.

Psychological field theory was certainly vague as to how the hypothesized forces functioned, the status or nature of such forces, and their interaction. Attempts to make it more precise by the adoption of notions from physics or biochemistry tended only to make it seem absurd, even as analogies. The Gestaltists were not blind to this but nevertheless regarded the concept of the field as vital to the understanding of mental processes, and so adopted it as a working hypothesis. Certainly the concepts of organization and simplicity as guiding forces became central to their discussion of thinking.

Another important principle believed to be operating within the field was the division into 'figure' and 'ground'. This is best illustrated by examples from perception, Rubin (1921) producing much of the evidence: his well known vase figure is one example. The perceptual field will always be found to be divided into what is unified as the subject matter of the present observation (the figure) and its surroundings (the ground). This is not arbitrary but governed by simple laws provided again by the forces or Laws of Organization. However, there is not necessarily only one way of organization, and, as we shall see later, thinking may often consist of discovering new, better ways of organization. The introduction into the field of even a very minor new element may produce dramatic reorganization in order to maintain the 'best whole'. Thus we have a collection of basic tenets characterizing the Gestalt school: human experience is dynamic, directed towards achieving organization and balance, and has parallels with neuro-physiological events.

The Gestalt approach to thinking

During the period when their ideas were at their most influential, the Gestalt group were responsible for producing an extended series of experimental studies. One of their (many) ambitious hopes was that this would lead to a new system of Gestalt logic based on the study of 'living thought'. Collectively, their approach to thinking also inspired experimental work carried out by those who perhaps were not working self-consciously within the Gestalt framework (e.g. Maier). How were the vital but somewhat vague beliefs of the Gestalt psychologists applied to thinking? First of all, their approach to thinking was an expression of the principles we have outlined, emphasizing that 'understanding' was more crucial than merely collecting quantitative data. Thus Wertheimer was concerned to discover what sorts of things seem to happen during problem solving rather than to collect data on such matters as average speed of solution, number of trials to criterion, differences between sexes etc. Such questions are of interest but only in relative terms and to the extent to which they illustrate general principles. The Gestalt psychologists would probably have been sympathetic to the point of view adopted by Bolton in Chapter 10 – that individual pieces of factual research will not simply summate to produce an understanding of the essence of thinking.

Second, their belief in the commonality of the principles governing all processes, and the ease with which visual perception lends itself to the demonstration of such principles, gives a distinctly perceptual flavour to much of the Gestalt analysis of thinking. Problems are perceived, elements reorganized, the reorganization being governed by the same laws as are found in perception: laws such as closure and similarity. Many of their experiments have a distinctive quality and bear the unmistakable Gestalt trademarks. Although a lot of them are by now well known, having been widely discussed, since we are particularly interested in the relationship between their theory and their methods it will be useful to review them briefly once again concentrating on how they went about their task rather than on what they found.

Köhler's experiments

Köhler was director of an animal research station on the island of Tenerife set up by the Prussian Academy of Sciences when he carried out a series of experiments on chimpanzees designed to counteract the trial and error based account of problem-solving in animals epitomized by the earlier work of Thorndike. A small group of chimpanzees was presented with a series of sixteen problems, graded in difficulty from simple to complex, in which fruit was presented in a position where it was not always directly accessible. An important procedural aspect was that the problem field could be surveyed as a whole. In order to reach the food the animals had to stack boxes, fit sticks together etc., solutions which, according to Köhler, required perceptual reorganization of the elements in the perceptual field. For example, a stick lying on the ground had to be seen as connected with the fruit in order for it to be used as a rake. Animals (and children on whom Köhler later carried out a number of similar experiments) were considered eminently suitable as subjects since, unlike adult subjects, they would lack ready-made methods for solving the problems. Thus with animals it should be easier to study the processes of restructuring in a 'pure' form less contaminated by previous experience. The chimpanzees eventually solved all but one of the problems. The important point however is the manner in which they solved them. After an initial period during which unsuccessful attempts were made to reach the fruit (this initial period varied in length and occasionally was absent) the animal would cease activity and remain relatively quiescent for a time. Then it would produce the solution without further experimentation in a smooth and purposeful manner. Köhler proposed that during the period of quiescence restructuring was taking place, leading to insight as to the correct solution (this account is discussed in more detail later in this chapter).

Köhler's description (1925) of his subjects' performance illustrates some important points about the Gestalt approach. Qualitative aspects are regarded as most informative. The animals' behaviour is allowed to speak for itself. Köhler's interpretations are supported by appeals to simple observations which, it is implied, will confirm what, to him, was almost self-evident. Since the aim was to *understand* what the animal is doing, Köhler argued one should try always to relate its behaviour to the solution of the problem. The emphasis on a molar description is brought out well in Köhler's insistence that isolated aspects of behaviour should not be divorced from the context of the problem as a whole, for in doing so one risks concluding that the animal is not behaving intelligently. (For example, the detour element, built into many of the problems often required that the animal initially pushed the food further away from itself in order to manoeuvre it into a more accessible position.) Köhler would almost certainly have argued that it is just as harmful to risk denying 'higher-order' processes to animals where they might actually exist as it is to infer them when alternative explanations might be possible. This attitude undoubtedly helps to give the whole description a rather anthropomorphic quality.

Wertheimer's experiments
Köhler carried out the pioneering work on problem solving but subsequently he became more interested in perceptual processes and memory, as did Koffka. It was Wertheimer who eventually applied the Gestalt procedures to problem solving in human subjects, and whose experiments have by now probably become as famous as Köhler's. Wertheimer's monograph *Productive Thinking* (1945), contains discussion of a wide variety of problems and anecdotal examples, including the discoveries of Einstein and Galileo, and brings out the eclectic quality of the Gestalt approach. Wertheimer was an inventive practitioner who possessed an apparently unlimited supply of anecdotes. However, his best known studies were conducted with children. The choice of children as subjects reflected not only the Gestalt preference for relatively naive subjects but was prompted by the belief held by the Gestalt group that their ideas had great significance for educational methods. Wertheimer, in particular, ridiculed teaching methods which relied on blind, mechanical, drill-like procedures and encouraged mere

repetition rather than a grasp of structural relationships. In one of his experiments children were asked to find the areas of various figures, beginning with a simple rectangle. After the rectangles came a parallelogram, followed by other parallelograms in unusual orientations. Finally a number of irregular shapes was presented, some having been formed by removing, say, a triangular portion from one side of a rectangle and tacking it on to the other, others being assymetrical shapes whose areas could not be calculated using the basic method. At each stage the aim was to see exactly what had been learned by working through the preceding examples. It was found that many children both failed to recognize that particular shapes were simple transformations of more basic ones and also frequently applied a previously learned rule blindly to cases where it did not fit. Thus a grasp of the problem's structure – the essence of the 'genuine solution' – cannot be taught by mere repeated exposure to a series of stereotyped problems, nor adequately tested unless a number of unfamiliar problem figures is also used.

Wertheimer's method had a Piagetian quality. The aim was to 'diagnose' what sort of understanding lies behind behaviour, so individual subjects were questioned in depth about the reasons for their answers. The limits of understanding were examined by presenting critical test stimuli, the procedures being varied to suit individual needs. When they got stuck the children were given clues as to what they might consider next. Throughout, the emphasis was overwhelmingly on qualitative aspects of behaviour. Looking at the various figures used one can appreciate the close relationship between perceptual factors and the process of solution – it is often a sort of visual 'twist' which is required. For example, a parallelogram can be seen to be the same sort of shape as a rectangle if a right-angled triangle is cut from one end and fitted on to the other. There are also points of comparison with Köhler's studies: the problems were presented as a series beginning with the most straightforward, and some of the children were casually presented with scissors to see if they would think of rearranging the shapes by cutting them to form a rectangle from a parallelogram. This brings to mind the tool-using aspect of Köhler's experiments.

Experiments of Duncker, Maier and Luchins
Some of the features which distinguish Wertheimer's approach to problem solving are also to be found in other experimental work

inspired by Gestalt ideas. In Duncker's experiments for example (1945, English translation) subjects were required to find solutions to realistic problems such as that of discovering (hypothetically) how to use X-rays to destroy an inoperable stomach tumour without damaging the surrounding healthy tissue. The subjects, this time adults, were asked to think aloud and the data consisted mainly of edited verbal protocols designed to illustrate the gradual progress of the subjects towards insight. The parallels with Wertheimer are fairly close – the subjects were given hints and helped along by sympathetic prompting; they were not allowed to spend too long exploring unprofitable leads. The main difference is that Duncker was perhaps more concerned than Wertheimer to provide a detailed stage-by-stage analysis of the actual process of 'reorganization' (see Chapter 8 for an information-processing view of Duncker's work).

Many of these elements are also to be found in the work of Maier (e.g. 1931; see also Maier, 1970) and Luchins (e.g. 1942; see also Luchins and Luchins, 1970). Maier, whose early experiments stemmed from Gestalt principles, although he was not actually satisfied with their theoretical account, used practical problem solving situations. Subjects, working in groups, were asked to construct rather curious contraptions using various props such as clamps and lengths of wood, in order to fulfil some specified function; for example to make two pendulums, with chalk attached, which would mark two particular places on the floor. Subjects were often asked to give more than one solution. Talking aloud was encouraged and prompting was used. In fact Maier was especially interested in the role of hints in problem solving. One factor investigated was whether having learned part of the solution in advance made any difference; for example, subjects were shown how to construct a plumb-line, or how to clamp two sticks together so as to make one long one. It was found that generally such experience did not help unless the subjects were also given some sort of hint which set their thought processes in the right direction. This process is still not well understood. There is a greater emphasis on quantification in this work, data being expressed, for example, in terms of percentages of solutions. Control groups were also used.

Quantitative methods were also adopted in Luchins' famous experiments on 'Einstellung' effects (a term used by the Würzburg psychologists). The basic format of these studies is that by solving a series of related problems involving volume, subjects are tricked into using a more elaborate formula than necessary for solving one or more critical test problems placed at the end of the series. The procedure clearly lends itself to more systematic investigation of independent variables such as the type and number of problems in the series etc. In the Luchins' experiments use is still made of verbal reports but these have more of an auxiliary status and are commonly taken from post-experimental interviews.

From this brief discussion it can be seen that the Gestalt psychologists brought a particular set of methods to the study of thought processes. Rather than being guided by theory, their research was often triggered by an apparently simple, practical problem or everyday observation which, in line with their phenomenological orientation, was considered as far as possible on its own merits without methodological or theoretical preconceptions. Highly detailed studies were carried out using those methods which were suggested by and considered appropriate to the phenomenon itself – hence the eclectic quality of their approach. The Gestaltists were largely unsystematic, they proceeded by example and anecdote, relied often on a qualitative, selective analysis, avoided jargon (in the main) and were reluctant to talk in terms of rigid laws of behaviour. However, from the chimpanzee experiments of Köhler to the (continuing) series of Einstellung experiments (see e.g. Luchins and Luchins, 1969) there has been a shift of interest in Gestalt research on thinking as their ideas have been modified by and absorbed into other psychological traditions. This has been accompanied by inevitable changes in the techniques used and the way in which observations are collected and presented. There is a close relationship between the theory, the research issues it generated and the experimental methods adopted to tackle them. We have looked briefly at the methods of the Gestalt group and at some of the research they carried out. Now it is important to examine in more detail the theoretical account of problem solving that the Gestalt psychologists actually proposed.

Structure

'Structure' occupies a central position in the Gestalt theory of thinking. Wertheimer is reported to have said that in order to understand thinking, psychologists might need to develop new mathematical, logical and psychological methods for dealing with structures. To solve a problem we need to appreciate its structure, since the solution will be determined by the inner requirements of the problem. As we have seen, according to the Gestalt view a problem exists when it is recognized that the various elements contained in the perceptual field are not arranged in a balanced, harmonious, or perhaps the simplest relationship to one another (Law of Prägnanz). The dynamic interplay of forces within the problem space is accompanied by structural stresses and strains which must be resolved so as to achieve equilibrium. We experience 'insight' and things fall into place when we reorganize or restructure the perceptual field according to the vectors which are present, thereby eliminating the tensions and creating a new and balanced organization of the parts. Thus in 'genuine' solutions there is a natural continuity between the problem and its solution, the latter being directed by the structural features of the former. Another important feature of genuine solutions is that they are transposable to problems which share the same structure. For example, in the parallelogram problem described by Wertheimer, the 'best' solution to the problem is the formula which fits all possible examples – length of base × perpendicular height. Other solutions are sometimes possible (e.g. where the area is, by chance, equal to the sum of the two sides) and may fit a limited number of cases but they are essentially structure blind and do not entail real understanding. The genuine solution fits the problem as a key fits the lock.

Insight

The concept of insight has been the subject of a great deal of controversy. It is defined by Köhler (1929) as 'our experience of definite determination in a context, an event or development of the total field'. The experience is usually subjectively compelling, but it has proved extremely difficult to set up the sort of criteria which one might use in studying problem solving experimentally. To begin with there is the danger of circularity if structural requiredness is taken as the defining characteristic of insightful solutions and, at the same time, is the only evidence offered for such solutions. One of the most widely held beliefs about insight is that it always occurs rapidly. In the *Mentality of Apes* (1925) Köhler certainly describes insightful solutions as occurring 'suddenly' but in the reconstructions of Wertheimer's seminars published by Luchins and Luchins (1970), Wertheimer seems anxious to refute this oversimplified view. It is proposed that insightful learning may sometimes be slower than learning by other methods. Perhaps we should avoid confusing behaviour and experience. The experience of which Köhler speaks may be characteristically 'sudden' yet there may also be a relatively extended period of behaviour leading up to the actual moment of 'illumination' during which behaviour possesses the dynamic, integrated qualities which Köhler also considered important (cf. Duncker, 1945).

In the *Mentality of Apes* Köhler also proposes continuity and smoothness as the behavioural criteria for insight and stresses that the solution should appear in a complete form often after a period of 'perplexity or quiet'. We can appreciate the relationship between these criteria and the original theory but it is difficult to see how such qualitative features might be harnessed for the purposes of experimentation. Several writers, notably Berlyne (1965), have also objected to the idea that such qualities of behaviour are necessarily indications of 'insight' at all. For example, the relative quiescence of the animal before it solves the problem may be a special case of *reactive inhibition* (a Hullian concept referring to the tendency not to repeat a response that has just been made; a sort of internal fatigue effect) brought about by lack of success. Köhler was very concerned, as were all the Gestalt psychologists, to contrast trial and error with insightful solutions. They did not deny that problems might be solved by trial and error but argued that genuine solutions did not possess these features. Thus by using problems in which it was extremely unlikely for chance solutions to occur, since such a long sequence of responses was required, Köhler hoped to provide evidence for an alternative account of problem solving to that proposed earlier by Thorndike (1898). From the viewpoint of a more advanced stimulus-response framework than Thorndike's, however, Berlyne argues that the alternative to insight is not, as Köhler supposes, simply random trial and error behaviour. He makes the point that the animal's reaction to the problem will reflect its learning history. There is no reason, in principle, why continuity and smoothness of behaviour should not be consistent with prior reinforcement processes. There is no need to postulate mechanisms such as insight. If it turns out that in complex problem situations the animal responds to 'structural relationships', we can say that the animal responds to configurations of stimuli rather than individual ones. According to Berlyne, therefore, alternative stimulus-response analyses of problem solving are possible. (Wetherick, however, in Chapter 3, argues that such attempts will always be ultimately doomed to failure except in very limited circumstances.)

Factors affecting insight

These difficulties aside, however, a loosely connected set of principles based on this general approach advocated by the Gestalt psychologists began to emerge during the 1930s and 1940s as a guiding influence in research. Yet 'insight' remains an intractable concept and even though the focus of interest has tended to shift away from the essentially mentalistic formula proposed by Köhler, we are still a long way from answering some of the basic questions about it.

In Köhler's experiments with chimpanzees we are told that there are three different kinds of change in the phenomenal field which may occur: first, unification, as when two short sticks are combined into one long one; second, analysis, which occurs, for example, when a branch is broken from a tree to be used as a tool; third, articulation, involving the recognition, say, that a rope must be uncoiled as part of the solution. Apart from the difficulty of deciding how far these are actually overlapping processes, we know very little about the factors which determine these forms of restructuring and do not know, either, how to recognize them when they occur. Köhler puts forward some very general suggestions. For example, the chimpanzee will be more likely to use the stick if it is placed near the bars. This could mean that the tensions within the perceptual field may reach critical threshold levels when particular spatial arrangements of the materials are present. Köhler also noted that, in the box-stacking problem, the box was less often used if it stood in the corner of the room (or if another animal was lying on it!). This is highly reminiscent of the 'functional fixation' effect eventually to be studied at great length by Maier, Duncker and others who carried out much of the early research on the role of 'directional' factors in problem solving (see Scheerer, 1963). In general terms the effect is that an object embedded in a particular context or having a conventional fairly clear-cut function will not be used readily by subjects for solving a problem in which the object must play a different role. Personal experience probably contains many anecdotal examples. Scheerer found that more than half of a group of subjects requiring a piece of string did not make use of the only available piece, which was holding up a calendar on the wall. In 'control' conditions almost all subjects took down the string when it was just hanging alone on the nail or when it was holding up a calendar which was out of date. Such effects seem closely related to the *Einstellung* effects of Luchins and are often referred to as instances of 'negative set'.

Such experiments, like the earlier ones of Maier, are rather loosely defined, for example lacking control of independent variables, and often seem to create more questions than they answer. This is probably one of the reasons why psychologists are increasingly studying problems which are less realistic but which have more readily identifiable logical and linguistic structures (see Chapter 5). Nevertheless there are one or two potentially important implications about how insight occurs. In Gestalt theory terms, what seems to be necessary for reorganization in problem solving is that, to begin with, the existing 'unbalanced' representation of the problem actually needs to be disrupted. There is a vast literature devoted to the 'strategies' which it is claimed can help the process along. We do not have sufficient space to discuss these methods here but most of them seem to operate by oiling the associative machinery so that the flow of ideas is improved. One relevant example may be taken from Adams (1974). Subjects were required to list possible functions of various simple objects (as in Guilford's *Uses for Objects* tests). A higher level of originality was found (although no firm data are supplied) when subjects were asked to set aside the names of the objects and to concentrate instead on the objects' properties, i.e. rather than responding to, say, a brick, the subject thinks of hardness, porosity, conductivity, heaviness etc. What is happening in experiments like this is anybody's guess but, arguably, the Gestalt theory provides as good an account as any of the likely processes. Perhaps 'disequilibrium' is actually self-induced by deliberately breaking up the organized *Gestalts* of familiar stimuli. Restructuring processes also seem to be the basis of other creative problem solving techniques such as are described in *Synectics* (Gordon, 1961). Wertheimer himself apparently did not approve of such techniques (Luchins and Luchins, 1970). One reason for this is probably that they smack suspiciously of associationist mechanisms. Another is that the whole focus of the Gestalt theory of problem solving is on the structural representation of the problem. Undirected fluency and originality would not necessarily bring any light to bear on this.

Past experience

The mechanisms surrounding insight therefore remain obscure. We have quite a lot of evidence on various factors which tend to inhibit the emergence of successful solutions by producing fixations of one sort or another. But it has not been possible so far to integrate this knowledge in a workable hypothesis about the processes involved in restructuring. However, we cannot leave the matter without discussing another major issue concerning insight in the Gestalt theory. This is the role played by the past experience of the subject in the restructuring of the problem field. That so much attention was devoted by Gestalt psychologists to 'Einstellung' effects of different types (Luchins and Luchins, 1970) should be sufficient evidence to refute the familiar jibe that Gestalt psychology 'ignores the role of previous experience'. The Gestalists certainly rejected the idea that previous experience 'explained' problem solving. Other (situational) factors are also at least as important and, anyway, we also need to know *how* previous experience is used, not simply whether it is or not. Birch (1945) found that the solution by chimpanzees of stick problems of the type used by Köhler was directly related to the opportunity the animals had to play with the sticks beforehand. This experiment does not 'disprove' the Gestalt theory, though it may pose some problems; nor does it indicate, as is sometimes thought, that the animals necessarily solved the problems by some fortuitous trial and error process. Moreover, Köhler seemed conscious of the animals' past experience when he described some errors as 'good errors'. Essentially these are near misses or, '. . . the after effects of former genuine solutions' appearing ' . . . secondarily in later experiments without much consideration for the special situation'. Nevertheless, a persistent criticism of the Gestalt theory has been that, on balance, it underestimates the influence of the individual's past experience in thinking since the theory undoubtedly places greatest emphasis on current perception (in the widest sense) in the determination of thinking. The motivational conditions and the directional forces involved in restructuring are held to be the direct product of psycho-neural processes operating at the level of perceptual awareness.

Bolton (1972) comments that in this analysis the thinker still appears to remain remarkably passive, a mere bystander to whom the end product of thinking is presented. It is as if the total structured configuration of the problem is seen as a *sufficient* condition for the problem's solution. This is a valid criticism but it seems unlikely that the Gestalt psychologists intended this literal interpretation. For one thing it would imply that all problems should automatically be solved! Of all the Gestalt theorists, Wertheimer was probably the most conscious of this issue. The role of forces that do not enter immediately into the dynamics of the problem itself, i.e. 'the totality of conditions that affect the problem solving process', is a constantly recurring theme in the edited Wertheimer seminars (Luchins and Luchins, 1970). Here it is stressed that the perception of a problem's structural requirements is not inevitable but is influenced by the attitudes, assumptions and motivations of the subject. The difficulty, as Bolton (1972) also suggests, is that the Gestalt theorists were not explicit about what the various factors were and how they interacted with the inner dynamic field conditions during thinking. One of the most important propositions made by the theory is that the structural configuration of the problem-as-represented contains, in principle, all the information that is necessary to solve it. There are no 'extra' factors of the type envisaged by earlier accounts of thinking such as were proposed by the Würzburg theorists. If, as Wertheimer seems to imply, additional selection processes, governed by factors outside the problem, are also at work during thinking, then we need a more complete account of what such factors are and how they operate. The Gestalt psychologists did not give it but they were not necessarily unaware of the basic need to do so.

The contribution of Gestalt psychology

One is not really assessing a living movement in considering the Gestalt school's contribution to the study of thinking. Boring (1950) points out that movements in psychology can die of success and actually puts the Gestaltists in this category on the grounds that the old enemy of Gestalt psychology, Wundtian analysis of experience into sensory elements, had disappeared by the 1920s and, with it, the *raison d'être* of the movement. Perhaps it would be better to say not so much that they succeeded but that they were superseded. The intellectual climate of the period from around 1930 to 1950 was largely against phenomenological psychology and in favour of the experimental psychology of behaviour not experience. The Gestalt principles were not expressed in sufficiently precise a form to suggest an obvious programme of experimental research, the usual way of keeping a movement alive. The important research that they had contributed was easily absorbed into the main stream of psychology; and the system of beliefs that had produced it was largely ignored.

Perhaps the Gestaltists' greatest contribution has been their cautionary role. Köhler (1959) said:

In American psychology it is rightly regarded as a virtue if a man feels great respect for method and for caution. But, if this virtue becomes too strong, it may bring forth a spirit of skepticism and thus prevent new work . . . not in all parts of psychology can evidence be immediately clear . . . we may be forced to form new concepts which, at first, will often be a bit vague. Most experimentalists, therefore, refrain from observing . . . the phenomenal scene. Yet this is the scene on which . . . the drama of ordinary human living is being played all the time.

The current dissatisfaction being expressed by some of both trainee and established psychologists at the apparent aridity of much present day psychology, and the reawakening in recent years of interest in 'cognitive psychology' – the aspects of behaviour the Gestaltists were most concerned with – may reflect a recognition of the very points they were trying to make. Of course, it is impossible to trace a direct influence; but the fact that a few isolated workers continue to adhere to the Gestalt viewpoint and that textbooks on a variety of subjects (including this one!) have nearly always found it obligatory to provide a section on Gestalt psychology, suggests that their ideas may not be entirely dead, but survive to provide a necessary counterbalance not just to the original enemy, but to the continuing 'threats' of behaviourism and excessive methodology.

Certainly the Gestaltists were no slaves to methodology. Their approach was catholic. They were not against experimentation or quantification – Wertheimer's work on the phi-phenomenon, the attributed starting point of the movement, was a well-controlled experiment into the conditions necessary to produce optimal movement; but they gave equal weight to qualitative data especially in the studies of thinking. Qualitative aspects of performance continue to play an important role in current research on reasoning (see Chapter 5, and also Wason and Johnson-Laird, 1972). The Gestalt psychologists also relied on demonstrations and appeals to reason, not surprisingly since they claimed to be dealing with experiences which are common to all and available to all. The various articles and books in which their views and observations were recorded are in the form more of rational essays than the research reports to which many of us are accustomed. However, while this catholicism in methodology may have led to some imprecision, it yielded a wealth of suggestions and revealed phenomena that are now widely recognized.

We have suggested that the Gestalt tradition no longer survives in an active form; however, it is possible to identify several parallels between their ideas and more recent developments. Piaget's theoretical system is clearly in the structuralist tradition; there are interesting similarities between the Law of Prägnanz and Piaget's concept of equilibration. Equally the Law of Prägnanz can be seen to be paralleled in balance theories and cognitive dissonance; and also to foreshadow the limited capacity concept of information processing theory. Indeed the Law of Prägnanz could be viewed as an early homeostatic model.

Lewin (1951), who has applied field theory to a system of personality and social behaviour, obviously drew much inspiration from the Gestaltists; and though the current status of his theory is uncertain it has produced a significant research tradition in social psychology. Fritz Perls's (1965) Gestalt therapy might also be mentioned, though whether Wertheimer would actually recognize many of his doctrines in it is debatable! And restructuring perhaps provides a simple description of the processes operating in such techniques variously called brain-storming, block busting and synectics.

However, the Gestaltists must be assessed not just for what they achieved but for what they hoped to achieve, assessed, that is, in principle as well as in practice. As Humphrey (1951) says, one is being presented with a programme rather than its fulfilment. We have tried to indicate how helpful some of their principles may still be today, even though they may create more problems than they solve. Indeed the problems they tried to deal with still remain largely unsolved. One must admire the courage of Wertheimer in tackling subjects such as thinking at a time when there was little intellectual sympathy. Carini (1970) has likened Wertheimer's contribution to psychology to that of Copernicus' to astronomy – both reversed the prevailing way of looking at their subject matter, thus revealing new and productive perspectives.

In practice the Gestalt achievements were less satisfactory. Many of their theoretical constructs were vaguely stated. We have already discussed, for example, the difficulties of assessing the exact status of *insight*. The Laws of Organization by which structures are formed were presented only in qualitative terms, no guidance being given to their relative strengths or possible interactions. The role of language was largely neglected. On the positive side however they have contributed some important constructs and some useful terminology for the study of thinking. The recognition of the continuity of psychological processes and the stress on intelligence rather than rote behaviour, on the structure behind mental processes and the functional relations between them, reflect an approach that is now widely incorporated in cognitive psychology. Terms such as 'insight' and 'functional fixity', though poorly defined, have become part of familiar psychological terminology and a convenient shorthand for describing complex behaviour. One should mention, too, Wertheimer's concern with education: though his work may not have produced a revolution in teaching, the value of insightful as opposed to rote learning is by now commonly acknowledged. It is characteristic of the Gestalt psychologists that they never forgot they were studying *people*.

Psychology would have been, and certainly would still be, able to survive without Gestalt theory. But psychology would lose a rich source of insights, and a commonsense orientation that may be vital for its future success. They gave and can continue to give us pause for thought. A. S. Luchins' recollections (Luchins and Luchins, 1970) of Wertheimer at the State University of New York include the following: 'After class some students were seated in the cafeteria hoping that Wertheimer would walk in.'

If nothing else, it would be nice to think that students could say at least this about psychologists.

References

Adams, J. L. (1974) *Conceptual Blockbusting: a Guide to Better Ideas*. San Francisco: Freeman.
Berlyne, D. E. (1965) *Structure and Direction in Thinking*. New York: Wiley.
Birch, H. G. (1945) The relation of previous experience to insightful problem-solving. *J. Comparative Psychology 38*: 367–83.
Bolton, N. (1972) *The Psychology of Thinking*. London: Methuen.
Boring, E. G. (1950) *A History of Experimental Psychology* (2nd ed.). New York: Appleton-Century-Crofts.
Carini, L. (1970) A reassessment of Max Wertheimer's contribution to psychological theory. *Acta Psychologica 32*: 377–85.
Duncker, K. (1945) On problem solving. *Psychological Monographs 58*: No. 5 (Whole No. 270).
Gordon, W. J. (1961) *Synectics: The Development of Creative Capacity*. New York: Harper and Row.
Humphrey, G. (1951) *Thinking: an Introduction to its Experimental Psychology*. London: Methuen.
Köhler, W. (1925) *The Mentality of Apes*. New York: Harcourt, Brace.
Köhler, W. (1929) *Gestalt Psychology*. New York: Liveright.

Köhler, W. (1942) *Dynamics in Psychology*. London: Faber and Faber.
Köhler, W. (1959) Gestalt psychology today. *American Psychologist 14*: 727–34.
Lewin, K. (1951) *Field Theory in Social Science*. New York: Harper.
Luchins, A. S. (1942) Mechanization in problem solving: the effect of Einstellung. *Psychological Monographs 54* (Whole No. 248).
Luchins, A. S. and Luchins, E. H. (1969) Einstellung effect and group problem solving. *Journal of Social Psychology 77*: 79–89.
Luchins, A. S. and Luchins, E. H. (1970) *Wertheimer's Seminars Revisited*. 3 volumes. Albany, New York: Faculty-Student Association, State University of New York at Albany, Inc.
Mach, E. (1886) *Die Analyse der Empfindungen und das Verhältnis des Psychischen Zum Physischen*. (Eng. trans. 1897 and 1914).
Maier, N. R. F. (1931). Reasoning in humans: 2. The solution of a problem and its appearance in consciousness. *Journal of Comparative Psychology 12*: 181–94.
Maier, N. R. F. (1970) *Problem Solving and Creativity in Individuals and Groups*. Belmont, California: Brooks/Cole.
Perls, F. S. et al. (1965) *Gestalt Therapy* New York. Dell.
Rubin, E. (1921) *Visuell wahrgenommene Figuren*. Copenhagen: Gyldendalska.
Scheerer, M. (1963) Problem solving. *Scientific American 208*: 118–28.
Thorndike, E. L. (1898) *Animal Intelligence*. New York: Macmillan.
Von Ehrenfels, C. (1890) Über Gestaltqualitäten. *Vtljsch. wiss. Philos. 14*: 249–92.
Wason, P. C. and Johnson-Laird, P. N. (1972) *The Psychology of Reasoning: Structure and Content*. London: Batsford.
Wertheimer, M. (1912) Experimentelle Studien über das Sehen von Bewegungen. *Zeitschrift Psychologie 61*: 161–265.
Wertheimer, M. (1945) *Productive Thinking*. New York: Harper and Row.

3 How the sins of the fathers were visited on the children: Behaviourism

N. E. Wetherick

The origins of behaviourism

The emergence of behaviourism as a force in psychology may be dated precisely. In a paper entitled 'Psychology as the behaviourist views it' Watson (1913) called for a radical change of emphasis in the subject. He did so from the point of view of a behaviourist because that is what he then was; a specialist in animal behaviour concerned principally with sensory capacity as determined by experiments using discrimination box methods. His analysis of the situation then prevailing in psychology suggested that a dead-end had been reached. The standard investigatory procedure involved introspective analyses to isolate 'mental structures', followed by the development of psychological theories based on the results of the analyses. Disputes had however largely degenerated into mutual accusations of lack of skill or persistence in introspection. Psychologists practising the introspective method were exclusively concerned with problems of consciousness, and it irked Watson particularly that they regarded work with animals as interesting only as a basis for speculation on how far different species of animals possessed consciousness analogous to that of human beings.

The problem of consciousness was at the time central, in philosophy as well as in psychology. Watson would certainly have encountered it during his initial training (in philosophy). He subscribed to the then widely held motor theory of consciousness which maintained that for a state of consciousness to come into existence a complete arc had to be established between a stimulus and a response. If no system of effectors was available to respond to it, then an impinging stimulus simply did not come into consciousness. Watson, however, held additionally that 'in a system of psychology completely worked out, given the response, the stimuli can be predicted; given the stimuli, the response can be predicted' (p. 167). Consciousness in effect merely ran parallel to what the organism was actually doing, which was responding to stimuli. Responses were essential though they could be either explicit or implicit; in the latter case they involved sub-threshold movements, usually of the speech organs. Watson was prepared at this time to assert that the laryngeal mechanisms were essential to thought!

In view of his known philosophical sophistication and his research background in animal behaviour it appears reasonable to suppose that Watson was advocating the adoption of a thoroughly mechanistic account of human and animal nature and of a theory of consciousness consistent with mechanism. He would not have claimed this approach as original to himself. He was merely trying to bring psychology into line with what was, in his view, the most satisfactory philosophical teaching of the day. Against psychology as it was then practised was the absence of applicable results and the likely impossibility of reaching any agreed theoretical positions on the basis of individual introspection. In favour of behaviouristic psychology was the likelihood of applicable results and the existence of objective methods developed for use with animals. Nothing had been said as yet of the conditioned response. Pavlov's work was then little known outside Russia. Lashley had however recently joined Watson's laboratory and he had interests in human salivary and motor conditioning.

Koch (1964, pp. 8–9) reports Lashley as having told him in conversation that, after publishing his 1913 paper, Watson spent much time trying to obtain photographic records of implicit speech movements (which for him constituted thought) but without success. His intention was to present his results in a presidential address to the American Psychological Association in December, 1915. (Koch wrongly gives the date as 1916.) Since no results were forthcoming

Watson wrote up Lashley's work on conditioning and presented that, with acknowledgements to Lashley (Watson, 1916). It appears however from Lashley (1916) that they disagreed on the significance of Lashley's work. Watson emphasized motor (as against salivary) conditioning, and its value as a more efficient substitute for the discrimination box in the study of human and animal sensory capacity. Lashley however considered salivary conditioning as of greater significance mainly because he was not satisfied that genuine motor conditioning could be distinguished from voluntary responding. Salivary responding was definitely not under voluntary control and he regarded the classical conditioning of this response as a pure paradigm case of associative learning in which all the factors involved could be independently varied. Conditioning theory subsequently figured mainly in studies of learning, not in studies of sensory capacity, and indeed played so central a role in learning theory that it seems reasonable to bracket Lashley with Watson as joint founding fathers of behaviourism. Lashley however soon returned to his first love, experimental neurophysiology, and Watson, though he lived on till 1958, was obliged to withdraw from academic life in 1920 as a result of an action for divorce.

Theoretical developments in relation to thinking

Tolman (1922) testifies that 'the idea of behaviourism is abroad . . . its lingo, if not its substance, is spreading like wildfire'. In that paper Tolman was concerned to establish the possibility of a behaviourism that was not mere physiology. In a retrospective review of his work (Tolman, 1959) he writes 'what I wanted was a behaviorist psychology which would be able to deal with real organisms, in terms of their inner psychological dynamics'. He rejected the extreme peripheralism of Watson, later taken up by Hull and then by Skinner.

Hull became interested in learning theory in the late 1920s and controversies arising between him and Tolman dominated the literature for the next twenty years. Both were concerned with what Rozeboom (1970) calls 'experience residues' – hypothetical states of the organism by which past experience is enabled to influence present responding. For Hull these residues were 'habits'. When the stimulus S evoked a response R, the response might be unconditioned but it might also be a habit-consequence of the reinforcement history of the organism. For Tolman the residues were 'expectancies'. The organism entertained an expectation that performance of response R to stimulus S_1 would be followed by S_2, perhaps a rewarding stimulus. In Tolman's formulation there is something 'in the mind' of the organism which determines its behaviour. In Hull's formulation there is nothing 'in the mind', there are merely S–R links which are however modifiable by selective reinforcement. Tolman had little to say about thinking but clearly thinking, as a process going on 'in the mind', is compatible with his general outlook and incompatible with that of Hull. Hull accepted from the beginning that he was under an obligation to offer an account of the higher mental processes in his own terms i.e. as fully determined interactions between the internal concomitants of stimuli and reponses which resulted in observable responses – responses which would ordinarily have been accounted for by reference to 'higher mental processes' intervening between stimulus and response and involving initiation of the response by the organism. Hull (1930) is a typical early statement of this view, in which he offers an account of 'knowledge' and 'purpose' as habit mechanisms. Imagine a sequence of states of the world ($S_1, S_2, S_3 \ldots$) in which each S evokes an R ($R_1, R_2, R_3 \ldots$) in an organism. Feedback from each successive R will provide the organism with a sequence of internal stimuli $s_1, s_2, s_3 \ldots$ each of which will become linked with the next R in the series. Thus the organism may learn to get from S_1 to R_2 via s_1 (feedback from R_1) without actually experiencing S_2 at all. Intermediate R's (e.g. R_1) may moreover become 'vestigial' (symbolized as $r_1, r_2, r_3 \ldots$); they may be 'pure stimulus acts' – responses which have no function as responses except to provide stimuli for the next response in the sequence, which may of course be another 'pure stimulus act'. In this way, Hull maintained, an organism could acquire habit-mechanisms which enabled it to respond to the 'not-here' and the 'not-now', corresponding to the popular notions of knowledge and purpose. Hull (1935) offered an account in similar terms of 'the assembly of behaviour segments in novel combinations suitable for problem solution' which explained the appearance of insight in problem solving (as distinct from trial-and-error learning). Spence (1936) tackled a related problem arising in animal discrimination studies. Lashley had drawn attention to the fact that, prior to mastering a discrimination, the animal characteristically behaves as if it were testing hypotheses, e.g. that the positive stimulus is 'always on the right' or 'alternately right and left' or 'dark rather than light'. Krechevsky (e.g. 1935) had conducted a series of investigations of this phenomenon. Spence's reply was to show how such behaviour can be accounted for strictly in terms of habit-mechanisms.

Hull presented two versions of a behaviour system (1943, 1952), the second incorporating modifications to allow for latent learning. (Rats who have explored a maze containing no food show that they have learned a great deal about it by mastering it very quickly once food is made available in it. They show 'latent' learning which was not allowed for in the 1943 system.) The development of the system to account more fully for higher thought processes in human subjects was continued by Maltzman (1955) who took over Hull's concept of the *habit family hierarchy*. Hull had introduced this concept to account for the organism's capacity e.g. to approach a goal from different spatial positions; by climbing, jumping, running etc. The stimulus evoked not one but a hierarchy of responses and if the most dominant response was ruled out by circumstances the next most dominant would take its place and so on. Maltzman adapted the concept to cover a temporal rather than spatial hierarchy. The dominant response was not ruled out by circumstances, it was simply extinguished because it did not lead to the goal; a less dominant response took its place and so on until a response occurred which did lead to the goal. This response then became dominant in the hierarchy as a consequence of reinforcement.

The notion of the habit family hierarchy gives Hull's behaviour system significant extra flexibility. Infinitely more flexibility follows, however, from the developments proposed by Berlyne (1965). He proposed to symbolize r_1, s_1 (that is the vestigial response, including its function as a feedback stimulus) by u_1, 'a situational thought'. He then distinguished directed from autistic (non-directed) thinking by supposing that 'transformational thoughts' (symbolized by ϕ_1, ϕ_2, ϕ_3 ...) are interposed between u's in the former but not in the latter. A transformational thought constitutes a 'legitimate step'. In a logical or mathematical argument a legitimate step is a step which obeys the rules of inference of the system. In science it is a step from one situation to another which succeeds it in accordance with the laws of science. In a game it is a step consistent with the rules of the game. Berlyne makes a good case for supposing that all varieties of thinking can be encompassed by Hull's system (as refined by Maltzman and himself) without violating Hull's original premise, that is his insistence on the need to 'maintain a thoroughly naturalistic attitude towards the more complex forms of human behaviour' (Hull, 1930).

Criticisms of the theory

Criticism of Hull's theory has almost always been presented in the form of sets of observations of behaviour which the theory could not account for (we have looked briefly at 'hypotheses' in rats and at 'latent' learning). The Hullian defence was always to show how the theory could account for observations without self-destructive modification. It seems clear that the system as elaborated by Berlyne is proof against this type of criticism. The logician Turing showed that arguments of the form 'you will never get a machine to do ...' are bound to fail, because specification of what it is that you will never get a machine to do amounts to a design for a machine to do it! I suspect that this applies also to Hullian behaviour theory. It is not however an argument in favour of the theory. In retrospect, any sequence of behavioural events can be cast in the form of a sequence of R's evoked by specified S's in accordance with specifiable laws linking S's and R's. (See, for example, Child and Waterhouse's (1952) reworking of Barker, Dembo and Lewin's (1943) data on frustration and aggression in children.) Some versions of behaviourist theory (e.g. Dollard and Miller, 1950) appear to recognize that this can only be done in retrospect by defining a stimulus as anything that evokes a response and a response as anything evoked by a stimulus. It is by no means a pointless exercise to develop a technical language which is internally coherent and in which all forms of behaviour can, in retrospect, be aptly and adequately characterized. However, behaviour theorists have usually seen themselves as doing more than this, as developing a theory in which 'given the response the stimuli can be predicted, given the stimuli the response can be predicted'. The degree of stimulus control over behaviour implied by this ambition can easily be simulated in the laboratory. This can be done with animal subjects by impoverishing the experimental environment so that there is literally nothing to engage the attention except what has been designated as the stimulus by the experimenter. With human subjects a similar effect can be achieved by asking the subject to attend only to the stimulus aspects of the situation.

Outside the laboratory however both animal and man are constantly inundated with potential stimuli and have to choose among them. Subsidiary S–R processes may (retrospectively) be postulated to account for the choice. But in the last analysis that choice is in principle unpredictable. It depends on the organism. Any law purporting to provide a basis for prediction will take the form 'stimulus S_1 evokes response R_1 in organism A'. Some at least of these laws must presumably be applicable to human organisms and the scientist formulating the laws is a human organism. It is, of course, possible that a human organism could know a law of this kind but nevertheless be unable to override its consequences as they apply to him. The law that relates the stimulus 'acid in the mouth' to the response 'salivation' is such a law but for the behaviourist case to be established it is necessary that all laws linking stimuli and responses should be of this type. It is easy enough for the behaviourist to assert of his subject that he is mistaken in supposing his behaviour to be under his own control, that this may be how it appears to him but that in fact he is under the control of stimuli operating in accordance with laws known to the behaviourist but not to the subject. Can the behaviourist say as much of himself? 'I am under the control of stimulus S_1 (a light flash) which evokes in me response R_1 (pressing a button).' If challenged most behaviourists would not deny that they might not produce R_1 as a response to S_1, they would assert that, if they did not, this was because they were under the control of other stimuli (unknown to them) which had overridden S_1. We might then call in a colleague of the behaviourist who would conduct an investigation and establish a new law 'S_1 evokes R_1 but $S_1 + S_2$ does not evoke R_1'. But the behaviourist could of course override this law too, once he was told of it, and so on . . . His assertion that his behaviour is under the control of S–R laws reduces to the assertion that a retrospective account of his behaviour can always be given in S–R terms. He is however always and necessarily one step ahead of any law of whose existence he is aware. It is not necessary to deny that some people, some of the time, are under the control of S–R laws of whose existence they are not aware. For this to be a universal truth however it would be necessary that no member of a species to which such a law applied could become aware of its existence. A non-member of the species, say an extra-terrestrial intelligence, to whom the law did not apply might discover it; though it would then have to be the case that the discoverer could not communicate his findings to a member of the species to which the law applied.

Experimental work on thinking arising out of behaviourist theory

The ambition of behaviourist theory to predict responses from stimuli and vice versa turns out to be unattainable simply because the human organism can take into account the reported existence of a law predicting his response to a stimulus as a reason for not responding in the predicted fashion. This however detracts little from the magnitude of the achievement of Hull and his followers in systematizing behaviour. This is an activity that has gone temporarily out of fashion but the need for it cannot in the long term be avoided. As Rozeboom (1970) points out 'Of course Hull was imprecise, inconsistent and all the rest – but his work is still the finest expression of clarity and explicitness that psychological theory has yet managed to achieve' (n. 56, p. 109). Perhaps the two most important conclusions Rozeboom draws are that as Hullian-type learning theory (emphasizing habit-strength) is elaborated, it becomes progressively less easy to distinguish it from cognitive theory (emphasizing expectancy); and that neither theory can deal adequately with discrimination learning for lack of 'a means by which irrelevant input is suppressed'. His insistence that 'it is absurd to pretend that mediational hypotheses are any more scientific or tough-minded than are frankly mentalistic interpretations' (p. 122) is also welcome, and leads us on to consider the work on concept shifts associated with the Kendlers which was designed to furnish experimental support for the behaviourist analysis.

The issues the Kendlers were and are concerned with (Kendler and Kendler, 1962) arise directly from Spence (1936) and they employ methods whose ancestry can be traced back to Watson's pre-1913 discrimination boxes. The initial formulations of learning theory proposed a direct relationship between observable S's and R's but Hull had from 1930 onwards been prepared in certain circumstances to postulate internal (unobservable) s's and r's (Berlyne's u's) which mediated the relationship between S and R. It seemed reasonable to the Kendlers to suppose that direct S–R relationships might be characteristic of relatively primitive organisms and mediated S– (r-s) –R relationships, of more advanced organisms. The concept shift paradigm offered a possibility of determining whether an organism was employing direct or mediated S–R connections. In a concept task where instances consist of red or green, squares or circles, the subject may initially be required to learn to respond to red instances as positive but may then have to shift his concept either to the other value on the same dimension i.e. 'green' (reversal shift) or to a value of the other dimension i.e. 'square' or 'circle' (non-reversal shift). This is the R/NR paradigm. Its importance lies in the fact that a direct S–R responder can be supposed to have formed only a direct connection between S (red) and R. When the concept shifts this connection will be extinguished, but the organism has at that stage never been reinforced for approaching 'green' whereas he has frequently been reinforced for approaching 'square' and 'circle' (whenever these were associated with 'red'). He will therefore find it easier to transfer to 'square' or 'circle' (i.e. to make an N–R shift) than to 'green' (an R shift). A mediated S–R responder will, on the other hand, have formed a connection between S (red) and a mediating link which might be characterized as 'colour' as well as a direct connection between S and R. When the concept shifts, the existence of the mediating link will make it easier for him to transfer to 'green' (R shift), which is associated with the same mediator, than to 'square' or 'circle' (N–R shift), which are not associated with that mediator.

When the R/NR paradigm was introduced the subject was required to learn the second concept to a criterion and the measure was the number of trials required. From Kendler, Kendler and Learnard (1962) onwards an 'optional shift' paradigm was introduced in which instances were presented in such a way that the subject could shift either to the reverse of his original concept (R shift) or to a value of the other dimension (extradimensional (ED) shift) and the measure was the number of subjects who were R, ED or N responders. (N responders are subjects who do not make a consistent shift in either direction). Using these paradigms the Kendlers established that animals and young children were on the whole direct S–R responders (i.e. they made NR or ED shifts) whereas older children and adults were mediated S–R responders (i.e. they made R shifts). These paradigms were criticized by attention theorists among others on the ground that they were biased against the R shift and by Smiley and Weir (1966) on the ground that no account was taken of the dimensional preferences of subjects. (An R shifter might be so simply because he preferred to work in terms of the dimension involved and an NR or ED shifter might be so because he still preferred the NR or ED dimension even though the first concept had involved what was for him a non-preferred dimension). A new paradigm was introduced in which the second part of the task presented the same dimensions but different dimension values from the ones that had been presented in the first part. An ID (intradimensional shift) was now one in which the same dimension was used in the second part of the task as the first even though the dimension values were different. An ED (extradimensional shift) was one in which a different dimension was used. With this new paradigm it was possible to show that both younger children and higher animals made intradimensional (i.e. reversal) shifts and could consequently be regarded as mediators. The Kendlers' response was to show (in the traditional fashion) that S–R theory could account for the results of attention theorists that were supposed to be inconsistent with it (Kendler, Basden and Bruckner, 1970); to drop the suggestion that mediating responses could be identified with language; and to change the emphasis from one in which each individual organism was regarded as either a mediator or a non-mediator to one in which virtually all organisms were regarded as potential mediators though the probability that mediation would be employed on a particular occasion differed from organism to organism and could be associated with a degree of maturity in human organisms. Kendler and Kendler (1970) and Kendler and Hynds (1974) maintain their basic S–R orientation but hold only that the incidence of mediated as against non-mediated behaviour has been shown to increase with age (in human subjects) and phylogenetic complexity. Other workers in the area (e.g. Gollin and Rosser, 1974; Cole and Medin, 1973) agree and continue to use the term 'mediator' for an R or ID responder. The problem is now seen as one of establishing the precise conditions in which subjects of different ages produce R/ID responses as against NR/ED responses. The original research objectives have however been lost sight of. There is no doubt that the behavioural differences exist but their interest lay in the implications they were believed to have for S–R theory. If virtually all higher organisms are potential mediators then these implications no longer hold. The differences have no special relationship to S–R theory and it is not clear why they deserve the amount of attention they have been and are still being given. No new theory has emerged to lend them new significance.

Both the Kendlers and Levine (to whose work we shall now turn) use the method of simultaneous presentation in which two instances are presented at a time; it is given that one instance will be positive and one negative and both are withdrawn immediately the subject indicates which he thinks is positive. In the real world nature does not present the organism with pairs of instances, certainly not with a guarantee that one will be positive and one negative. There would appear to be no justification for using this method with human subjects though it has some practical value in animal studies.

Levine initially employed mathematical methods to extract evidence indicating the use of hypotheses from data on the pre-solution behaviour of animal subjects (following Krechevsky). He later developed the 'blank trials' technique for which he is now best known. In this technique instances typically vary along four well-defined dimensions, each dimension taking one of two values. Feedback is given only on every fifth trial but on every trial the (human) subject has to indicate which of the two instances presented he thinks is positive. There are, of course, eight possible hypotheses (only one-value hypotheses are considered) and each hypothesis entails a particular pattern of four choices during each sequence of four presentations without feedback (known as blank trials); it is consequently possible to determine from his responses what hypothesis the subject was entertaining, or that he was not consistently entertaining any hypothesis. Levine (1966) showed that adult subjects entertain consistent hypotheses about 90 per cent of the time and that some of their inconsistencies are what he calls 'oops' errors, recognized as such by the subject as soon as they are made. Children show basically the same behaviour but are less accurate and more liable to stereotyped response sets (Gholson, Levine and Phillips, 1972). Levine (1966) showed further that when a hypothesis is entertained by a subject but shown to be false on a feedback trial it is dropped from consideration i.e. there is almost no chance that the falsified hypothesis will be used again in the next series of blank trials. Karpf and Levine (1971) found that asking the subject what hypothesis he was entertaining produced exactly the same results as the blank trials procedure but the procedure has nevertheless continued in use. These examples indicate the extent to which Levine has been influenced by the common behaviourist assumption that one must never rely on the data of consciousness, even for guidance as to likely experimental hypotheses. He has laboriously demonstrated what most people (including many psychologists) accept without demonstration; it is as if Galileo had dropped weights off the leaning tower of Pisa to show that they fell down not up!

Experimental work on thinking influenced by behaviourist assumptions

During the ascendancy of behaviourism, psychologists were on the whole preoccupied with what they considered to be the fundamental problems of learning. They assumed that thinking would in due course prove to be explicable in terms of the simpler events with which they were directly concerned. Hull and others made suggestions how this might be expected to come about but for the behaviourist the problem of thought was essentially one of theoretical reduction, not one demanding experimental investigation. As Bourne (1966) writes, 'not many years ago there was no experimental psychology of conceptual behaviour' only 'isolated bits of empiricism and speculation'. In the late 1940s and 1950s things had, however, begun to change. Papers appeared suggesting how problems of thinking might be approached from a behaviourist point of view (e.g. Galanter and Gerstenhaber, 1956; Marx, 1958), followed by papers in which actual experimental work was reported. During the 1960s interest in theoretical behaviourism declined and today the only avowed behaviourists are the Skinnerians who have nothing to say about thinking, except that there is nothing worth saying about thinking. The remainder of this chapter will be concerned not with behaviourist theory but with the legacy of behaviourism, the influence that behaviourism exerts on the way experiments are conducted and, more important, on the way that hypotheses are selected for test – even by psychologists who might indignantly deny that they were behaviourists!

One of the changes that Watson (1913) wished to bring about in psychology was 'a return to a non-reflective and naive use of consciousness'. He desired that consciousness should play the role in psychology that it played in chemistry and physics, as a tool of science. Whether the tool was used properly was to be a question for philosophers not for psychologists. Watson used his consciousness as a tool to arrive at metatheoretical decisions on what was the appropriate subject matter of psychology and what methods of investigation could usefully be employed. He totally rejected introspection of conscious contents as a scientific procedure designed to supply the raw data of psychology. He did not however reject thinking as a preliminary procedure in psychology as in all the other sciences, designed to delimit the field of investigation. When interest in theoretical behaviourism lapsed what was valuable in it was however rejected. All that remained was a prejudice against any resort to 'non-reflective and naive consciousness'. Behaviourists were obsessed with the need to do the right thing scientifically and referred back constantly to the prescriptions of philosophers of science. (It is unfortunate that the philosophy of science was at rather a low ebb in their time.) The successors of the behaviourists dropped their metatheoretical assumptions but retained their methods in the name of 'science'. They may justly be accused of having thrown out the baby and kept the bath water.

Bruner, Goodnow and Austin (1956, p. 246) point out that 'virtually all cognitive activity involves and is dependent on the process of categorizing'. Laboratory investigation of this process raises in an acute form the general problem of the relationship between laboratory experiments and the real world. Experimentation in any science involves abstraction. A simplified model is set up believed to be analogous in important respects to the segment of reality that is the object of investigation. If the analogy fails then phenomena may occur in the real world that do not occur in the laboratory or vice versa. In the former case the laboratory model must be elaborated and a closer analogy with the real world achieved but it is the latter possibility that will concern us more. The process of categorizing derives its overwhelming importance from the fact that (in the most general formulation) for all organisms some aspects of the real world are to be approached and some to be avoided. It is absolutely vital to the survival and well-being of any organism that it should be able to distinguish such states from neutral states which are of no special significance. Moreover this distinction must be made in advance on the basis of associated predictive cues. Whether a thing is 'good to eat' or not may be established by eating it and observing the consequences; likewise whether a thing is a 'predator' or not may be established by waiting to see whether it attacks. But it is more conducive to survival to act on the basis of predictive cues and such cues may be derived from the experience of other organisms as well as from one's own and (in the case of human organisms) may be passed on in the form of instruction. To possess the concept of 'good to eat' or 'predator' means to know that 'any object having such and such attributes may be regarded as a member of the category of things that are . . .' the attributes being of a kind that can be observed in advance or at a distance, without putting the observer at risk. Notice that many concepts are what are technically known as disjunctions; some fruits, bread, meat etc. are all exemplars of 'good to eat' though they have little else in common. Notice also that while useful concepts will usually have been given a name this is not essential. Any defined category of instances constitutes a concept.

Hull (1920) proposed a simplified laboratory model of what he called the evolution of concepts[1] in which the instances were Chinese ideograms. Chinese ideograms are complex shapes consisting of a root character and accidentals modifying the meaning of the root. For Hull's purpose their importance lay in their perceptual complexity, in their unfamiliarity to his subjects and in the possibility of grouping them in categories defined by possession of a common root. Thus a category of ideograms might be given the name 'dax', applicability of the name being signalled by possession of a particular root character. The subject had to learn that any ideogram possessing that root character could appropriately be called a 'dax'. Hull's subjects demonstrated a capacity to do this without becoming consciously aware of the root character and they benefited little from exposure to negative instances of the concept. This established what Hull had set out to establish, which was that consciousness is not necessarily involved in conceptual activity, the implication being that it might one day be possible to account for all conceptual activity without reference to consciousness.

A subject unfamiliar with the Chinese writing system cannot determine either the number or the nature of the dimensions of variation of Hull's ideograms and it can be argued that this rules out the possibility of bringing consciousness to bear on the problem. For Hull or any behaviourist this criticism is beside the point since a metatheoretical decision has been taken to ignore consciousness – as irrelevant at best and potentially misleading. Hovland (1952) however proposed that the dimension structure of the materials used in concept tasks ought to be transparent and from then on it became customary to use instances exemplifying different numbers of different shapes in different colours . . . Bruner et al. (1956) used materials of this type. They introduced a distinction between selection tasks (in which subjects select their own instances) and reception tasks (in which instances are selected by the experimenter). This is parallel to a real-life distinction between the formation of concepts by active search for instances having particular characteristics and subsequent test to see whether these instances exemplify the concept and the relatively passive procedure which is all that is available when it is not in the power of the subject to generate his own instances for test. Bruner et al. introduced a further distinction between two broad classes of strategy in the formation of concepts: 'focussing' and 'scanning'. Suppose instances consist of cards bearing one, two or three; red, blue or green; squares, circles or triangles. The first instance presented is IRS (one red square) and is positive. If the second instance chosen is

IBS and is negative then 'red' is certainly part of the concept since changing 'red' to 'blue' has changed a positive instance to a negative. In choosing IBS after IRS (positive) the subject has varied one dimension only. Whatever the concept is, it can by this method be established for certain in three trials. This however follows only if the subject assumes that the concept will be defined by some combination of the values of the dimensions to which his attention has been drawn. This is a reasonable assumption in the experimental situation but it is a respect in which the analogy fails between the experimental model and the segment of reality which is the object of investigation, for in the real world instances vary along an indefinitely large number of dimensions. Limitations on the subject's perceptual capacity will oblige him to consider only a fairly small number at a time but he will not be entitled to assume that the concept is definable in terms of values of the dimensions he happens to be considering. Without this assumption all that can be shown is that a dimension does not contribute to the definition of the concept. This follows if the dimension is varied and the new instance is positive.[2] It is not possible to conclude that a dimension does contribute to the definition if the dimension is varied and the new instance is negative. The dimension may simply have covaried on that occasion with a defining dimension that was not being considered. In the laboratory 'focussing' is maximally efficient. Outside it can, at best, only enable the subject to eliminate dimensions one by one from an indefinitely large set.

The alternative strategy, 'scanning', involves selecting a hypothesis from the values of dimensions exemplified by the initial positive instance and predicting that new instances will be positive if they exemplify this hypothesis. If the prediction is falsified then a new hypothesis has to be selected. In the laboratory this strategy is hopelessly inefficient but outside it is the only one possible. The subject is rarely a neutral observer of new instances; he has, in most cases, to make a decision to approach (or avoid) or not and needs a hypothesis on the basis of which to make this decision.

Bruner's experimental task may be tackled in one of two frames of mind. The subject may see it as a kind of game, like a crossword puzzle, having no essential relationship to any significant real-life activity, or he may try to treat it as a paradigm case of the real-life activity involved in inductive concept formation. In the former frame of mind, he may light on focussing since that is undoubtedly the most efficient way to play the game. In the latter he will be likely to scan since that is what he would have to do in real life. Only in the latter case, however, can the experiment be legitimately regarded as an investigation of the real-life process. Bruner is not entitled to regard focussing as somehow superior to scanning.

The fact that in the laboratory there is at least an implicit guarantee that the concept will be definable in terms of values of the dimensions to which the subject's attention has been drawn and that this guarantee has no analogy in the real-life activity which is the object of investigation has consequences for many other types of experimental result. Freibergs and Tulving (1961) showed that subjects asked to derive a two-value concept from four instances could do so very quickly if the instances were all positive. Where the instances were all negative the subjects failed initially but practice on a series of problems enabled them to find the concept almost as quickly from negative instances as from positive. However, no series of negative instances in the real world can define a concept; this is only possible where the guarantee operates.

Walker and Bourne (1961) showed that increasing the number either of relevant or irrelevant dimensions increased the difficulty of a concept task. The finding that the more irrelevant dimensions the more difficult the task is odd, on the face of it, since it seems to imply that a real-life task (where there are an indefinitely large number of irrelevant dimensions) will be virtually insoluble. In the light of the preceding discussion however it is reasonable to conclude that, where his attention has been drawn to a certain number of dimensions, the subject may feel obliged to consider them all, but that the finding has no direct bearing on real life since there the subject scans and the question of irrelevant dimensions does not arise.

Most recently Bourne and his associates have been concerned with concept rules and with the distinction between rule learning and attribute learning. In any real-life concept task, forming the concept is said to involve learning which attributes (i.e. values of dimensions) are involved and which rule relates these attributes to membership or non-membership of the concept category. Suppose instances consist of red or green, squares or circles. There are four possible instances RS, RC, GS, GC. It may be that the attributes 'red' and 'square' are the ones involved but these attributes may be involved in different ways depending on the concept rule. The rule may be affirmative (e.g. 'red') in which case RS and RC will be positive, and the rest negative; it may be conjunctive (i.e. 'red and square') in which case only RS will be positive; it may be disjunctive (i.e. 'red or square') in which case RS, RC and GS will be positive; it may be conditional (e.g. 'red implies square') in which case RS, GS and GC will be positive or it may be bi-conditional (i.e. 'red if and only if square') in which case RS and GC will be positive. There are, in addition, five complementary rules in which the instances described as positive above become negative and vice versa.

Subjects may be told which attributes are involved and required to learn the rule, or told the rule and required to identify the attributes involved, or they may have to learn both rule and attributes. Some of the rules are easily recognizable. Suppose we substitute 'Black or White race' for 'red or green' and 'Protestant or Catholic' for 'square or circle'. We can easily imagine a club open only to Whites (affirmative rule) or to White Protestants (conjunctive rule). It is not so easy to imagine a club open only to White Protestants and Blacks whether they are Catholic or Protestant (conditional rule), still less one open only to White Protestants and Black Catholics (bi-conditional rule). The latter two rules are more naturally interpreted as disjunctions of one and two-value concepts. It is not surprising to discover that they are more difficult to learn than the rest. Bourne (1970) shows that practice on a series of problems involving the same concept rule enables the subject to learn how to solve them efficiently, so that after practice on different rules the difference in difficulty between rules disappears. He adopts Bruner's suggestion that experience of the real world prejudices the subject in favour of affirmative and conjunctive rules. The subject is familiar with categories, membership of which is defined by possession of a set of one, two or more attributes and with categories defined by a disjunction of such sets. The real world interpretation considered above shows however that conditional and bi-conditional rules involve prima facie irrational bases of categorization. Nevertheless, subjects can learn very quickly to cope with them. The question one may ask is, what is the object of investigation in these experiments and in the theoretical models proposed to account for the results obtained in them (e.g. Bourne, 1974)? Ostensibly, they are concerned with the process of concept formation because this process is of fundamental importance for human thinking in the real world outside the laboratory. But the experimental paradigm itself offers innumerable possibilities of development and each new development poses a new and interesting problem for the subject. Since human subjects are known to enjoy problem solving for its own sake results are obtained, but these results do not necessarily shed light on the nature of thinking. They risk showing no more than that human subjects can, in principle, solve any problem that a human experimenter can devise.

Conclusions

It should be emphasized that none of the experiments considered here is open to serious criticism if the method employed is once accepted as valid. The arguments presented seek only to show that there has been a breakdown at the pre-experimental, conceptual level. All sciences start out from what is known. That is not to say that what is 'known' is true: science may have to persuade us that what is 'known' is in fact false (once upon a time everyone 'knew' that the sun revolved round the earth). Behaviourism set out to show that much that was 'known' about human and animal behaviour was false – organisms did not originate their behaviour and their thought processes were mere effectless epiphenomena. This end was to be achieved by a two-pronged attack involving critical argument that the generally accepted view was logically untenable and experimental demonstration that all the phenomena could be accounted for in terms of laws linking observable stimuli and responses. Thought processes, being regarded as epiphenomenal, were to be explained away in terms of simpler processes and not subjected to experimental investigation in their own right. The attempt may be judged to have failed, for it proved necessary in order to save the phenomena to postulate complex internal events whose resemblance to cognitions was too close to be coincidental. The effort was not however wasted and when systematic theories of behaviour come into fashion again it will be found that Hull, Berlyne and the rest left behind them much that is of value. (It is unfortunately this part of their work that has been most decisively rejected.)

Having judged, on what they took to be reasonable *a priori* grounds, that the contents of consciousness were epiphenomena providing no reliable insights into the causation of behaviour, the behaviourists tried so far as possible to act in the laboratory as if they had none and this aspect of their behaviour came somehow to be identified with 'science' in the minds of other psychologists. It makes little sense to hold that conscious mental processes, being more than mere epiphenomena, are legitimate objects of scientific study and at the same time that the scientist must make no use in the laboratory of the ones that happen to be available to him personally. Nevertheless this view has been widely acted upon if not knowingly subscribed to. One consequence has been that laboratory paradigms have been manipulated as if they were objects of study in their own right and the relationship between the paradigm and the segment of reality which is the real object of study has been neglected. (This relationship can be investigated only in the mind not in the laboratory!)

Behaviourism was a theory from which followed an appropriate laboratory method. The theory was abandoned on the grounds that it was logically and empirically inadequate but the method was retained, with consequences that were unfortunate for the psychology of thinking in particular. Current 'cognitive' theory (though it has not yet been articulated with anything like the precision of behaviourist theory) has quite different implications for method and the psychology of thinking may be expected to progress in so far as it succeeds in relating its methods to the kind of theory to which it now subscribes.

Notes

1 In the literature concepts are variously formed, evolved, attained, learned and identified. I shall stick to 'formed' because it seems to me that the use of the other terms is based on a misconception. It is argued that if a subject learns e.g. to call cards with red squares 'positive', he cannot be said to have formed the concept 'red squares' because this concept has been part of his repertory for years. In this situation, however, 'red squares' is not the concept involved; 'red' and 'square' are the attributes predicting membership of the category of instances that constitutes the concept. The concept is something like 'called positive in this experimental situation' and does not form part of the subject's repertory; the subject can therefore legitimately be said to have formed it. 'Red' and 'square' are of course concepts in their own right but here they play only a defining role. No concept can be defined except in terms of other concepts already understood.

2 Even this does not follow if the possibility is allowed of a disjunction of concepts each independently predicting membership of the class of positive instances. An unobserved dimension may then have remained positive, or changed from negative to positive as the varied dimension was changed from positive to negative!

References

Barker, R. G., Dembo, T. and Lewin, K. (1943) Frustration and regression. In R. G. Barker, J. S. Kounin and H. F. Wright (eds) *Child Behaviour and Development*. New York: McGraw-Hill.

Berlyne, D. E. (1965) *Structure and Direction in Thinking*. New York: John Wiley.
Bourne, L. E. Jr. (1966) *Human Conceptual Behaviour*. Boston: Allyn and Bacon.
Bourne, L. E. Jr. (1970) Knowing and using concepts. *Psychological Review 77:* 546–56.
Bourne, L. E. Jr. (1974) An inference model for conceptual rule learning. In Robert L. Solso (ed.) *Theories in Cognitive Psychology: the Loyola Symposium*. Potomac, Maryland: Lawrence Erlbaum Associates.
Bruner, J. S., Goodnow, J. J. and Austin, G. A. (1956) *A Study of Thinking*. New York: John Wiley.
Child, I. L. and Waterhouse, I. K. (1952) Frustration and the quality of performance: I. A critique of the Barker, Dembo and Lewin experiment. *Psychological Review 59:* 351–62.
Cole, M. and Medin, D. (1973) On the existence and occurrence of mediation in discrimination transfer. *Journal of Experimental Child Psychology 15:* 352–5.
Dollard, J. and Miller, N. E. (1950) *Personality and Psychotherapy*. New York: McGraw-Hill.
Freibergs, V. and Tulving, E. (1961) The effect of practice on utilization of information from positive and negative instances in concept identification. *Canadian Journal of Psychology 15:* 101–6.
Galanter, E. and Gerstenhaber, M. (1956) On thought – the extrinsic theory. *Psychological Review 63:* 218–27.
Gholson, B., Levine, M. and Phillips, S. (1972) Hypotheses, strategies and stereotypes in discrimination learning. *Journal of Experimental Child Psychology 13:* 423–46.
Gollin, E. S. and Rosser, M. (1974) On mediation. *Journal of Experimental Child Psychology 17:* 539–44.
Hovland, C. I. (1952) The communication analysis of concept learning. *Psychological Review 59:* 461–72.
Hull, C. L. (1920) Quantitative aspects of the evolution of concepts; an experimental study, *Psychological Monographs 28:* whole no. 123.
Hull, C. L. (1930) Knowledge and purpose as habit mechanisms. *Psychological Review 37:* 511–25.
Hull, C. L. (1935) The mechanism of the assembly of behaviour segments in novel combinations suitable for problem solution. *Psychological Review 42:* 219–45.
Hull, C. L. (1943) *Principles of Behavior* New York: Appleton-Century-Crofts.
Hull, C. L. (1952) *A Behavior System*. New Haven, Conn.: Yale University Press.
Karpf, D. and Levine, M. (1971) Blank-trial probes and introtacts in human discrimination learning. *Journal of Experimental Psychology 90:* 51–5.
Kendler, H. H. and Kendler, T. S. (1962) Vertical and horizontal processes in problem solving. *Psychological Review 69:* 1–16.
Kendler, T. S., Basden, B. M. and Bruckner, J. B. (1970) Dimensional dominance and continuity theory. *Journal of Experimental Psychology 83:* 309–18.
Kendler, T. S. and Hynds, L. T. (1974) A reply to Brier and Jacob's criticism of the optional-shift methodology. *Child Development 45:* 208–11.
Kendler, T. S. and Kendler, H. H. (1970) An ontogeny of optional shift behavior. *Child Development 41:* 1–27.

Kendler, T. S., Kendler, H. H. and Learnard, B. (1962) Mediated responses to size and brightness as a function of age. *American Journal of Psychology 75:* 571–86.

Koch, S. (1964) Psychology and emerging conceptions of knowledge as unitary. In T. W. Wann (ed.) *Behaviorism and Phenomenology.* Chicago: University of Chicago Press.

Krechevsky, I. (1935) Brain mechanisms and 'hypotheses'. *Journal of Comparative Psychology 19:* 425–62.

Lashley, K. S. (1916) The human salivary reflex and its use in psychology. *Psychological Review 23:* 446–64.

Levine, M. (1966) Hypothesis behavior by humans during discrimination learning. *Journal of Experimental Psychology 71:* 331–8.

Maltzman, I. (1955) Thinking: a behavioristic point of view. *Psychological Review 62:* 275–85.

Marx, M. H. (1958) Complex intervening variables in problem solving behavior. *Journal of General Psychology 58:* 115–28.

Rozeboom, W. W. (1970) The art of metascience, III. In J. R. Royce (ed.) *Toward unification in Psychology.* Toronto: University of Toronto Press.

Smiley, S. S. and Weir, M. W. (1966) The role of dimensional dominance in reversal and non-reversal shift behavior. *Journal of Experimental Child Psychology 4:* 211–16.

Spence, K. W. (1936) The nature of discrimination learning in animals. *Psychological Review 43:* 427–49.

Tolman, E. C. (1922) A new formula for behaviorism. *Psychological Review 29:* 44–53.

Tolman, E. C. (1959) Principles of purposive behavior. In Sigmund Koch (ed.). *Psychology: a Study of a Science,* Vol. 2. New York: McGraw-Hill.

Walker, C. M. and Bourne, L. E. Jr (1961) Concept identification as a function of amounts of relevant and irrelevant information. *American Journal of Psychology 74:* 410–17.

Watson, J. B. (1913) Psychology as the behaviorist views it. *Psychological Review 20:* 158–77.

Watson, J. B. (1916) The place of the conditioned-reflex in psychology. *Psychological Review 23:* 89–116.

4 Thought and things: Piaget's theory

George Butterworth

Over the past fifty years, Jean Piaget has elaborated a theory of cognitive development based on the premise that thought derives from action. His method, 'genetic epistemology', explains how knowledge is acquired by examining its evolution in childhood. The aim is 'to comprehend how, from elementary forms of cognition, superior levels of intelligence and scientific thinking come about' (Piaget, 1953).

It is impossible to encompass all the research which has been inspired by the theory in a short chapter. This essay will concentrate on Piaget's description of the origins of thought in infancy. Contemporary research raises important problems which have not been discussed widely. To the extent that the acquisitions of the sensorimotor period lay the foundations for later cognitive development, any conclusions drawn may have implications for the theory as a whole.

Piaget's assumptions

For Piaget, thought and action are related by force of necessity. James Mark Baldwin, a major influence on Piaget, expresses the underlying assumption: 'In the absence of alternative considerations, reflections, the child acts and act it must, on the first sensation which has any meaning in terms of its sensations of movement' (1894, p. 5).

Piaget maintains that the precursors of thought are to be observed in the infant's actions. He outlines the theory in the trilogy *Origins of Intelligence in the Child* (1953), *Construction of Reality in the Child* (1954), and *Play Dreams and Imitation in Childhood* (1951). From detailed observations of his own three babies, he maps a theory of cognitive development which has its origins in the reflex activities with which the newborn is endowed biologically.

The philosopher Immanuel Kant believed the concepts of space, time, causes, and objects to be *a priori* categories of experience; innate constraints on the interpretation of sensory information. Piaget concludes from his studies that these categories are not innate but are constructed by the infant during the first eighteen months of life. The newborn infant is a solipsist, making no distinctions between events which are contingent on his own activity and events which are independent of action. The world comprises a series of 'perceptual tableaux' which come and go with no meaningful connection between them. 'Things' enter the child's experience but they are not perceived as 'objects' which are substantial, permanent, and unique. Separate experiences are not connected in space and time.

The problem for Piaget is to extricate the infant from solipsism, a task which requires the baby to structure experience according to the Kantian categories. Piaget's solution is to argue that the motor programmes (schemes) directing action are organized in time and space, even though there is no direct perception of external reality. The infant gradually frees himself from his subjective point of view as he coordinates separate action schemes, such as looking, listening and grasping, into higher order motor programmes which take into account progressively more of the objective properties of reality. Increasingly complex sequences of action are constructed from earlier, simpler actions at each of the six substages in sensori-motor development. The infant's knowledge of objects is constrained by the particular action patterns at his disposal (i.e. objects are assimilated to patterns of activity). In turn, actions become adapted to accommodate to particular properties of objects. This interaction between the processes of assimilation and accommodation is known as equilibration and is characteristic of cognitive development at all stages of Piaget's theory.

Acquiring the object concept is the major intellectual achievement of the sensori-motor period. To have the object concept is to 'conceive of things as permanent, substantial, external to the self and firm in existence even though they do not directly affect perception ... and to conceive of them as retaining their identity whatever the changes in position' (Piaget, 1954, pp. 5 and 7). The object concept is acquired by a process of 'constructive deduction' (Piaget, 1954, p. 94). The constructive aspect lies in the coordination of action schemes which enable the infant to engage in active experiments on objects. The deductive aspect arises from the results of that experimentation. The ability to engage in constructive deduction at the representational level marks the beginning of thought.

This process is compared to the history of scientific method in unravelling the nature of physical phenomena. Just as the scientist has been freed from subjective impressions by experimentation and application of measurement systems, so the coordination of actions subsuming more and more complex sets of spatial relations (logico-mathematical groupings) eventually leads to objective knowledge of space, time, causes and objects (Piaget, 1971, p. 305).

The development of the object concept

Different objects can be at the same place at different times and the same object can be at different places at different times. But an object can only be in one place at one time. The conjunction of these spatial and temporal properties defines a unique object and requires a unitary space in relation to which objects can move. Table 4.1 shows the action schemes characterizing each of Piaget's six sensori-motor stages, the corresponding object concept and concept of space. The reader may wish to supplement this description with Piaget's own writing (1950, 1953, 1954) or with one of the summaries by Wolff (1960) or Dé Carie (1965).

Stages I and II: Practical space, o to 3 months
At birth, there is only a practical space, comprised of separate reflexes. The infant is not aware of objects as distinct from the actions which they elicit. When an object disappears the infant does not search for it but stares at the place where it vanishes. If the infant should rediscover an object, he is said to recognize his own action rather than the object as such. The infant merely repeats the action which gave rise to a particular experience.

When two separate motor schemes become coordinated, e.g. when

Table 4.1   Piaget's stages of sensori-motor development

Stage	Age (approx.)	Action pattern	Object/space	Search
I	0–6 weeks	Reflex	Practical	No search
II	6 weeks–3 months	Primary circular reactions	Practical	Repetition of action, no search
III	3–9 months	Secondary circular reaction (Procedures to make interesting sights last)	Subjective	Extension of movements but no search for hidden objects
IV	9–12 months	Coordinated secondary circular reactions (differentiation of action into means and ends)	Subjective/ Objective	Search where action was successful
V	12–18 months	Tertiary circular reactions (application of established means to new ends)	Objective/ Subjective	Search where object was seen last
VI	18 months Preoperational period	Representation, mental combination of means-ends relations	Objective	Persistent and successful search

the infant brings his hand to his mouth in order to suck it, this is known as a primary circular reaction. This mechanism was first described by Baldwin (1894) to explain why babies repeat activities over and again. Piaget adopts it as the device for introducing order into experience. He notes that to repeat an action, it is necessary to return to some point of departure. The motor response and the stimulus which elicits it form a closed system which can be described in spatio-temporal terms (the logic of groups). Any action system which can return to a point of departure has an invariant spatial structure. During the period of practical space, the spatial structure remains locked into action because the child is learning about his own activities through repetition, rather than about the objects to which the activity is applied.

Stage III: Subjective space, 3 to 9 months
Insofar as the primary circular reactions are applied jointly to an object, they become coordinated among themselves to form higher order schemes, the secondary circular reactions. The sensory modalities are united within a unitary space and consequently an object which is seen is known to have tactual properties, an object heard to have visual properties, etc. The infant's interest is captured by objects to which activity is applied, the secondary circular reactions being procedures for making interesting sights last.

Nevertheless, space and the concept of the object remain subjective, linked in the child's awareness to his own activity. The ability to grasp objects merely introduces a new set of action schemes to which the infant can perceive objects as subordinate. Piaget's son, Laurent, at seven months dropped a cigarette box which he had been swinging to and fro: 'far from considering the loss as irremediable, he begins again to swing his hand, although it is empty, after this he looks at it once more ... it is impossible not to interpret such behaviour as an attempt to make the object come back' (Piaget, 1954, p. 22).

Toward the end of the third stage, the infant will remove the cover from a partially hidden object but not from a completely hidden object. As far as the infant is concerned, the half hidden object is in the process of disappearing and the completely hidden object has ceased to exist. In immediate perception, the infant does not perceive shape or size constancy. The best known example is Laurent's inability to recognize the wrong end of his feeding bottle (Piaget, 1954, Observation 78, p. 126). Even as late as 8 months, objects are not perceived as permanent, they remain 'a reality at the disposal of action'.

Stage IV: Subjective/Objective space, 9 to 12 months
The first intentional adaptation to the properties of objects takes place with the coordination of secondary circular reactions. In manual search for a hidden object, the infant differentiates the means (the action) from the end (the object). Removing a cover to retrieve an object demonstrates some objectivity since the infant must take into

account the spatial relation between cover and object. However, the object concept still retains a subjective element since the infant locates the object only in relation to his own activity.

Having retrieved an object from an initial location, A, the infant continues to search at that place after seeing the same object hidden at a new location, B. This is known as the $A\bar{B}$, or stage IV error. The infant does not take visible movements of the object into account when searching. 'Faced with the disappearance of the object, the child immediately ceases to reflect and merely returns to the place where action was successful the first time' (Piaget, 1954, p. 61). The infant does not truly localize the object at A or B, the cover acts as a sign of the presence of an object. The infant only understands the relation of object to cover, to the extent that this is related to him. The object is not yet understood to move in a space independent of action and so its spatial mobility is limited. Piaget argues that objects are not sufficiently individualized to be dissociated from the global behaviour which has made them reappear at the initial position, A.

Perceptual constancy is achieved during the fourth stage by relating perceived changes in shape and size to constant dimensions specified through touch, a process of cross-modal correspondence. Like permanence, constancy is not specified directly in perception. This interpretation of stage IV is crucial for Piaget. Objects remain tied to actions even though infants are quite capable of searching. This is definitive proof that lack of search in earlier stages can be attributed to failure to perceive objects as permanent.

Stage V, Objective/Subjective space, 12 to 18 months

By the fifth stage, the infant learns to take into account the spatial relation between images perceived successively because the pragmatic strategy of searching at A fails. However, search remains a practical achievement, since the infant cannot take into account the movements of an object which he does not observe directly (invisible displacements). The infant cannot imagine movements which take place outside direct perception.

Invisible movements are discovered by systematically varying means and ends in intentional motor exploration (tertiary circular reactions). By throwing things about, rolling them and so on the baby discovers the spatial groups formed by an object whose path of movement remains unseen.

Stage VI, Objective space, 18 months onward
The final criterion for objectivity is that the infant should be able to represent a hidden object and its movements. By interiorizing the tertiary circular reactions the object concept is acquired. Representation, 'making an absent object present to the senses' finally frees the infant from his egocentric perspective. This 'Copernican revolution' allows the child to represent himself as an object in a world of objects.

The development of thought

The object concept is the 'first invariant' of thought. Its acquisition marks the beginning of the preoperational stage (two to seven years). The child now engages in mental activity on a representation of reality, in lieu of the overt motor activity which characterized problem solving in infancy. Thought remains closely linked to its sensori-motor origins, it is egocentric (tied to the child's perspective) and tends to centre on perceptually salient but misleading stimulus attributes.

Although the preoperational child understands that objects retain their identity through time and space, he does not understand that properties of objects such as mass, weight, volume or number remain invariant. Instead, the child bases judgements of e.g. number on perceptual attributes such as length. Having judged two rows of counters in one to one correspondence to be equal in number, the preoperational child changes his judgement when one of the rows is lengthened and says the longer row contains more. Thinking is unconcerned with logical justification and is irreversible. The child cannot reverse mentally an observed sequence of events to arrive at the conclusion that e.g. number must remain equal despite a change in appearance.

Yet a form of reversibility is available during the sensori-motor period because the baby of 18 months can reverse the effect of a change in an object's position with respect to himself to leave the fundamental identity of the object invariant. This is an example of 'vertical décalage' or repetition, in cognitive development. At succeeding stages, cognitive structures must be reacquired at higher levels of abstraction. Although there is reversibility at the level of action, reversibility does not characterize thought until the child enters the concrete operational stage (eight to twelve years).

During the concrete operational stage, represented actions become coordinated into a unitary system so that thought becomes reversible. The essential limitation now is that thought remains concrete and tied to context. Although the logical processes required are identical, conservations of mass, volume and weight are acquired separately. This is an example of a repetition within a single stage, a horizontal décalage. The repetition occurs because the concrete operational child deals with one aspect of reality at a time; thought is intrapropositional. Reversibility occurs only within the context of the particular object property being conserved.

It is not until the period of formal operations, beginning in adolescence, that thinking becomes interpropositional. Formal thinking operates on concrete operations, and integrates them into a unitary system from which further abstract properties can be derived. Now the child first considers abstract possibilities and then tests them against concrete reality. Reasoning follows the hypothetico-deductive method, whereby the child holds constant all elements of a problem save the one being tested to arrive at a logically necessary solution. Formal operations repeat at the highest level of abstraction the deductive processes which enabled the infant to construct the object at the level of action in the sensori-motor period (see Flavell, 1963 for a full account of the theory).

Research based on Piaget's sensori-motor theory

Thus, the sensori-motor period lays the foundation for all later stages in cognitive development. One of the consequences of Piaget's emphasis on instrumental action in cognitive development is that he gives very little attention to perceptual processes. For Piaget, perception is a static, 'figurative' process which depends on action schemes to provide continuity of experience. The assumption is that gaps in object perception must be bridged by representation (memory) before objects can be perceived as permanent. An alternative view is that the perceptual system has evolved to detect basic invariants directly. Piaget considered this but dismissed it as 'structuralism without genesis'. Nevertheless, a great deal of research on the perceptual capacities of young infants has reopened the issue. The roots of this approach lie in the work of Koffka (1935), Michotte (1950) and Gibson (1966).

Contemporary research suggests Piaget overestimated the problems the infant must overcome in arriving at knowledge of reality. Space

precludes discussion of all the studies which have revealed hitherto
unsuspected abilities in infants, but an extensive literature can be
consulted in Cohen and Salapatek (1975) and Stone et al. (1975).
Accounts more specifically concerned with object permanence can be
found in Harris (1975) and Gratch (1975). These include reviews of
work in the psychometric tradition, which is omitted here.

Object permanence

Consider the problem of object permanence. Michotte (1950) argued
that the experience of permanence (or impermanence) is determined
by the psychophysical conditions of object disappearance. The
continued existence (or annihilation) of an object is specified directly
by the spatio-temporal conditions of disappearance. He drew an
analogy with the figure-ground effect where the phenomenal array is
perceived in two parts. The spatial boundary belongs exclusively to
the figure and the ground extends indefinitely behind the figure. The
ground is perceived as 'existing', even though it is hidden. (N.B. The
distinction between figure and ground seems to be made from birth.
Salapatek and Kessen, 1966).

A similar distinction is said to obtain in perception of the temporal
aspects of an event. When a room is suddenly illuminated, the
illumination is perceived as being created at that moment, while the
objects in the room are perceived as pre-existing their moment of
illumination. The temporal boundary is attributed to the light and,
by contrast, the objects illuminated extend into an indefinite past.

It is important to note that these processes do not depend on the
capacity to represent hidden objects. The spatial and temporal
information in the visual field specifies permanence directly. For
example, the progressive occlusion of one surface by another specifies
a relation in depth between the surfaces (Gibson, 1966).

Michotte (1950) argued that perceptual functions of this kind are
innate but he offered no proof. Gibson et al. (1969) argue that infants
may have to learn to distinguish information specifying continued
existence from that specifying the opposite. Piaget (1969) disagrees
with both points of view. While admitting that perceptual effects of
this kind take place in adults, he argues that they are based on the
developing capacity to represent hidden objects from stage IV onwards.

Bower (1967) has linked the psychophysical and ontogenetic
approaches. In this study a conditioned sucking response was established

in babies eight weeks old to a 'bull's eye' stimulus which was then made to disappear in a variety of ways. Conditioned responding was maintained after a disappearance in which a screen was slowly drawn in front of the object (adults report this transformation as the disappearance of an object which continues to exist) but not after the object was made to disappear instantaneously by an arrangement of mirrors (adults report this transformation as an 'annihilation' of the object). If the visual information specified it, infants behaved as though the object continued to exist.

There was a temporal constraint on the conditioned response. If the object remained behind the screen for more than fifteen seconds, a decrement in sucking occurred when it reappeared. Bower maintains that the reappearance was unexpected, owing to the limited temporal span of the perceptual system. Analogous results were obtained in a later study (Bower, 1971) in which changes in heartrate were used as a measure of expectancy.

These studies suggest that the perceptual system specifies permanence directly, although the infant can hold the information in mind for only a limited time. Infants do not merely recognize an object which looks like the one which vanished. They seem to expect an object to be present even when it has been removed.

Bower and Wishart (1972) performed an experiment with infants of 6 months of age, who would not search for objects beneath a cover. In this study, the object was dangling on a string directly in front of the baby. Before the baby could reach, the lights were turned out and the infant's behaviour was filmed using infra-red television. After initial distress, infants would reach out and grasp the object. Out of sight was not out of mind. The same babies had great difficulty in retrieving an object from beneath a transparent cover.

To account for failure to search beneath a cover it seems necessary to make a distinction between space as perceived and as represented. When an object is covered, even if it is visible, the infant cannot traverse a direct path along the line of sight to retrieve it. Köhler (1925) and Bruner et al. (1973) suggest that detour problems require a representation of space in relation to which indirect movements can be plotted. The infant with limited ability to represent spatial relations (i.e. hold them in mind) may find the problem difficult because he cannot represent the indirect path which would allow retrieval. The transition from visually guided reaching to reaching based on a representation of space may be better described as an aspect of skill acquisition than as a problem of object permanence. Taken as a whole, the evidence suggests that object permanence may not pose the basic problem for the infant who fails to search.

Egocentric space and visual space

If we accept that the perceptual system specifies permanence directly, it follows that there must be perception of space, since the permanence of the object implies that it is located somewhere in space. It is one thing to assert this and another to prove it. The issue is complicated by a tendency in the literature to confuse two aspects of spatial perception. These are the spatiality of the infant's own body and the spatial properties of the external environment.

If the perceptual system specifies certain invariant properties of objects directly it implies that those properties do not change with changes in the position of the observer. Invariance is a relational term which specifies spatio-temporal properties held in common by observer and observed. As Gibson (1966) puts it, the observer 'resonates' to invariant information in the environment. This would seem to require a unitary egocentric spatial system in relation to which environmental events can be perceived.

Mounoud (1976) discusses this issue. He argues that even at the reflexive level it is a mistake to consider the behaviour of the newborn a heterogeneous collection of activities. The newborn displays complex intercoordinations in behaviour. For example, when the palm of the baby's hand is touched, the mouth opens (the Babkin reflex). There is a built in relation between the hand and the mouth. When the newborn hears a sound, he will turn his eyes in spatial coordination (Wertheimer, 1961; Butterworth and Castillo, 1976). This type of coordination ensures that information obtained from either of the senses maps onto a unitary egocentric space. There exist complex visuo-motor coordinations which support this argument. Bullinger (1976) has shown that neonates, when appropriately supported, will orient their bodies in a coordinated fashion toward a visual target. Maratos (1973) and Moore and Meltzoff (1975) have shown that neonates can imitate tongue protrusion, mouth opening, lip protrusion and certain finger movements in a specific fashion. There is also an early form of reaching which is visually elicited. Very young babies will reach toward an object in their visual field. This does not require continuous visual guidance of the hand (Alt, 1968; Bower et al.,

1970a). Rather than relying on the mutual assimilation of reflexes, it would be better to think of the newborn as an integrated organism from the outset.

With respect to external space, there is evidence that infants respond to the spatial properties of objects. Fantz (1961) showed that babies of one month fixate three dimensional objects in preference to two dimensional displays. Bower (1970) showed that babies perceive stereoscopic depth in Julesz random dot patterns. Campos et al. (1970) found that 2 month old babies show greater heartrate deceleration on the deep side of a visual cliff than on the shallow side, indicating that they may discriminate the difference in depth. Several studies suggest that infants perceive shape and size constancy long before 9 months of age (Bower, 1966; McKenzie and Day, 1972; Day and McKenzie, 1973). The problem is that infants could be responding to the retinal correlates of depth (proximal stimuli) without any appreciation of the spatial (distal) properties to which these stimuli refer. Yonas and Pick (1975) argue that convergence of data across a wide variety of stimuli and responses may give grounds for assuming spatial perception on the principle of parsimony. However, this would still remain a matter of faith. A collection of separate instances can no more prove that spatial perception exists than can any one instance.

The alternative strategy is to find a response which must take into account the distal properties of stimulation. Bower (1972) reported that infants in the first ten days of life would reach toward a thin rod or a thick rod with the fingers and thumb being appropriately extended to the diameter of the object. This would be very strong evidence for spatial perception from birth. However, Dodwell et al. (1976) failed to replicate the study. There is evidence for hand shaping prior to contact with an object in older babies. Bruner and Koslowski (1972) found that infants aged between 10 and 15 weeks made shaping movements of the hands which varied according to the size of spheres used as visual stimuli. Bower et al. (1970a) report that infants between 7 days and 4 months of age would reach for a 'virtual' object, a three dimensional illusion produced by a stereoscopic shadow caster. When they failed to contact the object, infants became upset. Gordon and Yonas (1976) used a similar technique with much older infants aged 20 to 26 weeks. They found that babies would adjust their reaching according to the apparent distance of the display. Yonas et al. (1977a) have devised a convincing test of depth

perception. The Ames trapezoidal window was used as a reaching
target with infants six months of age. The window was presented at
an angle of 45 degrees to the line of sight so that it projected a
rectangle at the retina. When viewed monocularly the side of the
window which appeared closer was actually further away. Infants
consistently reached toward the side specified as closer by the
misleading perspective cues.

Another approach has been to study the reaction of babies to
optical expansion patterns. Under normal circumstances, movements
of an observer provide visual information about external events
(exteroception) and about the organism's own activity (proprioception)
through optical flow patterns at the retina induced by the activity
itself. As an observer moves forward, for example, the retinal
projections of surfaces in the visual field grow outward from a
stationary central point. This form of optic flow is ordinarily
contingent on movements of the observer only, and so it can be used
to specify self generated movement.

Lee and Aronson (1974) showed that infants monitor the stability
of the upright posture through visual proprioception. Infants stood on
a floor which was stable, inside a 'movable room'. When the end wall
moved toward or away, infants would compensate for a non-existent
loss of balance and fall backwards or forwards according to the
direction of movement of the visual framework. This study does not
establish whether vision acquires its spatial properties as a result of
motor activity. Butterworth and Hicks (1977) compared the stability
of the seated posture in the moving room in an older group of infants
who could walk with a younger group who had not yet learned to
walk. Discrepant visual information disrupted the seated posture
equally in both age groups. Thus experience in walking could not
have been responsible for the effect. Bower et al. (1970b; and Bower
1977) and Ball and Tronick (1971) found optical expansion to elicit
postural adjustments in infants as young as 6 days of age, while Yonas
et al. (1977b) and Cicchetti and Mans (1976) found the cue to be
effective in normal and Down's syndrome infants respectively, at 2
months. The evidence suggests that there may be an innate link
between optic flow patterns and the observer's relation to external
space. Rather than motor activity giving rise to this particular
perceptual structure, the innate relation may act as a calibrating
device for the infant to gain control of posture.

Although debates about spatial perception in infancy remain

heated, the evidence now seems sufficiently strong to suggest that the infant functions from the outset in relation to an external space.

Object identity

Michotte (1950) described a phenomenon in adult visual perception which he called the 'tunnel effect'. Under experimental conditions, when adults observe a moving object enter a tunnel, to emerge at the far end after an appropriate temporal interval, they often report having seen an object in continuous movement, even though motion was not specified by any sensory information while the object was hidden. A number of studies have adopted this experimental paradigm to establish whether infants may perceive continuity of movement in the same way (Mundy-Castle and Anglin, 1969; Gardner, 1971; Bower, 1971; K. E. Nelson, 1971, 1974). They show that infants will extrapolate the trajectory of an object visually. Anticipation is not usually immediate but is acquired over several trials, even by infants over 9 months of age. If the path of movement is reversed, infants have to reacquire the pattern.

Mundy-Castle and Anglin (1969) showed that infants of 4 months would track along the apparent trajectory of an invisibly moving object. In their experiment, an object would move upward to disappear at one window in a large screen. Then an identical object would move downward at a second window to the right. Infants would first establish the contingencies of events. After a few trials, they would extrapolate a curved trajectory between the windows. If the sequence was speeded up or slowed down, the visual trajectory interpolated became appropriately shallower or steeper. Ball (1973) suggests that infants perceive such events as a causally related sequence. Once the infant registers the sequence, the perceptual system deduces that a movement has taken place to account for it.

This type of perceptual process is adequate to link separate experiences, although it may link events which are actually quite distinct. For example, Bower (1971) found that infants under 3 months of age did not take into account a change in the distinctive features of an object which passed through a tunnel. So long as the object emerged after the appropriate temporal interval, infants would track it undisturbed. This is not so illogical as it may appear. Features may serve to classify an object (together with many other characteristics) but no set of features can help to determine whether a single object has changed its locus. This requires spatio-temporal criteria. It would appear that the young infant makes use of such criteria in perception, integrating them with featural information later in development.

A spatial argument is also applicable to the pattern of search found to characterize stage IV of Piaget's sensori-motoi progression. Both longitudinal and cross sectional studies show that infants make errors searching for hidden objects. However, infants do not search only where a previous action was successful. Instead, they will search persistently at the initial location, A, or persistently at the final location, B: i.e. they will search either at one locus or the other. In longitudinal studies, the same infant may make a series of errors on one occasion of testing and be consistently correct on the next. In cross sectional studies half the infants in a sample search persistently at the initial location and half search at the final location (Gratch and Landers, 1971; Bower and Paterson, 1973; Butterworth, 1977).

A number of experiments suggest that the infant solves the stage IV problem on the basis of spatial information available to immediate perception. For errors to occur, it is necessary to have a delay between hiding the object and allowing retrieval (Harris, 1973; Gratch et al., 1974). Under these conditions, the features of the object do not contribute to the pattern of search. The equiprobable pattern occurs whether the same object is hidden at B or a distinctively different object is hidden (Evans and Gratch, 1972). The infant may have a limited ability to represent a specific object and delay may force him to rely on information which remains in the visual field to direct search. Although the object is hidden, the place at which it disappears is visible.

In fact the same pattern occurs when the object is visible at both A and B. When the object is covered with transparent perspex, search is divided between A and B, just as when the object is hidden (Butterworth, 1977). It is not even necessary to cover the object. It is sufficient to move the visible object directly between A and B for half the infants in a sample to search persistently at A while the remainder search at B (Butterworth, 1974). Even when a purely pragmatic procedure will work (i.e. search where an object can be seen), infants apply spatial criteria for identity.

Spatial position serves to define a unique object. The infant who functions in a perceived space is bound to rely on perceptual processes to judge identity in relation to the spatial context but this need not confer absolute properties on the object. It is assumed here that the infant locates the object in a duality of relations between the self and the visual field. It was argued earlier that the infant's body (egocentric space) should be considered a spatial totality. That is, it can act as a frame of reference in relation to which a stationary object can be located. For example, an object may be located to the right of the body midline. The egocentric component of the dual spatial reference system can specify an invariant position at which the object exists and retains its identity. The problem comes with object movement. If the object is to retain its identity, the egocentric code must be brought up to date when the object moves. Updating in turn requires the infant to assume that a single object has changed its egocentric location. This is a vicious circle which cannot be broken. A change of position with respect to the visual field is automatically perceived as the movement of a single object in space (Koffka, 1935). In particular the background specifies an infinity of stable positions through which the object can pass. It provides a stable external spatial reference system for movement which does not require updating. If egocentric space and the visual field are not congruent, the egocentric code specifies the initial locus as the place where the object retains its identity while the visual field specifies the place where the object was last seen. The problem for the infant is not that perception lacks the rule that an object can only be in one place at one time but lies in coordinating the frames of reference which give rise to the definition of place.

Further evidence that spatial factors determine where the infant will search comes from a series of studies by Butterworth and Hicks (in preparation).[1] Fig. 4.2 shows the design of one of these studies.

A standard procedure was adopted in which infants retrieved the object once from the initial location, A. Then the object was hidden at a new location, B, defined with respect to the cover, the background, and the infant (i.e. to the baby's left or right).

It was found that errors were eliminated if successive locations A and B were distinctively different and connected by a continuous background (condition IV). The other conditions result in the divided pattern of search. Further experiments have shown that the spatial stability of the A cover is crucial. If its position in the visual field is changed before the object is hidden at B, infants fail to solve the task. It is as if the original cover at its particular position serves as a distinctive landmark which coordinates egocentric and visual space. In much the same way, a landmark allows a map reader to relate his own movements to the geographical environment. Furthermore, another study showed that if the object is always hidden at the same absolute position beneath the same cover and the background is changed, the divided pattern reappears, even though the object does not move and the infant has the opportunity to repeat a successful response.

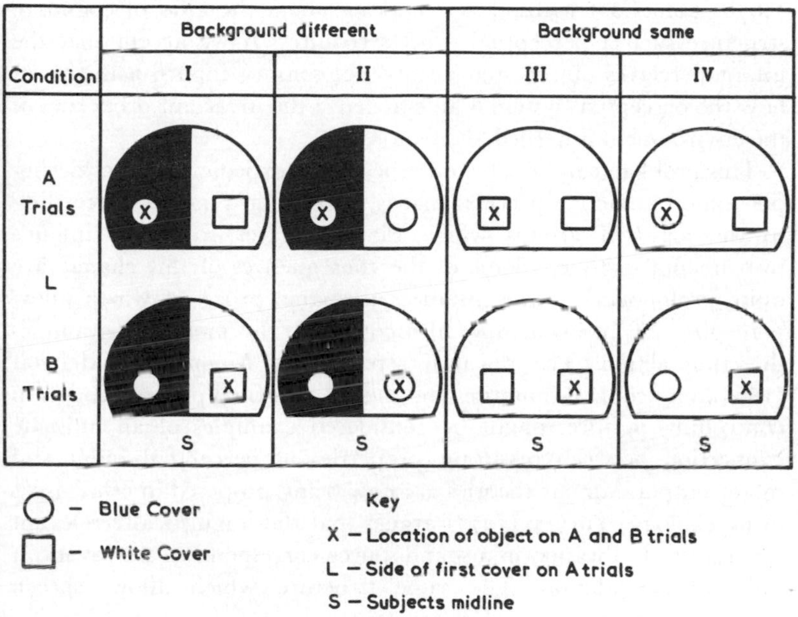

	Background different		Background same	
Condition	I	II	III	IV
A Trials	⬛️◻️ (X) □	⬛️○ (X) ○	X □	(X) □
L				
B Trials	○ X	○ (X)	□ X	○ X
	S	S	S	S

○ — Blue Cover
□ — White Cover

Key

X — Location of object on A and B trials
L — Side of first cover on A trials
S — Subjects midline

Fig. 4.2   Some spatial factors determining search in Piaget's stage IV task [Butterworth and Hicks]

Once the infant is provided with a landmark on which he can rely to monitor movements of the object, he demonstrates that he can search correctly. So, even if the infant's capacity to represent an object at a particular location is non-existent (which is probably not the case) the baby can rely on processes in immediate perception to connect the separate places at which the object disappeared through the spatial context. Even though the object is known in relation to the context, as Piaget argues, it can be identified when it is moved.

Implications

Taken as a whole, the evidence suggests that perception of the objective properties of the environment in infancy does not await the coordination of action schemes or the development of representation. If action does not structure perception in infancy, the implication is that perception provides direct information about reality. As Gibson (1966) argues, sensory systems have evolved to pick up invariant information that is objectively present in the world. But as Neisser (1976) points out, Gibson says nothing about the kind of cognitive structure such a perceptual process requires. If we accept that the infant perceives objects and events, not sensory inputs, a theory of how the perceptual system is able to detect the invariant properties of the environment is needed.

This problem can be solved by the simple expedient of considering perception an active process: that is, perception functions according to the logic of groups which Piaget derives from the infant's instrumental activity. Some of the consequences of this change are quite profound. In some instances the same processes which allow perception of an event may also constitute the motor programmes directing action. The research reported by Moore and Meltzoff (1975), on neonatal imitation and the role of visual proprioception in controlling posture, might be considered examples of an intimate connection between invariant properties of perceptual input and motor output. Similar theories are now being proposed in other areas of psychology. Turvey (1977) argues that the linguistically relevant invariants of vibration in a sound source correspond to the invariant units of articulation. The same structure which allows speech perception subserves speech production.

If perception is considered an active process, this has implications for Piaget's theory. It can be argued that thought reflects processes inherent in perception. Long ago, Dewey (1891) summarized the underlying developmental continuity by defining cognition as 'apperception of the apperceptive process' but as yet there is little developmental evidence that perceptual processes are transformed into cognitive structures. Butterworth (1976) found an asymmetry in performance when Piaget's stage IV task is arranged in the vertical plane. Infants who first found an object at the upper of two containers before it was moved to the lower made many more errors than infants who performed the task with initial and final locations in the opposite order. It was argued that positions which are 'up' are especially marked in egocentric space. Clark (1973) reports that the vertical dimension is also asymmetrical in the semantic space defined by the relationship between words. It is possible that the semantic asymmetry builds on the spatial asymmetry already present in infancy but this remains a speculation.

There is reason to suppose that instrumental activity is involved in cognitive development, although not quite at the structural level which Piaget envisaged. The problem with perceptual processes is that they remain tied to the context in which events occur, whereas what we choose to call conceptual rules are not tied to time or place. The transition from perception to thought may involve action in several ways.

As Gibson (1966) points out, action may make manifest the properties of objects to perception. It does not construct the object but it allows the properties of particular objects to be discovered. Many of Piaget's observations, in which infants manipulate objects in their own visual field, may reflect this process of discovery. Action may also serve to classify objects in terms of their functional properties, e.g. a ball rolls, although some of these properties can be perceived without action intervening. Functional properties may serve the same purpose in classification as visual features, auditory qualities, and so on. Nelson (1974) has shown that early vocabulary is composed of words describing both the perceptual characteristics and the functional properties of objects, so what the infant can do with an object may be important in how it comes to be categorized. Action may also be important in providing a metric for visual space, although action does not seem responsible for spatial perception as such.

However, none of this is sufficient to transform a perceptual process into a conceptual rule structure. Two further developments seem necessary. The first is to extend the child's understanding of object identity beyond the limited spatial confines of immediate perception. Once the infant comes to represent objects in relation to a generalized background, spatial limitations are removed. This development may take place by representing (interiorizing) the general properties of the background constantly available to immediate perception. From this point on, action may play an important role in the transition from perceptual to cognitive functioning. Awareness of the rules inherent in perceptual functions may require the infant to experience some 'resistance' of objects to the rules. In some stage IV studies, it has been found that older infants are more likely to make errors than younger infants (Butterworth, 1974, 1976; Harris, 1974). It is as if the younger infant works deductively on perceptual information which connects the present with the past and this leads to the equiprobable pattern described above. The older infant, who is very skilled in searching begins to anticipate the position of the object in egocentric space (this is known as a closed skill, Poulton, 1950). Consequently, the older baby often makes more errors than the younger child. Failure of such an action-based prediction may lead the infant to an awareness of the rules which govern the movements of objects.

The transition from a competence based on perceptual processes to performance based on conceptual rules is an important issue which recurs at all levels of Piaget's theory. For example, it has been shown that children between two and seven years of age (preoperational stage) perform competently on a variety of logical tasks which were thought to depend on the acquisition of concrete operations between the ages of eight and twelve. Bryant (1974) and Trabasso (1976) suggest that where memory factors are controlled and the task falls within the child's perceptual span, preoperational children display a basic competence in conservation, transitivity, and other concrete operational tasks. These theories are hotly disputed, partly because testing Piaget's theory inevitably raises complex methodological and theoretical problems (Miller, 1976).

Nevertheless, Bryant (1974) is quite clear that the competence which he describes is not the same as Piaget's conceptual competence in concrete operational problems. Bryant argues that the preoperational child relies on logical processes inherent in perception. The child is said to use external frames of reference to make unconscious deductive inferences about perceptual continua such as size and number. The perceptual solution involves none of the predictive qualities of concrete operational thought, rather the child makes deductions after the event. Thus for Bryant perceptual processes are prior to rather than consequent upon the acquisition of logical processes in cognition. The relation between the two is not made clear but he argues that children abandon external frameworks in favour of more flexible internal frameworks, such as number systems, as they get older. One possibility is that the developmental transition lies in mapping logic inherent in perception into language. This is not to say that language provides the child with the necessary logic but that language extends its range of applicability. Language can then act as a medium or frame of reference for cognitive processes (see e.g. Heber, 1977).

An extension of the 'frame of reference' argument can be made to the formal operational period. Strauss and Kroy (1977) argue that the capacity for scientific thinking depends on the ability to 'idealize'.

That is, to refer to a frame of reference in which interfering factors are eliminated. Only when the ideal model is available can individual propositions be tested. The result is a form of thought which can be paraphrased as follows: 'If it weren't for air resistance, a feather would fall as fast as a stone'. From this perspective cultural factors might be expected to influence formal operational reasoning to the extent that they define metaphysical or 'ideal' frames of reference.

Finally, it can be argued that the functional significance of perceptual competence in early infancy is to define social objects, so that the motorically immature baby can make contact with other people. If this is the case, there are implications for the role of social factors in cognitive growth. The subtle influence of social factors in the child's reasoning is illustrated by McGarrigle and Donaldson (1974/5). They found that preoperational children's judgement of the relative number of elements in two rows was influenced by whether they perceived the lengthening of one row as intended by the experimenter or as an accident. If the transformation was perceived as accidental, more children conserved number than if it was perceived as intentional. In a sense, the transformation is perceived as influencing number because the experimenter's behaviour defines length as a relevant attribute by which the child interprets the adult's questions about numerosity.

Conclusions

Piaget's description of development in infancy remains one of the most acute observational studies in psychology. Contemporary research raises basic disagreements over interpretation, rather than over the observations themselves. In particular, if infants can perceive invariant properties of objects directly, this must have profound implications for Piaget's constructionist model of cognition. This does not detract from the value of the Piagetian framework in confronting the psychologist with basic philosophical issues. Piaget's greatest contribution may let lie in reconciling the empirical method of enquiry with the philosophical assumptions on which psychology is founded.

Note

1 These experiments were financed by a grant from the Medical Research Council.

References

Alt, J. (1968) *The Use of Vision in Early Reaching.* Unpublished Honours Thesis, Harvard University.

Baldwin, J. M. (1894) *Mental Development in the Child and the Race.* New York: Macmillan.

Ball, W. A. (1973) *The Perception of Causality in the Infant,* Report 37, Developmental programme, Department of Psychology, University of Michigan.

Ball, W. A. and Tronick, E. (1971) Infant responses to impending collision: optical and real. *Science 171:* 818–21.

Bower, T. G. R. (1966) The visual world of infants. *Scientific American 215:* 80–92.

Bower, T. G. R. (1967) The development of object permanence: some studies of existence constancy. *Perception and Psychophysics 2* (9): 411–18.

Bower, T. G. R. (1970) Morphogenetic problems in space perception. In D. A. Hamburg and K. Pribram (eds) *Research Publications: Association for Research in Nervous and Mental Diseases 48.* Baltimore, Maryland: Williams and Wilkins.

Bower, T. G. R. (1971) The object in the world of the infant. *Scientific American 225* (4): 31–8.

Bower, T. G. R. (1972) Object perception in infants. *Perception 1:* 15–30.

Bower, T. G. R. (1975) Infant perception in the third dimension and object concept development. In L. B. Cohen and P. Salapatek (eds) *Infant Perception, from Sensation to Cognition,* Vol. II. New York: Academic Press, pp. 33–50.

Bower, T. G. R. (1977) Comment on Yonas et al., 'Development of sensitivity to information for impending collision'. *Perception and Psychophysics 21* (3): 281–2.

Bower, T. G. R., Broughton, J. and Moore, M. K. (1970a) Demonstration of intention in reaching behavior. *Nature 228:* 679–81.

Bower, T. G. R., Broughton, J. and Moore, M. K. (1970b) The coordination of visual and tactual input in infants. *Perception and Psychophysics 8:* 51–3.

Bower, T. G. R. and Paterson, J. G. (1973) Stages in the development of the object concept. *Cognition 1* (1): 47–55.

Bower, T. G. R. and Wishart, J. C. (1972) The effects of motor skill on object permanence. *Cognition 1:* 165–72.

Bruner, J. S. and Koslawski, B. (1972) Visually preadapted constituents of manipulatory action. *Perception 1* (1): 1–14.

Bruner, J. S., Kaye, K. and Lyons, K. (1973) *The Growth of Human Manual Intelligence, III: The Development of Detour Reaching.* Unpublished manuscript, Harvard University.

Bryant, P. E. (1974) *Perception and Understanding in Young Children.* London: Methuen.

Bullinger, A. (1976) *Orientation de la tête du nouveau né en presence d'un stimulus visuel.* Paper presented to the International Congress of Psychology, Paris.

Butterworth, G. E. (1974) *The Development of the Object Concept in Human Infants.* Unpublished D. Phil. thesis, University of Oxford.

Butterworth, G. E. (1976) Asymmetrical search errors in infancy. *Child Development* 47: 864-7.

Butterworth, G. E. (1977) Object disappearance and error in Piaget's stage IV task. *Journal of Experimental Child Psychology* 23: 391-405.

Butterworth, G. E. and Castillo, M. (1976) Coordination of auditory and visual space in newborn human infants. *Perception* 5: 155-60.

Butterworth, G. E. and Hicks, L. (1977) Visual proprioception and postural stability in infancy: A developmental study. *Perception* 6: 255-62.

Campos, J. J., Langer, A. and Krowitz, A. (1970) Cardiac responses to the visual cliff in prelocomotor human infants. *Science* 170: 196-7.

Cicchetti, D. and Mans, S. L. (1976) Down's syndrome and normal infants' response to impending collision. Paper presented to the annual meeting of the American Psychological Association, Washington, D.C.

Clark, H. H. (1973) Space, time, semantics and the child. In T. E. Moore (ed.) *Cognitive Development and the Acquisition of Language*. New York and London: Academic Press, 27-62.

Cohen, L. B. and Salapatek, P. (eds) (1975) *Infant Perception from Sensation to Cognition*, Vols. I & II. New York: Academic Press.

Day, R. H. and McKenzie, B. E. (1973) Perceptual shape constancy in early infancy. *Perception* 3: 315-26.

Dé Carie, T. G. (1965) *Intelligence and Affectivity in Childhood*. New York: International Universities Press.

Dewey, J. (1891) *Psychology*. New York: American Book Company.

Dodwell, P. C., Muir, D. and Di Franco, D. (1976) Responses of infants to visually presented objects. *Science* 194: 209-11.

Evans, W. F. and Gratch, G. (1972) The stage IV error in Piaget's theory of object concept development: Difficulties in object conceptualization of spatial localization? *Child Development* 43: 682-8.

Fantz, R. L. (1961) A method for studying depth perception in infants under 6 months of age. *Psychological Record* 11: 27-32.

Flavell, J. H. (1963) *The Developmental Psychology of Jean Piaget*. London: Van Nostrand.

Gardner, J. K. G. (1971) *The Development of Object Identity in the First 6 months of Life*. Paper presented at the meeting of the Society for Research in Child Development, Minneapolis, Minnesota.

Gibson, J. J. (1966) *The Senses Considered as Perceptual Systems*. London: George Allen & Unwin.

Gibson, J. J., Kaplan, G. A., Reynolds, H. N. Jr and Wheeler, K. (1969) The change from visible to invisible: A study of optical transitions. *Perception and Psychophysics* 5 (2): 113-16.

Gordon, F. R. and Yonas, A. (1976) Sensitivity to binocular depth information in infants. *Journal of Experimental Child Psychology* 22: 413-22.

Gratch, G. (1975) Recent studies based on Piaget's view of object concept development. In L. Cohen and P. Salapatek (eds) *Infant Perception, from Sensation to Cognition*, Vol. II. New York: Academic Press, 51-99.

Gratch, G., Appel, K. J., Evans, W. F., Le Compte, G. K. and Wright, N. A. (1974) Piaget's stage IV object concept error: Evidence of forgetting or object conception? *Child Development* 45 (1): 71-7.

Gratch, G. and Landers, W. F. (1971) Stage IV of Piaget's theory of infant's object concepts: A longitudinal study. *Child Development 42:* 359–72.

Harris, P. L. (1973) Perseverative errors in search by young children. *Child Development 44:* 28–33.

Harris, P. L. (1974) Perseverative search at a visibly empty place by young infants. *Journal of Experimental Child Psychology 18:* 535–42.

Harris, P. L. (1975) Development of search and object permanence during infancy. *Psychological Bulletin 82:* 332–44.

Heber, M. (1977) The influence of language training on seriation of five- to six-year-old children initially at different levels of descriptive competence. *British Journal of Psychology 68:* 85–95.

Koffka, K. (1935) *Principles of Gestalt Psychology.* London: Routledge and Kegan Paul.

Köhler, W. (1925) *The Mentality of Apes.* London: Kegan Paul, Trench Trubner.

Lee, R. N. and Aronson, E. (1974) Visual-proprioceptive control of standing in human infants. *Perception and Psychophysics 15* (3): 529–32.

Maratos, O. (1973) *Origins of Imitation in Early Childhood.* Ph.D. thesis, University of Geneva.

McGarrigle, J. and Donaldson, M. (1974/5) Conservation accidents. *Cognition 3* (4): 307–11.

McKenzie, B. E. and Day, R. H. (1972) Object distance as a determinant of visual fixation in early infancy. *Science 178:* 1108–10.

Michotte, A. (1950) A propos de la permanence phénoménale, faits et théories. *Acta Psychologica 7:* 298–322.

Miller, S. A. (1976) Nonverbal assessment of Piagetian concepts. *Psychological Bulletin 83* (3): 405–30.

Moore, M. K. and Meltzoff, A. N. (1975) *Neonate Imitation: A Test of Existence and Mechanism.* Paper presented to the Society for Research in Child Development, Denver, Colorado.

Mounoud, P. (1976) Revolutionary periods in early development. *Archives de Psychologie XLIV* (171): 103–14.

Mundy-Castle, A. C. and Anglin, J. M. (1969) Looking strategies in infants. Paper presented at the meeting of the Society for Research in Child Development, Santa Monica. Reprinted in W. Stone, H. T. Smith and L. B. Murphy (1974) *The Competent Infant.* London: Tavistock Publications, 713–17.

Neisser, U. (1976) *Cognition and Reality.* New York: W. H. Freeman.

Nelson, K. E. (1971) Accommodation of visual tracking patterns in human infants to object movement patterns. *Journal of Experimental Child Psychology 12:* 182–96.

Nelson, K. E. (1974) Infant's short term progress toward one component of object permanence. *Merrill Palmer Quarterly 20* (1): 3–8.

Nelson, K. (1974) Concept, word and sentence: Interrelations in acquisition and development. *Psychological Review 81:* 267–85.

Piaget, J. (1950) *The Psychology of Intelligence.* New York: Harcourt Brace.

Piaget, J. (1951) *Play, Dreams, and Imitation in Childhood.* New York: Norton.

Piaget, J. (1953) *The Origins of Intelligence in the Child.* New York: International Universities Press.

Piaget, J. (1954) *The Construction of Reality in the Child.* New York: Basic Books.

Piaget, J. (1969) *The Mechanisms of Perception.* London: Routledge and Kegan Paul.

Piaget, J. (1971) *Biology and Knowledge.* Chicago: University of Chicago Press.

Poulton, E. C. (1950) *Anticipation in Open and Closed Sensori-motor Skills.* Report No. 138, Cambridge, Medical Research Council Applied Psychology Unit.

Salapatek, P. and Kessen, W. (1966) Visual scanning of triangles by the human newborn. *Journal of Experimental Child Psychology 3:* 155–67.

Stone, W., Smith, H. T. and Murphy, L. B. (1974) *The Competent Infant.* London: Tavistock Publications.

Strauss, S. and Kroy, M. (1977) The child as logician or methodologist? A critique of formal operations. *Human Development 20* (2): 102–17.

Trabasso, T. (1976) The role of memory as a system in making transitive inferences. In R. V. Kail and J. W. Hagen (eds) *Perspectives on the Development of Memory and Cognition.* Hillsdale, New Jersey: Lawrence Erlbaum Associates.

Turvey, M. T. (1977) Preliminaries of a theory of action with reference to vision. In R. Shaw and J. Bransford (eds) *Perceiving, Acting and Knowing.* Hillsdale, New Jersey: Lawrence Erlbaum Associates, 211–65.

Wertheimer, M. (1961) Psychomotor coordination of auditory and visual space at birth. *Science 134:* 692.

Wolff, P. H. (1960) The developmental psychologies of Jean Piaget and psychoanalysis. *Psychological Issues 2:* 1–181.

Yonas, A., Cleaves, W. and Petterson, L. (1977a) *Sensitivity to Pictorial Depth in Infants.* Paper presented to the Annual Conference of the Society for Research in Child Development, New Orleans.

Yonas, A., Bechtold, G., Frankel, D., Gordon, F., McRoberts, G., Norcia, A. and Sternfels, S. (1977b) Development of sensitivity to information for impending collision. *Perception and Psychophysics 21* (2): 97–104.

Yonas, A. and Pick, H. L. Jr (1975) An approach to the study of infant space perception. In L. B. Cohen and P. Salapatek (eds) *Infant Perception from Sensation to Cognition,* Vol II. New York: Academic Press, 3–31.

5 The psychology of deductive reasoning: Logic

Jonathan St B. T. Evans

'Contrariwise', continued Tweedledee, 'if it was so, it might be; and if it were so, it would be: but as it isn't, it ain't. That's logic.'

(Through the Looking Glass)

Introduction

In this chapter I shall consider the contribution of formal logic to the study of human thinking, both as a normative or prescriptive theory of how we ought to think and as a descriptive theory of how we actually think. The former problem is, of course, mainly of interest to the philosopher and the latter to the psychologist. However, a number of psychologists have shown interest in normative theories in recent years, due partly to developments in artificial intelligence (see Chapter 8) and partly to the use of an analogy with the psycholinguistic distinction between models of 'competence' and 'performance' (see, for example, Osherson, 1975). Before consideration of the psychological issues involved, however, let us take a brief look at the nature of logic itself.

In general we may define a logical system as one which provides a set of *rules of inference* which permit conclusions to be drawn from assumptions in a manner which is *valid*. Validity is normally defined in terms of its consequence – namely that in any valid argument it is impossible to draw a false conclusion from assumptions all of which are true. In other words it is a system for ensuring that the conclusions of arguments based on true premises will themselves be true (it does *not*, however, preclude the possibility that false premises may lead to true conclusions). Mathematics can be seen as a logical system which provides rules of inference for the manipulation of numbers and symbols, and most mathematical proofs are of a logically deductive nature. A familiar example is Euclid's geometry in which a number of theorems (conclusions) are deduced from certain axioms (assumptions). Subsequent non-Euclidean geometries work within the same logical system, i.e. accept the same rules of inference, but hold slightly different axioms which necessarily generates different theorems.

Logic is fundamental to pure mathematics in that mathematical theories must be internally consistent. Scientific theories also must meet this requirement, but in science an extra element is added – an interest in *empirical* truth and falsity. But whilst certain basic propositions can be evaluated by direct observation (e.g. 'the rod will expand when heated') this is clearly not true of a complex scientific theory, such as Newtonian mechanics or Mendelian genetics. The corroboration of a scientific theory must somehow be *inferred* from the truth and falsity of empirically testable propositions. The view of Popper (1968) that the object of science is to seek falsification of its theories is widely accepted. This is actually accomplished by a form of logical reasoning known as *reductio ad absurdum* (RAA).[1] A RAA argument is one which permits one to infer the falsity of any assumption from which a logical contradiction is deduced. Hence, a scientific theory which generates predictions in the form of testable propositions, by a process of logical deduction, is subject to contradiction whenever such a prediction fails to fit with empirical observation. Such contradictions imply that at least part of the underlying theory is false, leading to consequent abandonment or revision of the theory.

In so far as a psychologist is a scientist he is interested in the above uses of logic in the construction and testing of theories. A psychologist of thinking is, however, interested in logic not only as a prescriptive model of his own behaviour, but as a descriptive model of how his subjects behave. Psychologists have most generally been interested in studying verbal reasoning process. (A possible point of confusion here is that philosophers and logicians use the term 'reasoning' to refer to the process of drawing inferences *according to the laws of logic* whereas psychologists frequently use the term to refer to the actual thought process by which inferences are drawn, whether logical or otherwise.) The main interest has been not in mathematical systems but in forms of logic developed for the purpose of drawing inferences from verbal statements or propositions. Such systems have a long history, and examples of the classical syllogism developed by Aristotle are probably familiar, e.g.

All dogs are mammals
All mammals breathe air
Therefore, all dogs breathe air.

Since Aristotle's time, more powerful and comprehensive systems of formal logic have been developed, such as the propositional and predicate calculi (see, for example, Lemmon, 1965). One of the most useful relationships dealt with in modern logic is the rule of *material implication* between some antecedent event or proposition p and a consequent q. Logicians often represent this relationship by the verbal formulation, *If p then q*, known as a conditional – although, as we shall see later, there are problems with this. For the moment, note that a class inclusive relationship such as the above 'All dogs are mammals' can be expressed as a conditional: 'If it is a dog then it is a mammal'. the conditional form is, however, very flexible and can be used to represent relationships with other semantic bases, for example causality: 'If the switch is turned then the light will come on'; or definitional relationships: 'If a person has an XY chromosome then that person is male'.

The notion that logic may be regarded as a model for human thinking has a long history in philosophy. Prior to the development of experimental psychology there was a tendency to assume an identity between the laws of logic and those of human thought, and dispute whether logic was reducible to psychology (psychologism) or *vice versa* (logicism). We are not concerned with such issues here, and the interested reader is referred to the scholarly reviews by Bolton (1972), Henle (1962) and Luchins and Luchins (1965). Our main concern will be to consider contemporary research into people's behaviour on logically structured tasks, and the kinds of theory which have been proposed to account for such behaviour.

Theoretical approaches

In an earlier article (Evans, 1972a) I classified psychological theories of reasoning into three categories:

(i) Logical

A 'logical' theory of reasoning is one which assumes that subjects draw inferences according to the laws of formal logic. Such a theory has been proposed by Henle (1962) to explain reasoning behaviour with problems constructed as Aristotelean syllogisms. She explains subjects' frequent erroneous conclusions by a tendency for them to misinterpret or alter the information presented in the premises of the argument.

(ii) Illogical

An 'illogical' theory is one which also assumes that the subjects reason with attention to the formal structure of the theory but adopt rules of inference deviant from those of formal logic: for example, an individual might accept logically fallacious inferences as valid. Chapman and Chapman (1959) have proposed a theory of syllogistic reasoning along these lines.

(iii) Non-logical

A 'non-logical' theory assumes that subjects' behaviour is determined by factors independent of the logical structure of the problems. The earliest theory of syllogistic reasoning, Woodworth and Sells's (1935) 'atmosphere effect' was of this type.

A second distinction discussed at length in the earlier paper (Evans, 1972a) is that of two kinds of factor which affect the reasoning process: *interpretational* and *operational*. Interpretational factors relate to the subjects' comprehension of the sentences forming the premises of the arguments. Operational factors are those pertaining to reasoning operations which must be carried out.

The distinction is also discussed by Smedslund (1970), who points out that one may deduce the nature of a subject's interpretation of a rule only if one assumes that he reasons logically. Conversely, we may discover whether a subject reasons logically only if we know how he has interpreted the sentence – reasoning and understanding are related in circular fashion. The Henle hypothesis, which is very influential among current researchers, makes the former assumption.

Her theory is in fact only *logical* at the operational stage and it is *non-logical* at the interpretational stage. The hypothesis is attractive because if one assumes reasoning to be logical, one can test psycholinguistic hypotheses about the subject's interpretation of different sentences used in reasoning tasks. If the hypothesis is correct then formal logic clearly can make an important contribution to the study of human thought. For this reason we will examine the Henle hypothesis critically in the light of current experimental evidence on deductive reasoning.

Contemporary studies may be classified into three main areas according to the kind of logical system on which the problems are based: (i) syllogistic reasoning (ii) transitive inference (three term series reasoning) and (iii) propositional reasoning. Owing to space limitations it will not be possible to deal in detail with the first two areas, which are well reviewed by Revlis (1975) and Johnson-Laird (1972) respectively. Propositional reasoning is chosen as our focus since research here has been particularly relevant to the problem of the role of logic in human thinking. Also, much of the interesting and important work in this area has been carried out since the last available review by Wason and Johnson-Laird (1972).

Logical background

Before discussing the experimental studies it is necessary to outline the basic features of propositional logic, upon which the structure of the problems is based. Among the propositions dealt with by logicians are the aforementioned conditionals (*If p then q*), disjunctives (*Either p or q*) and conjunctives (*p and q*). By far the most psychological research has centred on conditionals, the logic of which we must now look at more closely. The propositional calculus provides two alternative but equivalent methods for assessing the validity of arguments. There are certain rules of inference which permit a new proposition to be deduced from one or more previous propositions which are either assumed or themselves deduced. One such rule is *reductio ad absurdum*, defined above; the other procedure is known as truth table analysis. In this method the truth and falsity of each premise of an argument is permuted systematically and the resultant truth value of the conclusion calculated. If no combination exists where the premises are all true and the conclusion false then the argument is valid. The relation between truth and falsity is defined by negation: if *p* is true then *not p* is false and *vice versa*. Let us consider a simple example to illustrate the method of truth table analysis. Given the argument 'John is clever and rich, therefore John is clever' how can we determine its validity? We permute the truth values of the most elementary propositions 'John is clever' and '(John) is rich' and not the concurrent truth values of the assumption (only one here) and the conclusion.

Table 5.1

Truth table case	Assumption John is clever and rich	Conclusion John is clever
clever, rich	true	true
clever, not rich	false	true
not clever, rich	false	false
not clever, not rich	false	false

We see from the above that the conjunction 'John is clever and rich' is only true if both its constituent parts are true – in all other cases it is false. Clearly the conclusion is true for those lines in the truth table where John is assumed to be clever, and false in those lines where he is assumed not to be clever. Looking down the table we see that it is possible for the conclusion to be true when the assumption is false – but this is not forbidden. It is *never* the case that the assumption is true and the conclusion false, so our example is indeed a valid argument. Suppose we tried to reverse the argument and say that 'John is clever, therefore John is clever and rich'. This argument is clearly invalid because a case exists (John is clever and not rich) where the assumption would be true and the conclusion false.

The above example is trivial in the sense that the argument is intuitively obvious, but it serves to illustrate a formal method which is capable of dealing with very complex arguments. Now suppose we had an argument involving a conditional rule *If p then q*. In order to adopt the truth table method we would need to know what truth value we should assign to the rule as a function of the possible permutations of truth and falsity of its components p and q. This information we define as the truth table of the rule. Clearly the truth table we assign to the conditional rule should be both necessary and sufficient to characterize its logical nature and determine what inferences may be drawn from it. Unfortunately, it is far from clear what the nature of this truth table should be and we shall consider here four possibilities. (See Table 5.2)

Table 5.2

Truth table case	Truth value of the rule given			
	(a) Material implication	(b) Defective implication	(c) Material equivalence	(d) Defective equivalence
pq (TT)	T	T	T	T
pq̄ (TF)	F	F	F	F
p̄q (FT)	T	?	F	F
p̄q̄ (FF)	T	?	T	?

Notes: T = True; F = False; ? = Irrelevant (or indeterminate); p̄ = 'not p'; q̄ = 'not q'.

As stated earlier, the normal convention in formal logic is to assume that *If p then q* represents a relation of material implication between the antecedent *p* and the consequent *q*. The truth table for material implication is shown in Table 5.2(a). Under this truth table the rule is false if we have a true antecedent with a false consequent (the TF case) which occurs by the combination of *p and not q* (which we abbreviate as *pq̄*). For all other cases the rule is regarded as true.

If we recall a previous example of a conditional rule 'if it is a dog then it is a mammal' then under material implication the rule would be false only if we could find a dog which was not a mammal. However, the rule would be true not only for a dog which was a mammal, but anything which was *not* a dog whether it was a mammal (e.g. a cow) or not (e.g. a tree). Wason (1966) proposed that this part of the truth table is counterintuitive, and that people in fact have a defective implication truth table (Table 5.2 (b)) in which the rule is considered *irrelevant* to cases where the antecedent condition is not fulfilled. Thus, a third truth value 'irrelevant' is added to the 'true' and 'false' considered in standard logic.

Material equivalence arises if the implication is considered to go from *q* to *p* as well as from *p* to *q*. The logician assigns this relation *biconditional* rule, *If and only if p then q*, and describes it by the truth table shown in Table 5.2(c). This differs from material implication in that the FT case (*not p* and *q*) also falsifies the rule. People, unlike logicians, tend not to use the biconditional form to express equivalence. They use the conditional form to express equivalence as well as implication: the listener must disambiguate it according to his knowledge of the world. Hence, no one would take 'If it is a dog then it is a mammal' to mean also 'If it is a mammal then it is a dog'. On the other hand, we might well take a definitional rule to be an equivalence, hence 'If a person has an XY chromosome then that person is male' *does* suggest that 'If a person is male then that person has an XY chromosome'. Thus they would not see a mammal which was not a dog as falsifying the former rule, but would see a male person without an XY chromosome as falsifying the latter (each case is logically FT). An equivalence is regarded as 'defective' if the FF case (not an XY and not male) is regarded as irrelevant to the rule rather than a verifying case of it.

It was stated earlier that propositional logic contains rules of inference which are equivalent to, and hence derivable from, truth table analysis. For example, the simple argument formally proved in Table 5.1 is an accepted rule of inference known as 'And elimination' (Lemmon, 1965). Four accepted rules of inference associated with conditional rules are shown in Table 5.3. The Modus Ponens (MP) and Modus Tollens (MT) arguments are valid for either an implication or an equivalence truth table. In either table the case TF (p$\bar{q}$) is prohibited. Hence, if the antecedent is true (p) then the consequent must also be true (q): this is MP. Similarly, if the consequent is false ($\bar{q}$) the antecedent cannot be true, so one concludes, by MT that it is false ($\bar{p}$). Denial of the antecedent (DA) and affirmation of the consequent (AC) are valid only for equivalence truth tables in which FT case is also prohibited. Hence, a true consequent (q) necessitates a true antecedent (p) by AC, and a false antecedent ($\bar{p}$) necessitates a false consequent ($\bar{q}$) by DA. It is important to note that since the validity of inferences is determed from the *false* cases of the truth table, it is not affected by whether or not the truth table is 'defective' (Table 5.2).

To illustrate the nature of these inferences let us return to our previous examples of conditional rules. Given the implication 'If it is a dog then it is a mammal' we would accept MP (Dog implies mammal) and MT (not a mammal implies not a dog) but regard DA (not a dog implies not a mammal) and AC (mammal implies dog) as fallacious.

On the other hand, with our equivalence 'If a person has an XY chromosome then that person is a male' we would accept all four inferences: XY implies male (MP), not XY implies not a male (DA), male implies XY (AC) and not a male implies not XY (MT).

Table 5.3

	Given	Conclude	Validity	
			Implication	Equivalence
Modus Ponens (MP)	p	q	valid	valid
Denial of the antecedent (DA)	p̄	q̄	fallacious	valid
Affirmation of the consequent (AC)	q	p	fallacious	valid
Modus Tollens (MT)	q̄	p̄	valid	valid

Experimental studies of reasoning

Having looked in detail at the logic of conditionals, we are now in a position to look at some actual data on how people reason. In view of the above discussion of the linguistic ambiguity of conditional rules, it is clearly not very useful to ask whether people reason in the manner prescribed by formal logic. We will assess the evidence for *logical* theories of reasoning, such as that of Henle, by asking whether subjects reason *consistently* according to some particular interpretation of the rule.

It is particularly interesting to examine consistency between results obtained under different paradigms or methods of studying reasoning. In the case of conditional reasoning three main paradigms have emerged: (i) studies of the four basic inferences (Table 5.3); (ii) direct investigations of psychological truth tables (cf. Table 5.2); and (iii) Wason's 'selection task' or four-card problem (to be defined later).

(1) Inference tasks
In the first paradigm, subjects' tendencies to make or withhold the four inferences, MP, DA, AC, and MT are measured. There are several ways of doing this: the subject may be given the premises of the argument and asked what conclusion, if any, follows. More

commonly, he is given a choice of conclusions to choose from, including 'indeterminate', or given the likely conclusion (Table 5.3) and asked whether or not the inference is valid. These slight procedural variations tend to go unnoticed but might quite possibly exert some influence on the data collected.

Data from various sources reviewed by Wason and Johnson-Laird (1972) have tended to show that most adult subjects will make the 'valid' MP and MT inferences. The data for DA and AC are less clear, but most studies find that they also tend to be endorsed more often than not – a finding which has led various authors to suppose that subjects interpret a conditional rule as an equivalence.

Taplin (1971) conducted an experiment which looked not simply at the frequency of the four inferences, but also at subjects' consistency over repeated presentations of the same problems. Taplin was also interested in seeing whether subjects reasoned in a 'truth-functional' manner, that is, whether or not their reasoning was consistent with some kind of truth table. At a global level his results replicated earlier studies, i.e. all four inferences tended to be made rather than withheld. However, only 45 per cent reasoned in a consistently truth-functional manner, the great majority of these conforming to an equivalence truth table and only a few to an implication truth table.

The Taplin (1971) study had used thematic materials for the conditional sentences but an experiment by Taplin and Staudenmeyer (1973) produced essentially similar results with abstract materials, except that the degree of consistency was somewhat higher. However, a second experiment by Taplin and Staudenmeyer (1973) produced dramatically different results in which the frequency of DA and AC inferences was much lower: indeed, the majority of 'truth-functional' reasoners now conformed to implication rather than equivalence. The only difference between the experiments lay in the choice of conclusion given to the subject. In the early experiments the subject had to evaluate the conclusion as either true or false. In the last experiment he was also given an intermediate choice of either 'sometimes true' or 'sometimes false'. That such a small change of procedure can have such a large effect on results is clearly worrying. A plausible explanation is provided by our earlier observation that the syntactic form *If p then q* is ambiguous with respect to implication and equivalence. When materials are abstract, as in the Taplin and Staudenmayer experiments, the subject has no semantic basis for disambiguating the rule, so subtle demand characteristics may have a large effect on his reasoning. On a forced choice of 'true' and 'false' the subject apparently goes for equivalence on the DA and AC inferences. Once 'sometimes true' is presented as a possibility the subject then switches to this on DA and AC to express the implication/equivalence ambiguity.

The Henle hypothesis, that the subject reasons logically given his own interpretation of the rule, gains only equivocal support from Taplin's finding that half the subjects are consistently truth-functional whereas the other half are not. The hypothesis encounters further difficulties in accounting for the results of experiments on inferences about conditional rules into which negative components are introduced.

Now, how does the introduction of negative components affect the frequency with which subjects make the four inferences? Roberge (1971, 1974) observed that subjects make more 'errors' when the antecedent of the rule is negative. The use of the term 'errors' is inadvisable in view of our previous discussion of conditional rules – correctness is relative to the truth table assumed to apply. Roberge is actually assuming material implication. What actually occurs, as I have also observed (Evans, 1972c), is that subjects make fewer 'valid' MT inferences and more 'fallacious' AC inferences when the antecedent is negative rather than affirmative. Let us consider the first finding. Is the significant reduction of logically correct MT inferences explicable in terms of a change in the *interpretation* of the sentences caused by the introduction of a negative antecedent? This Henle-type position is hard to adopt because all of the alternative truth tables for conditional rules (Table 5.2) regard TF as falsifying, and hence require the MT inference to be valid. An alternative hypothesis is that a non-logical response bias acts against any inference in which the subject is required to infer the falsity of a component which is negative. According to this hypothesis subjects should also be less inclined to make DA inferences when the *consequent* is negative: this was predicted and observed by Evans (1977a). Evidence for this response bias is also found in a study of RAA reasoning (Evans, 1972d) and a study in which disjunctive rather than conditional rules were used (Roberge, 1976).

The tendency to make more AC inferences when the antecedent is negative suggests that there may also be a response bias in favour of inferences which affirm negative components. Evidence for this second bias in both Roberge's and my own experiments is much weaker, but it is interesting to note that both biases result in subjects preferring to accept the validity of arguments whose conclusions are negative rather than affirmative. Such a general bias was predicted long ago in the context of syllogistic reasoning, according to the 'caution' principle of Woodworth and Sells (1935).

In summary, then, the results of inference pattern studies do not support a simple Henle position and indicate a substantial contribution of non-logical factors. Let us now consider the second main paradigm, that of 'direct' studies of psychological truth tables.

(ii) Psychological truth tables

The inference pattern studies have often been regarded by their authors as indirect measures of truth tables, though perhaps without sufficient regard for the problem of response biases. In fact, as we shall see, response biases *also* affect so-called 'direct' measures. It is interesting to study this alternative paradigm, however, partly to see if reasoning is consistent with that observed in studies of inference patterns, and partly because the latter cannot differentiate between defective and non-defective truth tables.

As mentioned earlier, Wason (1966) proposed that subjects have a defective implication truth table for a conditional rule (Table 5.2 (b)). This hypothesis was first tested experimentally by Wason (1968) in an evaluation task. That is to say, subjects were shown examples of all four truth table cases and asked to evaluate the truth value of the rule in each case as 'true', 'false' or 'irrelevant'. Although a few subjects produced the defective implication table TF??, the most common pattern was TFF? which was defined as defective equivalence in Table 5.2(d).

Hence, we may interpret Wason's (1968) result as supporting his basic hypothesis with the condition that in this particular situation subjects would make a biconditional or equivalence interpretation of the rule. Direct evidence for defective implication as such came from a later study by Johnson-Laird and Tagart (1969). In this experiment, they varied the linguistic formulation of the rule expressing, in each case, the logical relationship of material implication. These rules were (1) *If p then q* (2) *Not p if not q* (3) *Not p or q* and (4) *Never p without q*. All rules referred to cards which had capital letters on the left and single digit numbers on the right. An example of a type (1) rule is 'If there is an A on the left then there is a 7 on the right'. Clearly, cards can be made to constitute each logical case: e.g. A7 (TT), A8 (TF), B7 (FT) and B8 (FF). As in Wason (1968) an evaluation procedure was used –

subjects sorted cards into categories 'true', 'false' and 'irrelevant' for each rule. Two important results emerged from this experiment: firstly, responding on the normal condition, *If p then q*, conformed closely to Wason's original prediction of defective implication, TF??. Secondly, the linguistic expression of the rule (all having the same truth table in formal logic) had a dramatic effect on responding. *Never p without q* was quite often associated with a defective implication table, but the other two rules produced no clear pattern of responding. Hence, the experiment shows that subjects' logical understanding interacts considerably with linguistic manipulations – a point to which we shall return.

A possible criticism of the use of an evaluation task is that subjects are given the 'irrelevant' category, and hence a strong demand characteristic exists for them to make use of it. In order to check this I conducted an experiment (Evans, 1972b) in which subjects were asked to *construct* verifying and falsifying cases of conditional rules. Since the procedure was exhaustive, i.e. the subject was told to construct all possible cases, any logical case not given either to verify or falsify could be inferred to be irrelevant. Hence, it was possible to measure three-valued psychological truth tables without ever mentioning the concept of irrelevance to the subject. It later turned out that this control was unnecessary, since the full pattern of the Evans (1972b) results were replicated with a near identical outcome using an evaluation task (Evans, 1976). In retrospect, the important feature of the Evans (1972b) study was the introduction of negative components into the rules.

On the affirmative rule, *If p then q*, results conformed reasonably to the defective implication pattern. However, inspection of the results as a whole suggested the influence of a non-logical operational tendency, which I called 'matching bias'. Essentially, on any given logical case there is a tendency for subjects to regard the case as relevant (T or F) as opposed to irrelevant (?), if the values to be selected match rather than alter those named in the rules. Consider, for example, a subject falsifying a rule of the form *If p then not q*, such as 'if there is a red triangle on the left, then there is not a blue circle on the right'. He would need, logically, to place a red triangle next to a blue circle – a double match. However, on an *If not p then q* rule, e.g. 'If there is not a green square on the left, then there is a red circle on the right', the subject would have to put something other than a green square next to something other than a red circle – a double mismatch

– in order to produce the correct TF case. Not only do subjects produce the correct case on the latter rule much less frequently, but they tend instead to produce the matching case pq (green square next to red circle) which is logically FT. FT, in turn, is rarely given on other rules where it does not match the named values. This matching bias is apparent throughout most of the results of the experiment.

The experiments we have looked at using the truth table paradigm suggest essentially similar conclusions to those drawn from studies of inference patterns. Data from both studies support the ambiguity of *If p then q* with regard to implication/equivalence, at least when abstract materials are used. In addition, the introduction of negative components allows the demonstration of systematic response biases of a non-logical nature. Before discussing the implications of the results we have seen so far, however, we must look at evidence from the third paradigm – Wason's selection task.

(iii) Wason's selection task

This problem, first introduced by Wason (1966) has attracted such a large amount of research, and has generated such interesting and varied results, that it must be regarded as a 'paradigm' in its own right. In one example of the problem the subject is given a rule which applies to four cards, each of which has a capital letter on one side and a single digit number on the other side. The four cards are showing the symbols 'D', 'G', '3' and '7' on their upward facing sides. The rule is 'If there is a 'D' on one side of the card, then there is a '3' on the other side of the card'. The subject is asked to name those cards and only those cards which he would have to turn over in order to find out whether the rule is true or false.

We may discover the correct answer to the problem by consideration of the underlying truth tables. Assuming implication, only the TF case, i.e. a 'D' paired with a number other than a 3 (D$\bar{3}$) could falsify the rule. The subject could discover such a falsifying case only by turning over the 'D' and the '7' (a number which is not a 3). In general, if the rule is of the form *If p then q* then the correct choice, given implication, is p and $\bar{q}$. Under equivalence the FT combination $\bar{D}3$, is also forbidden so the 'B' and '3' should also be turned over. In general terms, the correct solution, given equivalence, is to turn over all four cards, p, $\bar{p}$, q and $\bar{q}$. What makes the selection task interesting is the fact that *neither* of these response patterns is commonly observed. Most subjects choose either p alone, or p and q. Hence, from the viewpoint of any of the four truth tables (Table 5.2) the omission of $\bar{q}$ is an 'error'. The common selection of q is, of course, only erroneous if we assume one of the implication tables. This finding alone seems to cause problems for the Henle position although Bracewell (1974) has attempted an account based solely on interpretational factors.

The early research on the selection task has been reviewed in detail by Wason and Johnson-Laird (1972) and will be summarized only briefly here. What was essentially found was that the 'erroneous' response pattern was highly stable given various changes in procedure, and remarkably resistant to 'therapeutic' procedures such as enforced self-contradiction (Wason, 1969; Wason and Johnson-Laird, 1970). All the early experiments, however, used problem materials of an *abstract* nature, such as in the example given. When *concrete* or thematic materials were first employed by Wason and Shapiro (1971) a dramatic change occurred – the majority of subjects were logically correct. This result has been replicated many times, perhaps most strikingly by Johnson-Laird, Legrenzi and Legrenzi (1972). In the Johnson-Laird and Tagart (1969) study, discussed earlier, we saw how linguistic manipulations of a *syntactic* nature can have a considerable effect upon reasoning behaviour. (The introduction of negative components may also be classified as a syntactic manipulation, although the effects of negatives may be semantic in nature.) The research on the effects of concrete and abstract materials on the selection task indicates equally striking effects of *semantic* manipulations.

Although the phenomenon is restricted to abstract problem situations, it is nevertheless a psychologically interesting question to ask why subjects produce the erroneous response pattern, particularly with regard to the omission of the $\bar{q}$ card. Wason's early explanations were based on the supposition that subjects are motivated to attempt to verify rather than falsify the rule. Since he assumed a defective implication truth table, he regarded only the TT (pq with *If p then q*) case as verifying. Hence, subjects choose p and q looking for the verifying combination pq, rather than p and $\bar{q}$ looking for the falsifying combination $p\bar{q}$. This was later formalized into a flow chart model by Johnson-Laird and Wason (1970).

The Johnson-Laird and Wason model assumes subjects to be in one of three states of insight: NO INSIGHT, in which the subject attempts only to verify the rule – this leads either to the choice p alone or p, q according to whether or not the subject makes a biconditional interpretation of the rule;[2] PARTIAL INSIGHT, in which the subject

chooses cards which could verify and falsify – p, q, $\bar{q}$; and COMPLETE
INSIGHT in which the subject chooses only the cards which could falsify
– p, $\bar{q}$. (The last two states only occur with any frequency on abstract
tasks when 'therapeutic' procedures are introduced.) The theory
appears somewhat circular since the state of insight can only be defined
by observing the response which it underlies. Goodwin and Wason
(1972), however, found apparent support for the model by showing
that subjects' introspective accounts of their behaviour corresponded to
the state of insight predicted to accompany their response.

The Johnson-Laird and Wason model, and other more complicated
'insight' models of the selection task (e.g. Bree, 1973; Smalley, 1974)
are of the type classified as *illogical*. That is, they assume that the subject
responds to the logical structure of the problem but adopts erroneous
strategies. Following my finding of 'matching bias' in a truth table task
(Evans, 1972b), however, it seemed to me that this *non-logical* factor
could account for the selection task results. On the affirmative *If p then
q* rule, matching bias and the 'illogical' verification bias are confounded
– the verifying selections p and q are also those which match the values
named in the rules. When negative components are varied in the rules,
however, matching and mismatching values occur equally often in
each logical case (Table 5.4).

Table 5.4 The values constituting the different logical cases on Wason's
selection task when negative components are systematically varied.

Rule	Logical case			
	True antecedent	*False* antecedent	*True* consequent	*False* consequent
If p then q	p	p̄	q	q̄
If p then not q	p	p̄	q̄	q
If not p then q	p̄	p	q	q̄
If not p then not q	p̄	p	q̄	q

The crucial experiment was conducted by Evans and Lynch (1973).
The selection task was given with all four rules shown in Table 5.4.
Verification bias would have to predict that subjects would choose the
True Antecedent and True Consequent cases throughout. Matching
bias predicts that a given logical case will be chosen more often for

rules where it matches than rules where it mismatches. For all four cases highly significant evidence of matching bias was found. Over all rules, with matching bias cancelled out, the general pattern conformed to logical implication, for example, the False Consequent (equivalent to $\bar{q}$ on the affirmative rule) was chosen significantly *more* often than the True Consequent.

The Evans and Lynch result is clearly incompatible with verification bias and, consequently, the Johnson-Laird and Wason (1970) model. Why is it, then, that subjects in Goodwin and Wason's (1972) experiment produce introspective protocols apparently supporting the model? One possible explanation is that subjects are producing a *post hoc* justification or *rationalization* of their behaviour. The subject may be unaware of the matching bias tendency and when asked to justify his choices, produces an explanation consistent with what he has done, and *with what he was instructed to do*. Since he was told to make the rule true or false he gives verifying and/or falsifying accounts of his behaviour.

Some research which I conducted in collaboration with Wason appears to confirm this interpretation. In one experiment (Wason and Evans, 1975) subjects were given the selection task on the rules *If p then q* and *If p then not q* with abstract materials. The former rule should produce the usual 'no insight' responses. On the latter, however, *p* and *q*, the matching responses, are also logically correct. As in the Goodwin and Wason experiments, subjects were induced to give verbal justifications of their selections. Most subjects matched on both tasks but gave a verifying 'no insight' explanation of their behaviour on *If p then q* and a falsifying 'complete insight' explanation of their behaviour on *If p then not q*, where their choices were, of course, correct. Each subject did both tasks. It was not uncommon for a subject doing the negative rule first to exhibit apparent 'complete insight' which disappeared entirely on doing the subsequent affirmative task. This is consistent with rationalization but hard to reconcile with an 'insight' explanation. In a second experiment (Evans and Wason, 1976) subjects were given one of several alternative wrong solutions, purporting to be correct, and asked to explain the reasons for the solution. Not only did most subjects happily justify whatever solution they were given, but they expressed a high degree of confidence in the correctness of the reasons they gave.

In these papers Wason and I discuss the possibility of dual thought processes going on in these and related reasoning tasks. Discussion of this theory is beyond the scope of the present chapter, and we will leave this work with the observation that introspective data do not seem to constitute a suitable means for testing theories of reasoning behaviour. The selection task is still, however, stimulating current theoretical interest, as may be seen in the papers of Van Duyne (1976), Bree and Coppens (1976) and, perhaps most bizarre of all in the production of a mathematical model (Evans, 1977b).

Conclusions

It is time now to assimilate the essential features of the above review of research into propositional reasoning by three paradigms. In particular, what have we learned about the problem we started out with, namely the contribution of logic to the study of human thinking?

In all three paradigms we have considered there is good evidence that part of the behaviour is influenced by non-logical response biases, which are incompatible with the Henle hypothesis. The hypothesis encounters difficulties with other findings as well. For example, the usual selection task data are not compatible with *any* known truth table, nor are the inference task data of many of Taplin's subjects. Neither are data on the same rules collected in different paradigms very consistent. Most inference pattern studies suggest an underlying equivalence interpretation of conditional rules, whereas truth table tasks and selection task studies, if anything, suggest an underlying implication.

On the other hand there is an abundance of evidence that interpretational factors are also having a considerable influence upon the data, both at a syntactic and semantic level. Although the Henle assumption of logical reasoning makes the testing of interpretational hypotheses simple, it is not actually necessary. Having recommended that one can do this by making due allowance for operational tendencies or response biases (Evans, 1972a), I have at last got around to attempting to do just that (Evans, 1977a; Evans and Newstead, 1977). Deductive reasoning ought to be a useful method for testing psycholinguistic hypotheses; my own efforts have convinced me that such research is difficult, but not impossible.

Is logic, then, useful as either a competence or performance model of human reasoning? As a performance model, at least for abstract reasoning, it is clearly inadequate. Even if we interpret 'logical' in the broad sense of being consistent with some interpretation of the rules, only a part of the reasoning data can be described in these terms. What, then, of logic as a competence model? Does logic form a basis for human reasoning when performance factors such as response biases are removed? Osherson (1975) argues against this position on the grounds that 'standard' logic requires one to accept the validity of certain counter-intuitive arguments. Certainly, the data we have reviewed (for just one example, consider Johnson-Laird and Tagart, 1969) do not suggest an interpretational component based on standard logic.

If not standard logic, then does our reasoning behaviour have a basis in some alternative logical system – perhaps one embedded in natural language? An ingenious attempt to construct a competence model along these lines has been attempted recently by Johnson-Laird (1975). The problems of testing such competence models by experiment are, of course, profound and exactly analogous to those involved in testing the 'psychological reality' of Chomskian linguistics.

Any honest appraisal of research into human reasoning must acknowledge one very penetrating criticism, namely that the experiments to date have been very artificial. Most of the experiments we have discussed are based on problems of an abstract nature, unrelated to real life problems within the experience of our subjects. It is now generally acknowledged that the attempts to investigate human memory via meaningless nonsense syllables were misguided and largely unproductive: the study of meaning or semantics is central to the understanding of memory. Researchers of deductive reasoning may have been equally misguided. Like the memory men, reasoning researchers must now be prepared to grapple with complexities of semantics and natural language, leaving far behind the comparative simplicity of formal logic.

Notes

1 Strictly, philosphers regard RAA as an argument in which one assumes the contradiction of what one wishes to prove. However, the prior intentions of the reasoner do not affect the logical necessity of the inference.
2 There is a logical weakness in the theory here which is exposed by Bree (1973).

References

Bolton, N. (1972) *The Psychology of Thinking*. London: Methuen.
Bracewell, R.J. (1974) *Interpretation factors in the four card selection task*. Paper read at the Trento conference on the selection task.

The psychology of deductive reasoning: Logic 109

Bree, D. S. (1973) The interpretation of Implication. In A. Elithorn and D. Jones (eds) *Artificial and Human Thinking*. Amsterdam: Elsevier.

Bree, D. S. and Coppens, G. (1976) The difficulty of an implication task. *British Journal of Psychology 67*: 579–86.

Chapman, A. C. and Chapman, J. P. (1959) Atmosphere effect reexamined. *Psychological Review 58*: 220–6.

Evans, J. St B. T. (1972a) On the problems of interpreting reasoning data: logical and psychological approaches. *Cognition 1*: 373–84.

Evans, J. St B. T. (1972b) Interpretation and matching bias in a reasoning task. *Quarterly Journal of Experimental Psychology 24*: 193–9.

Evans, J. St B. T. (1972c) Reasoning with negatives. *British Journal of Psychology 63*: 213–19.

Evans, J. St B. T. (1972d) *Deductive Reasoning and Linguistic Usage*. Unpublished Ph.D. thesis, University of London.

Evans, J. St B. T. (1976) On interpreting reasoning data – a reply to Van Duyne. *Cognition 3*: 387–90.

Evans, J. St B. T. (1977a) Linguistic factors in reasoning. *Quarterly Journal of Experimental Psychology 29*: 297–306.

Evans, J. St B. T. (1977b) Towards a statistical theory of reasoning. *Quarterly Journal of Experimental Psychology 29*: 621–35.

Evans, J. St B. T. and Lynch, J. S. (1973) Matching bias in the selection task. *British Journal of Psychology 64*: 391–7.

Evans, J. St B. T. and Newstead, S. E. (1977) Language and reasoning: a study of temporal factors. *Cognition 5*: 265–83.

Evans, J. St B. T. and Wason, P. C. (1976) Rationalization in a reasoning task. *British Journal of Psychology 67*: 479–86.

Goodwin, R. O. and Wason, P. C. (1972) Degrees of insight. *British Journal of Psychology 63*: 205–12.

Henle, M. (1962) On the relation between logic and thinking. *Psychological Review 69*: 366–78.

Johnson-Laird, P. N. (1972) The three-term series problem. *Cognition 1*: 57–82.

Johnson-Laird, P. N. (1975) Models of deduction. In R. J. Falmagne (ed.) *Reasoning: Representation and Process*. New York: Wiley.

Johnson-Laird, P. N., Legrenzi, P. and Legrenzi, M. S. (1972) Reasoning and sense of reality. *British Journal of Psychology 63*: 395–400.

Johnson-Laird, P. N. and Tagart, J. (1969) How implication is understood. *American Journal of Psychology 82*: 367–73.

Johnson-Laird, P. N. and Wason, P. C. (1970) A theoretical analysis of insight into a reasoning task. *Cognitive Psychology 1*: 134–8.

Lemmon, E. J. (1965) *Beginning Logic*. London: Nelson.

Luchins, A. S. and Luchins, E. A. (1965) *Logical Foundations of Mathematics for Behavioural Scientists*. New York: Holt.

Osherson, D. (1975) Logic and models of logical thinking. In R. J. Falmagne (ed.) *op. cit.*

Popper, K. R. (1968) *The Logic of Scientific Discovery*, 3rd edition. London: Hutchinson.

Revlis, R. (1975) Syllogistic reasoning: logical decisions from a complex data base. In R. J. Falmagne (ed.) *op. cit.*

Roberge, J. J. (1971) Some effects of negation on adults' conditional reasoning abilities. *Psychological Reports 29:* 839-44.

Roberge, J. J. (1974) Effects of negation of adults' comprehension of fallacious conditional and disjunctive arguments. *Journal of General Psychology 91:* 287-93.

Roberge, J. J. (1976) Reasoning with exclusive disjunctive arguments. *Quarterly Journal of Experimental Psychology 28:* 419-27.

Smalley, N. S. (1974) Evaluating a rule against possible instances. *British Journal of Psychology 65:* 293-304.

Smedslund, J. (1970) On the circular relation between logic and understanding. *Scandinavian Journal of Psychology 11:* 217-19.

Taplin, J. E. (1971) Reasoning with conditional sentences. *Journal of Verbal Learning and Verbal Behaviour 12:* 530-42.

Taplin, J. E. and Staudenmayer, A. (1973) Interpretation of abstract conditioned sentences in deductive reasoning. *Journal of Verbal Learning and Verbal Behaviour 12:* 530-42.

Van Duyne, P. C. (1976) Necessity and contingency in reasoning. *Acta Psychologica 40:* 85-101.

Wason, P. C. (1966) Reasoning. In B. M. Foss (ed.) *New Horizons in Psychology I.* Harmondsworth: Penguin.

Wason, P. C. (1968) Reasoning about a rule. *Quarterly Journal of Experimental Psychology 20:* 273-81.

Wason, P. C. (1969) Regression in reasoning? *British Journal of Psychology 60:* 471-80.

Wason, P. C. and Evans, J. St B. T. (1975) Dual processes in reasoning? *Cognition 3:* 141-54.

Wason, P. C. and Johnson-Laird, P. N. (1970) A conflict between selecting and evaluating information in a reasoning task. *British Journal of Psychology 61:* 509-15.

Wason, P. C. and Johnson-Laird, P. N. (1972) *Psychology of Reasoning: Structure and Content.* London: Batsford.

Wason, P. C. and Shapiro, D. (1971) Natural and contrived experience in a reasoning problem. *Quarterly Journal of Experiment Psychology 23:* 63-71.

Woodworth, R. S. and Sells, S. B. (1935) An atmosphere effect in syllogistic reasoning. *Journal of Experimental Psychology 18:* 451-60.

6 Measurement constructs and psychological structure; Psychometrics[1]

W. E. C. Gillham

Experimental v. psychometric approaches

Psychologists have typically employed two fundamental strategies in investigating the variety of processes usually subsumed under the heading of thinking, processes which may be as diverse as problem-solving, concept formation, intuition and creative elaboration. One such strategy may be described as the more or less 'experimental' and systematic examination of individual/task parameters to illuminate one aspect of 'thinking'; such investigations are characteristically restricted in scope, complex in conception and organization, and sometimes highly ingenious. A good example of this approach is the work of Vurpillot (1976) investigating similarity/difference judgements in preschool children – in particular the criteria they used in judging whether pairs of pictures were the same or different. By the systematic manipulation of differences in the experimental material (e.g. position, size, presence-absence) Vurpillot was able to shed some light on the nature of the reasoning the children were employing making their judgements.

A second strategy, which is the concern of the present chapter, is what may be described as the psychometric approach. 'Psychometrics' is an extensive term covering all forms of measurement, for whatever purpose, in psychology. Techniques for the analysis of the relative contribution and interaction of the variables under investigation and the expression of the statistical significance of quantitative changes are in general use in experimental psychology. But however elaborate this statistical analysis might be its role is essentially subordinate to the purpose and design of the experiment; although the experimental design takes account of the statistics to be employed, its constructs are not defined by measurement, even if the evidence of measurement can upset them. The psychometric approach, I suggest, is characterized by a search for definition by measurement so that, for instance, 'intelligence' has been seen as adequately defined by tests that purported to measure it. The first intelligence tests came into widespread use during the second decade of this century at the same time as techniques of correlation and factor analysis were being developed. The application of these techniques to cognitive tests was seen as the ultimate in the scientific exploration of the cognitive domain. In the 1930s the identification of a 'new' factor was regarded as a discovery on a par with other scientific discoveries (Burt, 1940; Vernon, 1950), the definitive charting of unknown territory. The tacit assumption that factors had some kind of 'real' existence led to their being given causal, quasi-explanatory status – like 'ability'

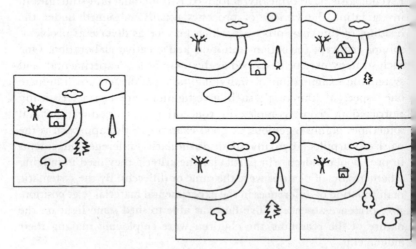

Fig. 6.1   Experimental material from E. Vurpillot, *The Visual World of the Child* (Allen and Unwin, 1976)

constructs in general but with the superimposed gloss of 'objective' measurement. The concept of factors as reflecting basic psychological elements led Burt (1940) to consider the 'metaphysical status of factors', and Guilford (Guilford and Hoepfner, 1971) to construct a 'search' model of the intellect based on an *a priori* assumption of the existence of 120 orthogonal (uncorrelated) abilities whose validity would depend on their independent measurement.

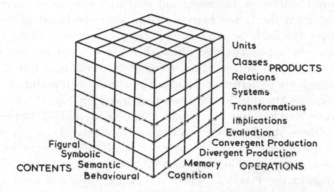

Fig. 6.2   The structure-of-intellect model (from Guilford and Hoepfner)

What we have to consider is the extent to which 'thinking' is usefully studied by means of cognitive tests yielding quantitative scores that can subsequently be manipulated in various ways (correlated, factor analysed, and so on). These cognitive tests, usually called intelligence tests, or tests of various abilities, or creativity, may or may not be standardized, i.e. related to population norms. What they have in common is that they are usually assumed to sample 'underlying' or 'latent' abilities, traits or processes, and that the test responses are coded in quantitative, 'equal unit' terms – these being the raw data for further processing.

This is a critical point of departure and one we must consider carefully. The distinction between the experimental and the psycho-metric approach to the study of thinking is not at the level of the kind of task with which subjects are presented. The experimental investigation of thinking has often involved items from intelligence tests and some cognitive tests have derived their items from experimental psychology. And experimental as well as psychometric psychologists specify test materials and standard instructions. Where they differ is in their reasons for giving the test items and what they do with, and as a consequence of, the subjects' responses to the test tasks. The experimental psychologist is using the test tasks to answer questions usually derived from theory. As a result of the subject's responses he may modify the tasks, develop supplementary ones, scrap the whole procedure and work out something better designed, or change his theoretical basis. The psychometric psychologist is more likely to be in search of data that will allow him to rank subjects in terms of presumed abilities or processes, and which may be given inferential support from the factor analysis of the intercorrelation of the test variables. Insofar as he can be said to have a theoretical model it will probably be a factorial one, although few tests (and none of those widely used) are constructed according to a factorial model. Guilford's tests which are so derived, by and large exist in the literature but not in practice. Attempts to construct tests based on Piaget's theory of cognitive development (e.g. Tuddenham, 1970; Pinard and Sharp, 1972; Elliott, 1975) are either not easily accommodated to psychometry where they have sought to preserve qualitative description and exploration in terms of stage-like shifts in ways of reasoning and thinking, or not Piagetian where precise test tasks and score values are specified. Piaget himself rejects psychometrics as a means of investigation (Tuddenham, op. cit.) and it is worth noting that his interest in cognitive development arose from his experience in using some reasoning tests by Burt in translation: he noted that some children gave the same 'wrong' answers and realized that this reflected how *they* were thinking about the problem.

Piaget advocates the use of exploratory techniques to gain insight into cognitive processes – the 'clinical method' or, latterly, the well-named 'method of critical exploration' (Inhelder et al., 1975) – and his work is testimony to the complicated procedures this sometimes involves. To become aware of this complexity, however, one has to probe for it, otherwise it is possible to see test responses as being simpler or more unitary than they really are; and, indeed, to remain in ignorance of the psychological processes that are actually involved. Bock and Wood (1971) in an article on test theory observe that 'considering the faith we place in test item responses as valid tokens of behavior it is surprising how little we know about the psychological properties of items'. And Olson in the discussion at the 1968 Toronto Symposium *On Intelligence* (Dockrell, 1970) remarked on the obliviousness of psychometricians to the real complexity of what they are dealing with. But it is in the very nature of conventional cognitive tests with the constraints and prohibitions of standardized administration and scoring of items that psychologists using them inevitably standardize and simplify the data they obtain. That this must be so is apparent in those studies which, using conventional tests, have sought to investigate the strategies of problem solution employed by testees – for example, Donaldson's (1963) study of children's errors on verbal reasoning test items.

Psychometric constructs and psychological structure

Donaldson's study showed that identical or very similar responses or 'products' were sometimes achieved by very different routes, and two of my own students (Westerman, 1973; Bennett, 1976) have found that this is true even with a figural reasoning test that is particularly homogeneous in content, viz. Raven's Progressive Matrices. If thinking is a product-related process, it is partly defined by its products but not adequately so. An apparently sensible classification of test responses (the 'products') as being of 'the same kind' may be some way from reflecting the nature of the processing that preceded them. The 'psychological properties of items', to use Bock and Wood's phrase, reside in the behavioural (and structural) features of subjects' responses to them. Measurement of qualitative characteristics must needs be based on a classification which reflects these features of the data.

But conventional tests do not classify responses so much as pass or fail them, coding them by assigning equal-value scores and thereby obliterating any variety they might display. It is not too much of an exaggeration to say that a great deal of information is discarded (given no score value) and the rest given uniform weight and identified in terms of the title of the test or sub-test variable (verbal comprehension, block design, and so on). For what test constructors usually do is to group together items that they presume will tap vaguely or broadly defined 'processes' or ability traits, and define normative score-ranges which will make it possible to rank individuals on the presumed trait dimension. This coding and classification means that already, within one test variable and before any correlating and factor analysing have taken place, you are a considerable distance from the psychological reality of the processes and strategies involved in producing the overt responses to the items making up the test. No subsequent psychometric magic can put back into the numerical data what has been excluded by the form of coding employed.

In the light of this it is quite surprising what has been expected of (and claimed for) the analysis of the intercorrelations of test variables scored in this fashion, although it is perhaps no more remarkable than what has been claimed for intelligence tests in general. Suffice it to say that the very construct of intelligence has been seen as having its main support via the 'construct validation' provided by factor analysis. Like 'internal consistency' methods of calculating reliability, test validity[2] has often been seen as something to be found within sets of test variables, rather than between tests and real-life competence in what might be considered criterial situations. Guilford, for example, is quite explicit about the status of factorial construct validity, claiming that 'Our way of using factor analysis has one great advantage in that we do not have to worry about the criterion problem. Factor analysis provides its own criteria' (Guilford, 1964).

Observing, as we have done, that test intercorrelation is usually given most attention in construct validation, Levy (1973) comments that 'Typically, we seem to want to understand the meaning of one test in terms of several other tests whose own 'construct validities' may not be well understood. Almost as a consequence of our frustration with the multiple meanings of the mass of data collected, we follow up with a factor analysis which may well confuse the issues more than it illuminates them'.

Levy considers alternatives to factor analysis and its correlational assumptions, in particular *facet analysis* which permits the systematic description of the process-related operations involved in test items. But although this approach may offer something for the future, the fact remains that it is factor analysis that has been the principal psychometric technique for inferring processes, or 'abilities', or 'latent traits' from test performances.

The nature of factor analysis

The basis of factor analysis is correlation, and linear correlation at that. This means that only linear relationships are reflected in the correlational matrix from which factors are extracted. Levy points out that 'a qualitative structure among variables is not always to be found by a structure of linear equations'. Donaldson (1972) refers to a number of cognitive skills in which qualitative changes result in a performance decrement, at least for a time, when strategies are initially adopted that will ultimately lead to an enhanced level of performance.

The more obvious correlational fallacy is to assume that a numerical relationship necessarily implies a psychological relationship (or lack of it). We are all familiar with anecdotes such as Thouless's observation of a high positive correlation between the rate of increase in the human population and the population of storks in Southern India; we tend to forget that a more plausible correlation may equally be fable. Numerical relationships are neutral and explain nothing: they have themselves to be explained, which is why a zero correlation may still reflect a psychological relationship of a kind which cancelled out or balanced up the numerical values.

But even if we accept that a positive correlation coefficient indicates a genuine psychological relationship there is a limit to a correlation-based statistic which is almost always overlooked. It is well expressed by Burt (1940) in his professorial prose:

> It would be truer ... (and) ... more instructive, to think of our tables of measurements, correlations, factor-saturation and the like as comprising a series of mutually equivalent matrices, each capable of being transformed into the other, and to note that each of those matrices, even if ultimately reduced to a single row or vector, can still enumerate only *relations between qualities and not the amounts of those qualities by themselves* ... (my italics).

There are some things about factor analysis[3] that I shall ignore, even assuming that I were fully competent to discuss them. So I give no consideration to different methods of factor analysis, different ways of referencing factors, to criteria for continuing, or not continuing to extract factors from a matrix, to techniques (and judgements) relating to factor rotation, and so on. Given a matrix of intercorrelations there are many things you can do with it mathematically – all justifiable although perhaps not equally so – and all affecting the resultant factor pattern, and therefore one's basis for making inferences. And how does one make these inferences?

Factors, like human beings, are born with no name although there is usually one waiting for them, which may not fit their character very well. But as with their human counterparts they soon become assimilated to their name-identity and the initial act of ascription, and perhaps its unsuitability, is often forgotten. Human beings, however, have the advantage over factors in that their meaning does not reside just in their name. Factors, like correlation coefficients, have no intrinsic psychological significance: meaning is ascribed to them by a psychologist with his preferences and presuppositions. And by a more or less careful scrutiny of the test variables which 'load' on a particular factor, the psychologist assigns a 'best-fit' descriptive label which may be of a 'content' or 'process' kind, or possibly both. Some test items appear to invite a process label more readily than others: a factor which loaded heavily on such test variables as repeating digits forward and backwards would be unlikely to escape being labelled as 'memory'. Thurstone (1938) in identifying his (usually) seven Primary Mental Abilities (Verbal, Number, Spatial, Memory, Reasoning, Word-fluency, Perceptual speed) gave some of them content labels and some process labels. Despite the 'illogicality' of this nomenclature, the terms Thurstone uses seem the obvious and sensible ones. What it does call into question is how 'process' these descriptions really are.

Factorial 'models' of psychological processes

More tidy-minded psychologists such as Eysenck (1967) and Warburton (1970) have proposed a two-dimensional content x process 'model', but tidy-mindedness is no guarantee of psychological veracity. If it were then Guilford with his 3-D content x process x product model of 120 discrete abilities (see Fig. 6.2) would have achieved a unique level of truth. Cattell (1971) criticizes the structure-of-intellect model as involving categories chosen on too rational, philosophic and *a priori* a basis. Cattell's work has largely been directed to the discovery of empirically derived but definitive factor structures which means that he does not entirely escape from his own criticism. However, Guilford's insistence on finding tests that will fit his model is the obverse of discovery: indeed, it is more like psychological invention.

The fundamental assumption of such *a priori* classifications is that, given construct validity, i.e. relatively independent uncorrelated factors, you can virtually guarantee the processes that subjects have employed in solving the test items. This presupposes, firstly, that one can identify definitive tests for a hypothesized factor structure and secondly, that processes can be regarded as a property of test problems rather than test problem solvers.

I am not suggesting that certain test tasks may not constrain, more or less severely, what we can do with them, that is, the kind of mental operations we will find necessary for their solution. But having some experience of investigating problem-solving strategies on a fairly narrow range of tasks, I am impressed by the perverseness and trickiness of the average problem-solver. I am also impressed by the difficulty of finding out how an individual is solving a problem even when he is doing so under your very eyes. To attempt to construct test items that 'require' a certain kind or level of thinking would seem to fly in the face of what cognitive psychology has taught us during the last fifteen years or so; which is presumably why attempts to construct 'Piagetian' tests always seem to peter out. Test items themselves have no psychological properties: they are only so characterized in relation to the cognitive operations of human beings, and individuals are likely to perceive, and process, the 'objectively' identical problem in different ways. Hence the myth of 'unambiguous' test instructions. Whilst some forms of test instructions are more likely to lead to multiple interpretations by testees than others, no test instruction can guarantee a uniform interpretation.

The cumulative significance of all this is that at the level of the factor matrix we are at a considerable distance from the psychological reality of cognitive processes: the chain of inference is long and the transformations in the data have been many. When you are operating at such a distance from your raw material, it is easy to come to believe in the primacy and explanatory power of such statistical abstractions. This seems to be characteristic of those psychologists, like Burt, Cattell, Eysenck and Guilford, who have used factor analysis as the basic technique for 'theory' or 'model' construction. It is not difficult to see the desirability of identifying (or prescribing) a definitive and stable factor structure for psychologists who have sought for their discipline the status and character of the 'discoveries' and 'laws' of the natural sciences. The relativity and reflexive character of psychological organization defeats such aims although it is possible to minimize confrontations with psychological reality by working with more or less restricted populations. P. E. Vernon, for example, has persistently criticized Guilford for using too homogeneous a population in determining factors for his search model of the intellect. Certainly Guilford's factor structure only applies to the test items used *with the test populations he has employed*. In other words, for substantially different populations the same sets of test problems might produce different patterns of inter-relationship, different *factorial* patterns. However, if we are interested in the possibilities of factor analysis as a tool for investigating broad aspects of psychological processing, such relativity immediately starts to look a little more promising.

Factorial relativity and psychological discovery

If factor structure is not objectively defined but defined relative to a population group, then comparative factor analyses of different group performances might tell us something about differences in the processes being employed, even if only at a gross and general level. Instead of a means of achieving a predetermined factor structure, factor analysis then becomes a technique of discovery amongst sets of test items assembled for other reasons, for example because they are educationally important, or culturally valued in some other way.

Even without between group comparisons, the element of discovery in factor analysis has always been in terms of an unexpected factor structure (that is, unexpected correlations). Thus Maxwell (1959) in a factor analysis of the WISC found that some 'performance' subtests loaded more heavily on a verbally referenced factor than they did on a 'space-performance' factor. This suggested that linguistic processes *might* be involved in the successful solution of these subtests. Such an inference would seem justified, but note that it is only possible because subtests of verbal content formed part of the correlation matrix. If factors, as Burt has pointed out, at the most reflect *relations* between qualities (rather than the qualities themselves), then the presence of a factor merely indicates that this is a source of variation (or co-variation) for the population producing the scores being analysed, since two or more variables have to vary together for correlation to be possible. A factor is only available for interpretation if such co-variation exists in the matrix.

Balinski (1941) carried out a factor analysis of the standardization data obtained for the Wechsler-Bellevue at the different (mainly adult) age-levels sampled. Overall the factor structure obtained was very similar but at two age-levels a factor appeared which Balinski identified as a *memory* factor. But this does not mean that recall processes were not involved at those age-levels where no memory factor was apparent – it is simply that they were not a major source of *variation* for that age population. This is one step further back from our earlier observation that factor analysis (necessarily) neglects non-correlational data: for correlation to be possible there has to be variation attributable to the inferred quality. We recall Vernon's

(1970) observation that 'for the psychometrist an ability must be something on which people vary'; without variation it cannot be measured, although operative.

Balinski was comparing factorial patterns of ability at different age levels; this poses some problems as to the continuity of the qualities involved in intellectual performance. There is some evidence that older people learn and solve problems somewhat differently from young adults, although performances may be comparable until that last, more or less dramatic declension into infantile forms of thinking. But if we consider the beginning of the life-span and the qualitative ascent of intellectual growth, it is clear that in comparing factor analytic patterns of adults and children we are up against discontinuity in many of the variables that might interest us. Being intelligent at the age of five or seven or ten is different in *kind* from being intelligent at twenty. Thus what may look like the same factors at different age levels may be nothing of the sort. But this doesn't prevent your making comparisons with such cautions in mind.

Factorial complexity and individual differences in cognitive organization

One very general finding is that fewer factors are apparent in analyses of children's test performances, the 'general' factor in particular being larger. Why this is so is not clear but it is reasonable to assume that in part it may be due to a qualitative differentiation in ways of thinking. Biological considerations apart it is evident that children have a much more standardized intellectual environment than adults: for purposes of comparison one would have to give all adults the same kind of job. The great variation in adult work experiences would seem likely to increase differences in ways of thinking and areas of attainment between individuals. The more complex factor patterns obtained when adults are given similar sets of tests as have been given to children may reflect greater process and strategy variations in the adult population as a result of their varying training and work experiences.

French (1965) makes a similar point for reasons that themselves merit our consideration. French has this to say:

It seems possible that the factorial composition of test problems involving higher mental processes often appears complex, not only because the problems require several different kinds of abilities in their solution, *but also because they measure something different for examinees who solve them by using different methods.* . . . an investigation of this situation (seems) likely to lead to worthwhile information about individual differences in problem-solving styles, an appreciation of the different things a test measures for different subjects, and an understanding of the extent to which factor analysis reflects qualitative differences in individuals' reactions to a test as well as to differences in the nature of the tests themselves (my italics).

French's comments are made in the introduction to a study in which subjects were grouped on the basis of their identified problem-solving styles and their performances on the *same* set of fifteen cognitive tests subsequently factor-analysed. Different factorial patterns were found for the groups pre-identified in this fashion. The styles of approach identified were broadly of the systematizing v. scanning and the analytic v. global way of perceiving problems. French's study is of interest because he identifies these as *characteristics* of cognitive operations rather than as 'ability' or 'operations' constructs *per se*.

The area of styles of thinking is marked by empirical and conceptual confusion, partly because of the semantic muddle that always arises when different terms are used in similar ways and partly from the mistaken assumption that such terms need to be given independent construct validity (i.e. independence in measurement terms): which they only do if they are considered to have that kind of existence. Factorial construct validity can usually be achieved, if that is desired, although the sorts of items making up the test content (and therefore the content validity) may violate common sense, and criterial validity (i.e. correlation with 'real-life' performance) be entirely lacking.

The attempts to distinguish 'creativity' from 'intelligence' exemplify this sort of muddle, starting with the familiar category error assumption that because we can characterize some individuals (or some activities) as 'creative' there must be something called creativity that those individuals have more of, or that particularly saturates some kinds of activity. It must be doubted whether 'creativity' tests have ever achieved content validity with items that, for example, require the subject to think of different uses for, amongst other things, a paper clip and a tin of boot polish: Lynn's description of creativity tests as 'tests of silliness' (quoted by Kline, 1976) would seem reasonable. The absence of an adequate way of scoring quality of response is general, although Wallach and Kogan (1965) achieved correlational independence from intelligence test items (the explicit aim of their project), an achievement which seems to have over-shadowed the other deficiencies of their assessment technique.

Guilford, who is commonly credited with providing the initial stimulus for recent research on creativity by his presidential address to the American Psychological Association (Guilford, 1950) claims that 'creative activity can be described in terms of fluent production of items of information, and elaboration upon what is given' (Guilford and Hoepfner, 1971). Such processes he suggests come within the category of divergent production – one of the twenty-four cell slices of his SI model, another slice being that of convergent production – the two corresponding approximately to our familiar tags of inductive and deductive reasoning.

Shouksmith (1970) observes 'Guilford's "divergent" and "convergent" thinking processes should not be regarded as distinct and different entities. This is not to say that they cannot be distinguished factorially . . .'. (One is tempted to add: 'if this is what you want'.)

Shouksmith's own work demonstrates the 'discovery' aspect of factor analysis. He reports on the basis of giving the same cognitive tests to men and women, that 'Factorially the female group is more complex than the male. . . . For females a much greater range of behaviour patterns appear to be mutually exclusive categories . . . for example, we see that "creative associating" is opposed to "deductive reasoning" in women, whereas it is not so clearly opposed in men'.

This seems a little too glib to be true and it is important to query Shouksmith's factor labels and the validity of the tests he used. Yet such comparative findings are suggestive since they might reflect, in a general way, differences in the organization of covert processes. What cannot be claimed is that different factor patterns for different groups on the same test battery necessarily always, or even usually, indicate such basic levels of organization. Different educational and social experiences will affect patterns of attainment (and therefore test intercorrelations) without revealing any deeper secrets.

The origins of factors

In order to test any hypotheses one might have as to the origins of observed factors, several conditions need to be met. Anastasi (1970) stipulates that 'The investigator must administer a fairly large number of suitable tests to sufficiently large groups; he must employ appropriate factor-analytic techniques: and he must have access to at least some data regarding relevant cultural and other experiential variables'. Anastasi's paper constitutes a substantial review of the factor analytic literature relating to the identification of psychological traits and she observes that in such studies the meaning of ability traits 'becomes essentially an inquiry into the causes of correlation among different behavioural samples, as represented . . . by test scores'.

Anastasi quotes Tryon (1935) as proposing three mechanisms to account for correlation among different psychological measures, such as test scores. Firstly, the extent to which they 'sample similar universes of conceptual components'; secondly, the correlation between the environmental fields in which the different psychological components originated, e.g. educational advantage enhancing performance on a range of different attainments; thirdly, the correlation of 'independent gene blocks' attributed to assortative mating. Such a breakdown would seem to be difficult to make in practice and those psychologists who have interested themselves in the theoretical analysis of factorial ability-trait formation have usually shown preferences: Jensen (1969) favouring explanations in terms of behavioural genetics, Ferguson (1954, 1956) proposing differential positive transfer as a result of cultural experiences, and Vernon (1969) citing contiguous educational experiences. But 'accounting' for the correlation is not the same as knowing the nature of the inter-relating behaviours that make up the correlation; the 'causes' of behaviour (including co-varying sets of test responses) do not determine the detail of their operation, either the form of the response or the nature of the processes involved.

Factor analytic comparison of groups: three studies

Up to now this chapter has been rather abstract – necessarily so because we were considering the nature of psychometric abstractions. Coming down to the level of practical research we have suggested that comparative factor analyses (same tests, different populations) might indicate differences in the way these groups handle test problems; it might even indicate what kind of tasks are most 'open' in this respect. It is not suggested that such factor studies would ever be adequate on their own for the elucidation of the processes involved, but that they might provide a point of reference for other kinds of investigations. I shall describe three comparative studies to illustrate the possible uses of such a psychometric perspective.

Dockrell (1966) (cited by Anastasi, 1970) administered a battery of ten tests dealing with verbal and non-verbal ability, linguistic and numerical skills, and practical/spatial ability to groups of children aged ten, twelve and fourteen years. He classified these children according to their social class as determined by the Registrar-General's classification of their father's occupation and (for the secondary school age children) the type of school they attended: grammar, technical or secondary modern.

Dockrell had hypothesized that there would be differences in the kind of factors and the degree of their differentiation as a function of social class and type of secondary school. He found, as have other research workers (e.g. Mitchell, 1956) that middle class children are more differentiated in their abilities than working class children; he also found that this differentiation occurred earlier in middle class children. It is relevant to note here that a number of psychologists (notably Garrett, 1946) have proposed developmental theories of intelligence based on a progressively greater elaboration and differentiation of abilities, a view which has its most formal expression in the work of Guilford.

In his comparison of the different secondary school groups Dockrell found generally greater differentiation amongst those attending grammar and technical schools, but in the former verbal abilities were more clearly differentiated whilst spatial and numerical skills were more highly differentiated in the technical school children. It is interesting to compare these sorts of findings with small-scale experimental studies of the effects of practice upon factor patterns – presumably a micro-version of what happens in social and educational settings. For example Fleishman and his associates have investigated the factor make-up of sets of perceptual-motor tasks at different stages of practice, revealing regular and progressive changes suggesting an increasing differentiation of function as learning proceeds (Fleishman, 1972). This is in accord with Ferguson's transfer theory referred to earlier since he concludes that 'as the learning of a particular task continues, the ability to perform it becomes gradually differentiated from . . . other abilities' (Ferguson, 1954).

It is possible to relate this increasing differentiation to Piaget's concept of operations which develop through the organism's interaction with his environment into a hierarchy of increasing complexity.

However, the data that Dockrell presents allow no more precise inference than that.

Two important cross-cultural studies are those of Irvine (1969) and Vernon (1969).

Irvine's investigation involved a large number of subjects – over 5000 children in a variety of elementary and secondary schools in Kenya, Zambia and Rhodesia. He used a large test battery classified as: reasoning in English; reasoning with low verbal content; language skills (English); numerical and mathematical skills; spatial and perceptual tests; information and knowledge. It is immediately obvious that there are two qualifications as to how far this can be regarded as a cross-cultural study: in the first place the sample, although large, was a selected one (by definition of school attendance) and therefore more westernized than those not attending school; secondly, the choice of tests designed to sample the skills and values of Western culture necessarily restricted the extent to which they sampled vernacular linguistic and cognitive styles (see Chapter 7). Irvine was, of course, well aware of these limitations and attributed the broad cross-cultural uniformity of the main factor loadings to the standardized English-model education in these African schools. The greatest degree of uniformity was in overlearned drill skills such as spelling and arithmetic. There was less factorial uniformity in tests where the materials were non-verbal but where internal verbalization was of some importance. Irvine followed up some of these differences with individual interviews, and comments that 'students reported switching back and forth from vernacular to English in working through items in tests of a "nonverbal" kind'. Irvine pursues the implications of this in relation to 'the common belief that verbal tests are more potent sources of culture differentiation than figural and nonverbal tests' and suggests that the nature of verbal problems is such that cultural bias is more easily identified. Irvine observes that 'In symbolic and figural tests, the limits of individual perceptual and verbal strategy differences . . . seem to be considerably extended, and are correspondingly the more difficult to map'. In a further study (Irvine, 1969b) of the performance of African students on Raven's Progressive Matrices he found individual variation in strategies when achieving the same score, a degree of item-group interaction across cultures, significant item-difficulty changes between cultural groups, and at least five factors. He concludes that 'figural tests may offer open-ended situations where between-groups differences in perceptual organization and learning opportunity operate in a complex fashion'.

Irvine's work is of particular interest to psychologists concerned with the study of thinking because he got behind the test performance and factorial patterns and took account of the educational and social milieu and the strategies that individuals brought to bear on the test problems. This is also characteristic of one of the most extensive cross-cultural studies carried out on school-children, that of P. E. Vernon (1969).

The size of the groups studied by Vernon was smaller than in Irvine's investigation but more geographically widespread, including schoolboys in England, the Hebrides, Jamaica, Uganda, and Indian and Eskimo boys in Canada. The range of tests used was also unusually diverse including a variety of tests aimed at assessing basic concepts and perceptual skills as well as tests developed as 'creativity' measures. The factor patterns obtained by Vernon were notable for their cross-cultural similarity but there were some interesting variations. Thus the verbal-educational factor ($v:ed$), which usually emerges as a broad group factor (i.e. loading on most but not all test variables) when a wide range of tests is used, was actually a general factor in the Hebrides and Jamaica having substantial loadings on tests other than those sampling conventional educational attainments. Vernon thought that this was because the cultural stimulus for all the skills tested was derived from school experience.

In Uganda, by comparison, no general factor was found, the largest group factor being $v:ed$ loading mainly on school-type subjects and apparently distinct from other cognitive tests, notably Raven's Matrices, the Draw-a-Man Test and Kohs Blocks. Vernon comments (1969, p. 186) that this means that such tests 'would have even less predictive value for school work than they do in Western cultures, since education depends so heavily on the specialized ability of acquiring the English language'. Vernon identified an additional group factor in his Uganda data which loaded on figural, perceptual and performance tests. He suggested that 'This factor may be interpreted as an ability for coping with perceptual analysis, concrete operations and the world of objects, quite distinct from educational attainments' (p. 187).

The three studies that have been described represent some of the best work using comparative factor analytic techniques to elucidate the organization of 'abilities'. Although they could perhaps have been improved by the use of more recent techniques for making factor comparisons across groups (Jöreskog, 1971; Sorbom, 1974), they do make clear the limitations of the factorial approach: without good information about the educational and social experiences of the testees and some insight into the strategies they employ in solving the test problems, the factor patterns themselves are almost meaningless. A belief in the construct validity provided by factor patterns alone, is one dimension of the myth of 'objective' testing which has persisted for so long.

It seems that only now, in the late 'seventies, are we able to get the mental testing movement into perspective. We can see it as remarkable in vigour, confidence and unselfconsciousness, which it maintained almost undiminished for half a century. Even as late as 1965 Holtzman writing about the concept of intelligence, could say that 'one of the most significant accomplishments of psychology has been the development of tests for measuring intelligence' (Holtzman, 1966). But at the time, such a claim seemed to many people, including the writer, perfectly reasonable; a decade later it is obvious that intelligence tests and their analysis by traditional psychometric manipulations obscure more than they reveal about the nature of intelligent behaviour and the processes that underlie it. Our expectations of psychometric constructs in terms of clarifying psychological functioning now seem rather curious, having the difficult-to-explain character of one's own personal recent past: it is hard to understand why we were not more critical. In contrast, it is now possible to see what needs to be done, even if we are unsure how to achieve it: to develop a psychometry – which may not look much like traditional psychometry – that reflects the qualitative aspects of our psychological data. Perhaps the writer with the clearest view of this is Guttman (1971), who provides a suitable concluding paragraph. He comments:

Just as we have learnt not to be subservient to the normal distribution, and just as we have begun to learn to treat qualitative observations with the same respect as numerical observations, let us try to be free of other *a priori* mathematical and statistical considerations and prescriptions ... Instead, let us try to think substantively during the initial stages of a problem of measurement, and focus directly on the specific universe of observations with which we wish to do business.

Notes

1 I am indebted to Professor Philip Levy of the Department of Psychology,
   University of Lancaster, and Dr Elizabeth Valentine of the Department of
   Psychology, Bedford College, for their comments on a late draft of this
   chapter.
2 For a good elementary account of 'reliability' and 'validity' see Cronbach
   (1970).
3 For an elementary account of factor analysis see Cronbach (op. cit.).

References

Anastasi, A. (1970) On the formation of psychological traits. *American
   Psychologist 25*: 899–910.
Balinski, B. (1941) An analysis of the mental factors of various age groups from
   nine to sixty. *Genetic Psychology Monographs 23*: 191–234.
Bennett, D. (1976) The invisible features: an exploration of children's
   difficulties in solving figural relation problems, namely matrices. Unpub-
   lished M. A. project, University of Nottingham.
Bock, R. D. and Wood, R. (1971) Test theory. *Annual Review of Psychology 22*:
   193–224.
Burt, C. (1940) *The Factors of the Mind.* London: University of London Press.
Cattell, R. B. (1971) *Abilities: Their Structure, Growth and Action.* New York:
   Houghton Mifflin.
Dockrell, W. B. (1965) Cultural and educational influences on the differentia-
   tion of ability. In *Proceedings of the 73rd Annual Convention of the American
   Psychological Association.* Washington, D. C. (cited by Anastasi, A., 1970).
Dockrell, W. B. (1970) *On Intelligence.* London: Methuen.
Donaldson, M. (1963) *A Study of Children's Thinking.* London: Tavistock
   Publications.
Donaldson, M. (1971) Preconditions of inference. In J. K. Cole (ed.) *Nebraska
   Symposium on Motivation 1971.* Lincoln, Nebraska: University of Nebraska
   Press.
Elliott, C. D. (1975) The British Intelligence Scale: final report before
   standardization, 1975–76. Paper presented at the Annual Conference of the
   British Psychological Society: Nottingham, England.
Eysenck, H. J. (1967) Intelligence assessment: a theoretical and experimental
   approach. *British Journal of Educational Psychology 37*: 81–98.
Ferguson, G. A. (1954) On learning and human ability. *Canadian Journal of
   Psychology 8*: 95–112.
Ferguson, G. A, (1956) On transfer and the abilities of man. *Canadian Journal
   of Psychology 10*: 121–31.
Fleishman, E. A. (1972) On the relation between abilities, learning, and human
   performance. *American Psychologist 27*: 1018–32.
French, J. W. (1965) The relation of problem-solving styles to the factor
   composition of tests. *Educational and Psychological Measurement 25*: 9–28.

Garrett, H. E. (1946) A developmental theory of intelligence. *American Psychologist 1: 372-8.*

Guilford, J. P. (1950) Creativity. *American Psychologist 5: 444-54.*

Guilford, J. P. (1964) Progress in the discovery of intellectual factors. In C. W. Taylor (ed.) *Widening Horizons in Creativity.* New York: John Wiley.

Guilford, J. P. and Hoepfner, R. (1971) *The Analysis of Intelligence.* New York: McGraw-Hill.

Guttman, L. (1971) Measurement as structural theory. *Psychometrika 36: 329-48.*

Holtzman, W. H. (1966) Intelligence, cognitive style and personality: a developmental approach. In O. G. Brim Jr, R. S. Crutchfield and W. H. Holtzman *Intelligence: Perspectives 1965.* New York: Harcourt, Brace and World.

Inhelder, B., Sinclair, H. and Bovet, M. (1975) *Learning and the Development of Cognition.* London: Routledge and Kegan Paul.

Irvine, S. H. (1969) Factor analysis of African abilities and attainments: constructs across cultures. *Psychological Bulletin 71* (1): 20-32.

Irvine, S. H. (1969b) Figural tests of reasoning in Africa. *International Journal of Psychology 4* (3): 217-28.

Jensen, A. R. (1969) How much can we boost I.Q. and scholastic achievement? *Harvard Educational Review 39: 1-123.*

Jöreskog, K. G. (1971) Simultaneous factor analysis in several populations. *Psychometrika 36* (4): 409-4.

Kline, P. (1976) *Psychological Testing.* London: Malaby Press.

Levy, P. (1973) On the relation between test theory and psychology. In P. Kline (ed.) *New Approaches in Psychological Measurement.* London: John Wiley.

Maxwell, A. E. (1959) Factor analysis of the Wechsler Intelligence Scale for children. *British Journal of Educational Psychology 29: 237-41.*

Mitchell, J. V. (1956) A comparison of the factorial structure of cognitive functions for a high and low status group. *Journal of Educational Psychology 47: 397-414.*

Pinard, A. and Sharp, E. (1972) I.Q. and point of view. *Psychology Today 6* (1): 65-8.

Shouksmith, G. (1970) *Intelligence, Creativity and Cognitive Style.* London: Batsford.

Sorbom, D. (1974) A general method for studying differences in factor means and factor structure between groups. *British Journal of Mathematical and Statistical Psychology 27: 229-39.*

Thurstone, L. L. (1938) Primary mental abilities. *Psychometric Monographs No. 1.*

Tryon, R. C. (1935) A theory of psychological components – an alternative to 'mathematical factors'. *Psychological Review 42: 425-54.*

Tuddenham, R. (1970) A 'Piagetian' test of cognitive development. In W. B. Dockrell (ed.) *On Intelligence.* London: Methuen.

Vernon, P. E. (1950) *The Structure of Human Abilities.* London: Methuen.

Vernon, P. E. (1969) *Intelligence and Cultural Environment.* London: Methuen.

Vernon, P. E. (1970) Intelligence. In W. B. Dockrell (ed.) *On Intelligence.* London: Methuen.

Vurpillot, E. (1976) *The Visual World of the Child* (trans. W. E. C. Gillham). London: Allen and Unwin.
Wallach, M. A. and Kogan, N. (1965) *Modes of Thinking in Young Children.* New York: Holt, Rinehart and Winston.
Warburton, F. W. (1970) The British Intelligence Scale. In W. B. Dockrell (ed.) *On Intelligence.* London: Methuen.
Westerman, I. C. (1973) An investigation of children's attempts to solve the problems of the Raven's Progressive Matrices. Unpublished M. A. project, University of Nottingham.

7 In search of a wider perspective: Cross-cultural studies[1]

J. B. Deręgowski

A caveat

In so far as the title of this paper conveys the impression that the discussion contained therein is concerned with purely cultural phenomena it is misleading. Had these notes been written fifty years ago they would have almost certainly had the word 'racial' or 'ethnic' in the place of 'cultural', but this too would not describe the content correctly.

The current usage arises, sadly, not from a vastly superior knowledge of the phenomena which psychologists have acquired in the intervening period (although we did progress somewhat) but rather from changes in fashion. This change can scarcely be said to have led to increased precision, since Kroeber and Kluckhohn (1952) in their review of the concepts and definitions of culture are able to examine over 150 ways in which the term 'culture' has been used.

It is perhaps both simpler and more instructive to look at the efforts made by a variety of researchers in their attempts to clarify how various aspects of thinking are related to their own, sometimes implicit, concepts of culture than to formulate a generally acceptable definition of the latter. This very pragmatic approach will be adopted here. It will be taken for granted that purely cultural psychological phenomena are virtually impossible to find, for even the most superficial skimming of the relevant literature shows that the three formative influences upon man's behaviour: genetics, ecology and culture, are interrelated in such a complex manner that proper experimental controls when investigating the effect of any one of these upon cognitive differences between various groups have seldom been attempted and that such attempts as have been made have not led to very conclusive results.

Thinking occupies a high position in the spectrum of cognitive activities and is affected by the functioning of both memory and perception. Since both show cross-cultural variation it is necessary to examine them in some detail before considering cross-cultural studies of thinking.

The cross-cultural approach and other approaches

The cross-cultural studies of thought processes do not fall under the exclusive aegis of any of the theoretical approaches described in the other papers. On the contrary such studies have been used to elucidate the theoretical schemata of all these approaches. Thus there are cross-cultural studies concerned with concepts of the Gestalt psychologists (such as, for example, the studies of Michael, 1953, and Berry, 1966); cross-cultural studies concerned with the Piagetian constructs (for a review see Dasen, 1972, and Heron and Dasen, 1979); cross-cultural studies of field-dependence inspired by Witkin's work (see Witkin and Berry 1975, and Witkin, 1977); and cross-cultural studies of abnormal thought inspired by Freud (e.g. Malinowski, 1937). Each of the major approaches has, with greater or lesser success, been used in the cross-cultural setting, often because such setting provided, in the eyes of the researcher, the optimal method of testing a particular prediction.

On the other hand, the contingencies of inter-cultural work have forced researchers to solve new problems not encountered within normal laboratory settings, and forced them to find new solutions. These solutions include the adaptation of apparatus and test materials to the field conditions, development of appropriate procedures and refinement of their original theoretical concepts.

In addition such work has led to sampling of populations lying well outside that traditionally dominant group of subjects (American college students) and in consequence forced psychologists to view in a

somewhat different light some almost sacrosanct *ex cathedra* pronounce-
ments and tenets. This effect is well illustrated by Jahoda's (1970)
comment about 'Guilford's (1959) brilliant essay in which he explicitly
claimed to be analysing *human* intelligence. Now one of the main
factors for classifying the structure of the intellect is symbolic content
"composed of letters, digits and other conventional signs". Thereby he
blithely ignores that part of the world population (which) is lacking
in literacy.'[2]

Cross-cultural comparisons: methodological issues

In order to facilitate discussion of some of the issues adumbrated a
simple impromptu model will be used (Fig. 7.1). The figure presents
schematically the relationship between various conceptual components
responsible for the processes globally described by the term cognition.
Such components have been both implicitly and explicitly put forward
in a large number of intercultural studies.

It is apparent that 'cultural' mechanisms are merely concerned
with preservation of certain 'established' ways and not with exploratory
transformations of information, so that they cannot by themselves
lead to a new mode of behaviour but can help in evolving such a
mode by affecting the manner in which the *immediate* mechanism
operates, by supplying it with information.

The various parts of the mechanism are not accessible to an
experimenter who can only note the entire organism's behaviour. In
addition, he has a limited control of the input of information to the
organism, and can of course record the environmental circumstances
in which the organism finds itself.

The essential differences between methodologies used by various
students of human behaviour in inter-cultural settings arise from
various treatments and combinations of these three factors: manipulation of the input, observations of the environmental factors, and
observations of output.

An unskilled observer lacks a systematic approach to either input
or output of the organism. His observations are related to each other
in accordance with a scheme either conceived impromptu or dictated
by previous experience and hence affected by his own cultural biases.
The greater the familiarity with the culture of his subjects the greater
the likelihood that the interpretation put forward will accord with
that which the subjects would be likely to give. The greater his

familiarity with the rules governing human behaviour in general, the greater the likelihood that the interpretation derived by him would have general scientific validity. The data gathered under such circumstances provide no inkling of the capacity of the subject to manipulate the stimuli. All the responses obtained may be attributable to the recall of past experiences and merely mirror the set of cultural values and culturally approved actions rather than an individual's ability to evaluate and manipulate data. Hence the persuasiveness of a legal argument and the high level of social skills which have often impressed observers (e.g. Cole, 1975) might have been purely a result of overlearned rituals and tell us nothing about the manner in which experiences are organized when active organization is called for.

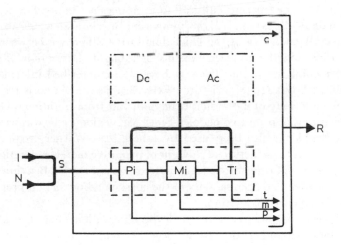

Fig. 7.1   The subject receives stimulus S composed of the general noise (N) and the information (I) especially injected by the experimenter. This stimulus is conveyed to the 'immediate' mechanism (suffix i) wherein perception (P) mnemonic processes (M) and thought processes (T) take place. The immediate mechanism is linked to the long term storage mechanism wherein cultural (suffix c) data (D) and algorithms (A) are stored. The influence of the two mechanisms is mutual. The experimenter assesses the processes by observing the response (R). Such a response may consist of various combinations of the ingredients shown (c, p, m, and t), and the experimenter, by adjustments of I, hopes to achieve a relatively 'pure' result reflecting the cultural beliefs and the processes of perception, memory and thinking. It is argued that asking a subject what he believes in leads to almost pure (c) response, asking him to respond to an illusion figure to a practically pure 'p' response and so on.

The distinction between the ability to reproduce, as and when appropriate, such overlearned rituals and techniques, and the ability to adopt analytic as well as synthetic strategies is clearly of importance. Failure to notice the distinction between the two is, however, common. Thus Lévy-Bruhl's (1966) thesis about the nature of the primitive mentality is based essentially on reports and descriptions of behaviour of the 'primitives'. Examination of such data led him to conclude that 'The primitive mind, like our own, is anxious to find reasons for what happens but it does not seek these in the same direction as we do. It moves in a world where innumerable occult powers are everywhere present and always in action or ready to act' (p. 437). Such a view is consistent with reliance on the part of the 'primitives' on the purely traditional wisdom acquired through experience and allocated, in our diagram, to the separate 'cultural' store. It does not imply, but neither does it deny, the existence of the 'innovative' mechanism whose absence in Lévy-Bruhl's view is the chief qualitative difference between the primitive and the civilized systems of thought. Derivation of such fundamental conclusions from such very circumscribed information attracted Boas's (1938) stricture: 'Lévy-Bruhl's conclusion is reached not from a study of individual behaviour but from traditional beliefs and customs of primitive people.' Since such evidence as was used by Lévy-Bruhl has also been used by others (e.g. Werner, 1948, who thought that the structure of thought of primitive man is syncretic and concrete; Lévi-Strauss, 1962; and, indeed, to some extent, Boas himself) much of what had been said about the corresponding mental processes seems to be open to question.

The essential difference between the observations described above and those characteristic of the experimental approach lies in the systematic variation of stimuli in the latter. The responses obtained are therefore the result of an interaction between the cognitive state of the mechanism and the two inputs. The specific 'experimental' input (I) is represented in the diagram by the upper of the two input arrows and the background input (N) which is generally present by the lower arrow.

Effect of experience

The key to cross-cultural differences must *ex definitione* lie in the results of cultural experience of an individual. Such social factors as the style of weaning, the strictness of upbringing, the nutritional habits and the language spoken have all been suggested to be responsible for the difference in behaviour; so have the nature of environment, its bareness and density, the nutritional limitations it sets, and the rigours of life imposed by it.

The extent of awareness on the part of a subject, that his reponses are influenced by the 'cultural' mechanism is not the same for all three parts of the 'immediate' mechanism. Simple perceptual tasks appear to be performed with lesser insight into such influences than cognitively more complex tasks. For example, a subject responding to a simple illusion figure is not likely to be aware of the cultural influence upon his decision, but he may well be aware of this when he is solving a problem by using a culturally tainted algorithm.

The extent of the influence of cultural factors upon current processes, would, one expects, depend largely upon the degree of similarity between the new material and the culturally established norms. This tenet is present in various guises in all the major current explanations of cross-cultural differences.

The simplest of all notions accounting for such an effect is that of familiarity. Those phenomena which are often encountered in a particular culture establish, by sheer attrition as it were, specific patterns within the cultural store. Thus experience with lots of objects embodying rectangular forms would lead to specific changes in the cultural store influencing the perceptual mechanism which would cause the people coming from such a 'carpentered' culture to perceive as right angles angles which are not right angles and hence lead them to make errors. This, of course, is the essence of Segall, Campbell and Herskovits's (1966) 'carpentered world hypothesis', which led to probably the most extensive cross-cultural experiment. In it, well known illusion figures (such as Müller-Lyer arrows and the Sander parallelograms) were used as stimuli, and the magnitude of the illusory effect served as a measure of the cultural influence. An analogous rationale led to the 'ecological hypothesis'.

The detailed results of the experiments carried out need not concern us here. It is sufficient to note that considerable cultural differences were found by the authors to support the hypotheses but that this support was not entirely free from ambiguity. Subsequent experimentation has broadened rather than clarified the issues.

Essentially the same rationale, that frequent experience leads to the presetting of the perceptual mechanism, is found in the studies on the Ponzo illusion carried out by Leibowitz et al. (1969) and Brislin

(1974). These workers demonstrate the presence of the effect by using three-dimensional as well as two-dimensional stimuli and extending it to full scale 'real world' test situations.

In conclusion it can be said that there is a body of evidence suggesting that cultural differences in perception may result in some part from adjustment of the individual's perceptual mechanism as a result of frequent exposure to certain types of stimuli. Whether such an effect also influences psychological functions such as memorization or classification of stimuli which involve to a larger extent a subject's deliberate participation, is less clear.

Okonji's (1971) work is frequently quoted as showing the effect of cultural familiarity on the use of superordinate concepts. But this conclusion can be questioned because his results show such effects for only one (the oldest) of the three age groups of children which he used in a cross-cultural comparison and because the sequence of the two tests used was not counterbalanced. The lack of counterbalancing has ensured that the Nigerian children were tested first on the more familiar materials whilst the opposite held for the Scots who, in consequence perhaps, performed less well.

More convincing evidence of familiarity is perhaps provided by Porteus (1931). In one of the earliest experiments to use materials which were familiar to remote subjects he compared Australian Aborigines and Caucasian subjects on the ability to match photographs of footprints. The idea was inspired by 'the well known skill of the Aborigines in tracking men and animals and their reputed ability to recognize individual tracks . . .' (p. 399). On this test, in spite of the difficulties which the use of photographs might have caused them, the Aborigines scored as well as their Caucasian counterparts although on other tests their scores were much lower than those of Caucasian samples. Porteus concluded thus: 'Allowing for their unfamiliarity with photographs we may say, then, that with test material with which they are familiar the Aborigines' ability to discriminate form and spatial relationships is at least equal to that of whites of high-school standards of education and better than average social standing' (p. 401). Further evidence is provided by Irwin, Schafer and Feiden (1974), who found that Mano farmers were superior in their performance to U.S. undergraduates when asked to sort rice but inferior when asked to sort geometrical forms. This observation as well as that of Porteus points to the difficulties which the concept of familiarity entails when examined more closely. There can be little doubt that the US students were familiar with rice, in the sense that they had seen and probably even eaten rice. Their poor performance is perhaps therefore more precisely attributable to the relative lack of the *salience* which rice has in the American culture, a distinction emphasized by the analogy which the study of footprints provides. The perceptually salient phenomena are those which are either ecologically or culturally significant and which therefore lead to a growth of expertise in recognition. That this effect is independent of familiarity resulting from the frequency with which the phenomena are encountered is convincingly demonstrated by the comparison of the classificatory abilities of any schoolboy given to car spotting with those of, say, his mother. This essential difference between familiarity with an object as a member of a class and familiarity with the features which make it possible to subdivide the class using one of the features as a criterion is probably responsible for the result reported by Greenfield (1974). She found that Zinacanteco children expert in arranging flowers in a culture in which the colours of flowers are irrelevant to arrangements did no better at a colour sorting task involving flowers than did a control group. The findings of Deręgowski and Serpell (1971) can also be interpreted in these terms. There can be little doubt that both Scottish and Zambian schoolboys tested by them were familiar with photographs, in the sense that both groups had encountered photographs before. There is experimental evidence which shows that both groups were about equally expert on sorting models. Yet when the models were depicted in photographs the Scots' performance was better. It seems that, like the US undergraduates, the Zambians in this circumstance did not attend sufficiently closely to the minutiae of the stimuli.

   The effects of both familiarity (resulting from cultural or ecological exposure) and of salience (resulting from skills fostered by culture or environment) can be said to follow directly from encounters with particular types of stimuli. There is, however, a specific theoretical orientation which makes cross-cultural comparisons between responses to visual stimuli whose relation to normal visual experience seems to be less direct. These are the studies inspired by Witkin's concept of *field dependence*. The extent of field dependence of an individual is indicated by his ability to respond to standardized tests which require perceptual isolation of the stimulus from the specially constructed distractors. Thus in the Embedded Figures test a subject is required to detect a simple geometrical figure hidden in an overlapping network.

In the Rod and Frame test the subject is required to adjust a rod to a vertical position, his task being made difficult by a frame which is presented at an angle. In the Blocks test the subject is requested to reproduce geometric patterns. To do this he has to recognize various components of these patterns and to assemble them correctly. A recent extensive review of the relevant findings is provided by Witkin and Berry (1975).

It is unlikely that these three tests of field dependence measure the same basic skill. The differences between the individual tests are far too broad for that. Hence either the tests sample different skills which appear to correlate or the effect is due to a general characteristic of an individual which may be influenced by his cultural exposure, but such influence is correspondingly diffuse and does not relate *directly* to the tests used in assessment of field dependence. Witkin favours the latter explanation. Whatever the origin of the variation of scores on the tests of field dependence, significant differences between scores have been observed when these tests were used for inter-cultural comparisons (Berry, 1966) and provide further support for the argument that cross-cultural differences in cognition exist.

Categorization

Allocation of stimuli to categories in accordance with their perceived characteristics forms an essence of all taxonomic systems. One would expect, since perceptual differences among cultures have been shown to exist, to find differences in categorization of both simple and complex stimuli.

All objects possess more than one characteristic and hence can be classified in more than one way. Furthermore resulting classes often overlap so that objects may fall in one or more of them. Thus a green ball and a pea share the attributes shape and colour but not of size, whilst a ball-bearing shares the attribute of shape with ball and the pea and may share the attribute of size with either of them. It is unlikely, however, to be green.

Such attributes as given in the above example are abstractions which seldom occur on their own in daily life. Man does not normally encounter disembodied colours or shapes. Every object encountered has in addition to these simple characteristics several others, some of these being more difficult to measure and define than others. The intersection of the variety of attributes defining an object can as a result be variously categorized depending on which of the attributes are taken account of. Furthermore the attributes tend to an extent to be interchangeable and this leads to a creation of a series of conceptual continua which cannot be defined in terms of simple physical measures. As a result one is rather surprised and unconvinced by the claims of the zoologists that a whale is not a fish and those of the Karam (Bulmer, 1967) that a cassowary is not a bird. Both these classificatory 'anomalies' arise from the different weighting given to various characteristics of the objects by different groups of people.

A form of stimulus intermediate between an abstraction (such as colour) and one grossly enmeshed in social values (such as the cassowary in the eyes of the Karam) probably provides a suitable nucleus for discussion of the problem.

Given such a stimulus, a subject, when responding to it, may pay greater or lesser attention to its position on the perceptual continuum. It is possible, in a laboratory, to present subjects with very simple stimuli which have only one variable characteristic. If this characteristic is not salient, then the position of the matching response on the continuum will be entirely unaffected by the position of the original stimulus. If, on the other hand, the characteristic has some salience then the position of the response will in some measure reflect the position of the stimulus. The two events are depicted diagrammatically in Fig. 7.2, in which orientation is used as an example of a continuum.

If a subject codes the figure as, say, 'inclined figure' then the idealized probability distribution of his responses (there is always a chance of random errors which for the present purpose are ignored) is as shown

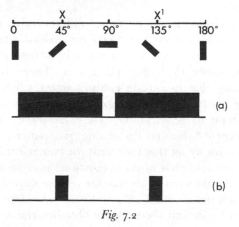

Fig. 7.2

in Fig. 7.2a. It consists of two rectangles separated by a narrow slot portraying the 'horizontal' orientation of the figure and stopping just short of the two ends of the continuum which relate to the 'vertical' orientations.

If the subject considers the stimulus inclined at $45°$ and its enantiomorph (symmetrically identical part) to be equivalent, then his responses will fall in either of the two zones shown in Fig. 7.2b. The two orientations of the stimulus which are objectively disparate are, as far as the subject is concerned, perceptually equivalent. When responding to such stimuli, therefore, a subject would appear to 'flip-flop' randomly from one orientation to another. Data of immediate cross-cultural relevance to this issue were obtained by Serpell (1971) in his study of discrimination learning. His results show considerable cross-cultural differences, the nature of which depends on the type of stimulus used. This finding suggests a culturally variable mechanism whose basic *modus operandi* can be described as follows. The perceptual continuum is divided into zones within which the responses fall and the zones where they do not fall otherwise than as a result of a random error. The former of these zones are further subdivided into the zones of objectively correct responses and the zones denoting various types of systematic errors. The likelihood of responses falling within various 'non-random' zones is not equal. The variety of cultural differences which this variation posits has been discussed by Deręgowski (1977a), who has suggested that such cultural differences can be used to argue that the cultural variation can be described in terms of differences in settings of a multistable perceptual mechanism (Attneave, 1976).

A manner of detecting inter-cultural differences in treatment of continua is offered by analysis of subjects' responses to a task requiring reproduction of a stimulus. This approach is best illustrated by considering responses to Kohs-type figures. There is a body of evidence showing that in certain cultures subjects, when presented with a square pattern in a 'diamond' orientation and asked to reproduce it, tend to perform the task correctly in so far as the pattern is concerned but err in setting the pattern in a wrong orientation, thus implying that they treat the two orientation settings, that of the model and that of their response, as equivalent. Such a response, however, does not imply that the relationship is symmetrical, i.e. that given settings S' and S", S' is as likely to be responded to with S" as S" is with S'. Indeed the evidence obtained shows that subjects given the stimulus in the diamond setting tend to respond by constructing a response with the figure somewhat closer to a 'square' orientation and if the latter figure is used as a stimulus the response is closer yet to the 'square' orientation (Deręgowski, 1977b). On the other hand, given a 'square' stimulus they show no such trends. This leads to a perceptual continuum on which every point contains information about two characteristics; its own objective orientation and the ideal orientation, and the subject responds to the combination of the two. Intercultural differences which arise in this context reflect differences in the resultant 'pull' towards the 'ideal' orientation. Analogous observations involving the constancy of implicit shapes, that is of figures so depicted that their shape as implied by the surrounding figure differs from their shape in the plane of the picture, also show cross-cultural differences. It is noteworthy that the trends observed in the two cases are not consistent. Whilst in the case of Kohs-type figures 'western' Icelandic subjects showed less tendency towards the 'ideal' than did their African counterparts (Deręgowski, 1972); in the case of implicit-shape constancy the trend towards the 'ideal' shape was stronger in western (Scottish) subjects than in their African counterparts (Deręgowski, 1976).

Ingenious experiments by Rosch offer an excellent example of the growth of the difficulties of interpretation with the increase in the number of variables. She (Rosch, 1975) used both colour and shape as stimulus characteristics for testing the categorization behaviour of the Dani of New Guinea. In the case of colour she used sets of Munsell chips varying either in hue or brightness and found that 'the presumed natural prototypes of colour categories' played a key role in defining how well her subjects performed on a task involving learning of colours.[3] Analogous results were obtained with geometric figures. However there is a potentially important difference between these two types of stimuli which suggests that the two sets of results are open to alternative interpretations. This is so because the transformations which were applied to the geometrical figures were not monotonic as were the colour transformations, and each figure used could have been a derivative of some other figure as well as of the 'source' figure employed. Thus for example two of the derivatives of a square used by Rosch are a trapezium and an irregular quadrilateral. Rosch presented these stimuli in the context of other derivatives of a square, finding that they were indeed seen as closely related to squares, the square being in effect the 'perfect' version of both. But the trapezium could also be seen as a derivative of a triangle. Furthermore the square could itself be seen as being a derivative of a circle by considering a series extending from a circle through a series of figures whose sides are chords of the circle and leading to a hexagon, a pentagon and a square. Since the number of such continua increases with the intricacy of the classified objects and since the salience of various continua varies from culture to culture the problem of classification grows greatly in complexity. This can be shown by the variety of reasons which can be given for sorting four such simple objects as: (1) A red plastic spoon (2) A white plastic bowl (3) A penknife with a red handle and (4) A smoker's pipe made of metal and wood. Some of the possible criteria and the resulting categorizations are listed below. In each case the criterion is followed by the resulting grouping of the objects.

1 COLOUR Red: Not red:: spoon and knife: bowl and pipe
2 SHAPE Bowl on stem: No bowl on stem:: spoon and pipe: bowl and knife.
3 MODE OF USE Inserted into mouth: Not inserted into mouth:: spoon and pipe: bowl and knife.
4 NATURE OF MANUFACTURING PROCESS Assembly involved: No Assembly involved:: knife and pipe: spoon and bowl.
5 POSSIBLE USE I Knife and pipe could be broken up and the metallic parts used for construction of a compass.
6 POSSIBLE USE II Knife, spoon and pipe could serve as a gnomon, not so the bowl.

It is apparent from the above sample that objects which can be categorized in accord with simple perceptual criteria e.g. colour and shape can also be categorized by a great variety of more complex rules. Sorting by simple perceptual criteria requires no previous knowledge of the objects. Sorting by more complex rules requires such knowledge. In addition there is a large number of categories derivable from considerations of how objects *could* be used which requires knowledge of *other* objects. Under these conditions the simple sorting task becomes a creativity task, and the subject is no longer tested on his culturally determined categories but rather on the subtleness of his thought. Such tasks require that the subject should be able to recall and rearrange his past experiences. In this context therefore cross-cultural differences in recall become important.

Studies of memory

There was in the late nineteenth century a widespread belief that 'primitive races' are unusually well endowed with mnemonic capacities. Puzzled by such reports and especially by those of the extraordinary feats of memory of the Swazi, Bartlett (1932) conducted several simple experiments. These led him to the conclusion that: 'What is initially outstanding and what is subsequently remembered are, at every age, in every group, and with nearly every variety of topic, largely the outcome of tendencies, interests and facts that have had some value stamped upon them by society.'

Probably the most interesting of the studies inspired by Bartlett are those by Nadel (1937a, b) He compared two tribes speaking different but kindred tongues and differing grossly in their cultural characteristics in spite of superficial similarity of their 'economic and political life'. The differences lay primarily in those aspects of culture which Nadel expected to be reflected clearly in the psychical attributes (Nadel, 1937c). The Yoruba religion Nadel observed was elaborate and had a rationalized system of deities. The Nupe religion has no such system; they believed in magic and impersonal power. The art of the Yoruba is rich, 'religious and mythical emblems play an important part in their life. Again, the Nupe have nothing of the sort, their art is imageless they have but crude wall-paintings, and their strength lies in ornamental, decorative art. The Yoruba have a strong gift for pantomime and drama, not so the Nupe.' Nadel concludes his description of the two tribes with an assertion that 'the essential difference between the two groups becomes manifest also in their folklore and mythology (except for a few folk tales which are common to both groups), in the structure of their music, in the motory pattern of their dances, even in the pattern of their normal, habitual everyday behaviour.'

Nadel used two experimental tasks involving recall of stories and of pictures. In the story experiment the two groups were found to differ in their attitude to logical coherence. The Yoruba tended to adhere to it, and indeed to strengthen it by inventing new logical links; not so the Nupe who tended to enumerate. The Nupe when recalling pictures were found to be more sensitive than the Yoruba to 'temporal arrangement and stressed unity of solution and emotional tone rather than facts of meaning and rational consistency.' They were also found to 'arrange their material very frequently in a spatial order working with such descriptive categories as top and bottom, left and right, front and back.'

A similar pattern of responding appears to be present in the Kpelle data collected recently by Cole et al. (1971). When they tested Kpelle and American subjects by using a series of objects and noting whether there was any evidence of clustering in recall, they found a significantly higher rate of clustering in the American control group than in the Kpelle. Puzzled by this they examined the correlation between the order in which the stimuli were presented and their recall, but no evidence that the subjects were trying to recall the stimuli in the original sequence was obtained. The Kpelle thus appeared to lack any obvious strategy and this was reflected in their poor performance at all ages and their small (when compared with the Americans) increase of accuracy of recall with age. However, when the procedure was modified and an opportunity for spatial coding provided, much higher scores were obtained. Verbal cueing such as telling them that the items fell into categories (clothing, tools, food, etc.) did not lead to improvement, but specific instruction that a given category has to be recalled (e.g. 'recall clothing') did do so.

In their attempt to explore the problem further, Cole et al. used Bartlett's story paradigm. In some of the stories used the information presented was already clustered, whilst in others it was not. In these circumstances the recall pattern was found to be much more influenced by the way in which the information fitted the story. It appears, and further work by Scribner confirms this (Cole and Scribner, 1974, p. 36), that although grouping and reorganization of material are resorted to by the Kpelle this is seldom spontaneous. 'It thus seems', Cole and Scribner conclude, 'that spontaneous structuring of material as a deliberate aid to recall is not a common technique in the repertoire of traditional Kpelle adults and that it is less common among Kpelle students than it has been found to be among American students.'

Another variation of Bartlett's procedure has since been used on the assumption that cultural difference in cognition could be detected by attaching different meaning to essentially meaningless symbols such as digits. The following story is taken from Deręgowski (1970). 'A boy called Johnny was eight years old when he went to a town nine miles from his village. He travelled by bus for four hours and paid two shillings for the journey. He arrived in the town at seven o'clock and saw his five nephews. He gave his nephews whom he had not seen for six years, three bananas which he brought from his village.' Of eight items of information presented in the story four deal with various aspects of time, a concept of little cultural salience in simple rural communities. The remaining items deal with concepts having, it was thought, relatively greater cultural salience. The results obtained with one of the samples used, consisting of forty-four rural Tumbuka women, show that they recalled, on average, twice as many of the 'non-time' numbers as the 'time' numbers, while in a sample of urban schoolboys recall of the two types of times did not differ materially. Thus, recall of a particular type of material appears to be affected by the cultural environment. Similar results using similar techniques have been reported by Price and Tare (1975) from Papua New Guinea.[4]

The work on memory done on Kpelle in Liberia has its parallel in Luria's (1976) work done in remote parts of the Soviet Union. Both studies suggest strongly that memory processes have considerable influence in thinking. This is dramatically shown by Luria's subjects' responses when requested to repeat a syllogism before attempting solution. Often such repetitions were so imperfect as to preclude correct solutions.

Thus both the perceptual mechanism and the mnemonic mechanism impose a heavy cultural imprint upon the stimuli. The effect of such imprint, as will be shown below, is more likely to be exacerbated than mollified by the processes of thinking, to which we shall now turn.

Thinking

As in other cross-cultural studies so here the primary impetus came from work done in the west.

In the important and virtually neglected field of inferential thinking, Cole et al. adapted the Kendlers' (Kendler and Kendler, 1967) technique to test Kpelle subjects in Liberia.

The subjects were asked to operate a simple apparatus. Correct operations consisted of pressing a button on a metal box to obtain a marble and placement of this marble in the opening of another box which caused the reward to be delivered. The two boxes together with another 'distractor' box formed a solid block of three. The subjects were taught (1) how to obtain the marble, and *separately*, (2) how to use it to obtain the reward. They were then faced with the task of combining these two operations in order to obtain the reward. This, it was observed, was difficult for them. A task of this type is usually analysed in terms of ability to infer and failure is thought to be indicative of either insufficient grasp of one of the two elements or inability to combine the two elements. The task can, however, also be analysed by adopting a work-study approach. Such an approach was not used by Cole et al. but will be used here since it appears to be helpful. According to this the task consists of three actions:

(Experiment 1) 1 Finger-push (**) button (*)
2 Pick (***) marble (*)
3 Drop (***) marble (*)

These actions each involve two elements, an act and a wherewithal, either of which may cause difficulties to the subjects as a result of cultural exposure. One can assign probable values to each of the elements to show how culturally acceptable they are, as indicated by the asterisks. The more acceptable the element the more asterisks. This analysis suggests that a considerable improvement could be obtained by replacing the moderately unacceptable action of finger-pushing by some other action and replacing the unfamiliar objects. This, indeed, was done by Cole and his collaborators, who ran another experiment as shown below:

(Experiment 2) 1 Open (***) matchbox (***)
2 Pick (***) key (***)
3 Open (***) lock (***)

This experiment led to about ten times the number of correct responses obtained in Experiment 1. Two more experiments were carried out. Actions involved in Experiment 3 were identical with those of Experiment 1, with the sole exception of the second action, which was: Pick (***) key (***). Experiment 4 differed from Experiment 2 in the last action only, which was: Drop (***) key (***).

The findings were that the tasks in the third experiment were about as difficult as those in the first, whereas the tasks in the second and fourth experiments were significantly easier.

Although the above analysis does not enable one to decide whether a characteristic of the physical elements or a characteristic of the actions is responsible for the results it does demonstrate convincingly that the illiterate Kpelle are quite capable of inferential thought. It further suggests that a description of a test in terms of two operations learned independently which have subsequently to be combined, although logically faultless, may not describe adequately the psychical processes used by the subjects, and that an 'ergonomic' description may be more apposite.

In commenting upon their experimental results Cole et al. (1971, p. 211) note the contrast between performances of a group of American first-graders on the first two of the experiments and remark that their subjects 'showed general improvement when they began dealing with matchboxes instead of the inference apparatus; this suggests that their generally poor performance in the Kendlers' studies may be much less a matter of general defects in "mediational" capacity than an inability to attend to relevant aspects of the problem involving a strange apparatus'. This is a particularly noteworthy observation for it shows clearly that much can be gained by studying cognitive problems cross-culturally.

Since inferential thinking is important to problem-solving, especially (as Cole et al. clearly show) to the solving of new problems, this would appear to be an important area for cross-cultural inquiry. It is not however the area on which most effort has hitherto been expended. The aspects of thinking which have so far attracted the attention of cross-cultural psychologists are largely those derived from Piaget's theories. Classification and conservation of various substances and numbers have been tested in a variety of cultures with mixed results. Dasen (1972) and Heron and Dasen (1979) review the field. It is sufficient to note that here as in other activities discussed cross-culturally differences are found. Dasen (1972) points out that on classification certain groups, for example Irani children tested by Mohseni, fall on the 'typical curve of "retarded" development', and that this result contrasts with the performance of Tiv children (Price-Williams, 1962), which was not found to differ from that of their European counterparts.

An experiment by Price-Williams et al. (1969) in which Mexican rural and urban children from potters' families were tested on conservation of quantities is of especial interest since it pertains to the transfer of learning. It was found that the potters' children showed superior conservation of substance but the extent to which this correlated with other conservation tasks was not well defined, there being a positive correlation between scores in the rural group but not in the urban group. The results therefore do not enable one to say whether in terms of the previous paradigm the activity or the material influences the performance. The rural result would support the argument of conservation as an ability independent of the physical materials involved. On the other hand, from the urban data it would appear that the physical substance plays a determining role, and hence that it was the strangeness of the apparatus rather than the unusual action of pressing the button which led to Cole et al.'s results. It would imply, therefore, that the processes described are essentially narrow skills. Such categorical description is, however, questionable, for both the nature of the task and the material may range widely in the extent of their cultural acceptability and the final result is likely to be influenced by an interaction of these two factors.

The matter is further complicated by the absence of differences due to 'strangeness' in the cases where such differences would be expected. Dasen (1974), for example, found that there was no difference in conservation scores between his two groups of Australian Aborigines differing in the extent of their contact with the European population, on a variety of Piagetian tasks. Spatial skills as measured by these tests were not found to differ in the way which their cultures would suggest. An even stronger and more discordant effect was observed by Berry (1966), who found that the spatial performance of Eskimos was not consistently inferior to that of Scots.

Such findings strike directly at simple notions of cultural influence and suggest that the processes tested, although affected by cultures, may lie too far from those aspects of culture which are postulated to influence them, and that other variables may intervene.

Bruner (1966) maintains that cultural influence can be envisaged as being the product of 'amplifiers'. He observed that in technological societies stress is laid on the importance of mapping various systems of respresentation onto each other. This is not so in simpler societies and hence Wolof children, for example, who were studied by Greenfield (1966), although perfectly capable of handling liquids in daily life, responded 'more' when a liquid was poured into a long and narrow glass. It is as if asking a question elevated the entire problem onto a different plane where different rules prevail. Western children, Bruner argues, are provided by their cultures with the means (the amplifiers) to deal with such problems. The cultural 'amplifiers' suggested are therefore those characteristics of culture which ensure that a particular style of responding is dominant. Bolton (1972) points out the essential difference between Bruner and Piaget which such an approach entails; the former treats culture as a provider of specific 'amplifiers', the latter might regard it as a provider of 'resistances' necessary for the development of operational thought in the sense that the resistances 'are particular manifestations to which an individual must accommodate in order that he develop *general* operational co-ordinations.'

The impact of culture on the processes of thought as revealed by verbal responses is also provided by studies of syllogisms. Cole et al.'s (1971) observation of the Kpelle when confronted with syllogistic problems in the form of stories, show that their subjects, when questioned about logical implications, were repeatedly trying to bring in 'real life' knowledge. The problem was not treated as a problem *per se*, the game, it seems, was not engaged in by the subjects. When the experimenter, after saying that the spider and the black deer *always* ate together and mentioning that the spider was eating now, asked: 'Is black deer eating?', the subject replied: 'Yes', and justified his answer by saying: 'Black deer always walks about eating green leaves in the bush. Then he rests for a while and gets up again to eat.' Having gained their not inconsiderable knowledge in the 'real world' the subjects were reluctant to jettison it in the somewhat strange circumstance of the experiment. Similar observations were made by Luria (1976) whilst analysing responses of illiterate peasants. Such influence of one's experience and beliefs upon one's way of thinking is not, however, confined to illiterate and remote populations, as Thouless's (1959) study shows. He tested a group of adult students and found that they thought those conclusions drawn from syllogisms to be sound which agreed with their beliefs, even if the conclusions were logically in error. They acted therefore in a manner similar to the Kpelle and Luria's subjects in that they allowed beliefs derived from their experience to influence their thinking in a 'laboratory' situation.

Luria observes also that when some of his subjects were given sufficient time and were told explicitly to derive their conclusions from the oral statement of the experimenter ('What do my words suggest?') they were able to do so. This observation, if it is generalizable to other samples, shows that the cultural 'amplifiers' do not entirely preclude the use of 'unamplified' strategies, but that such strategies are not resorted to in the first instance, and remain unexplored unless specifically called for. A degree of cultural rigidity is thus implied.

Indeed such rigidity has been reported by Kendall[5] (1977) in a series of extensive tests of African workers requiring extrapolation of a series of patterns; in some patterns the extrapolation can be made on a purely perceptual basis, but some patterns call for a conceptual-analytic approach. (Kendall likens the two strategies for which these items call to the 'global' and 'analytic' styles of perception associated with Witkin's studies of field dependence.) Kendall finds considerable resistance in his subjects to the shift from a purely perceptual style to a more analytic one and adduces Laroche's (1956) evidence to suggest that this indeed may be the essence of the difficulties which various tests show. 'Lack of flexibility and *not* lack of "mental ability" might be a major factor contributing to . . . poor performance.'

If this suggestion is correct then it has important implications as far as cross-cultural testing materials are concerned. For one cannot be certain to what extent familiarity would affect flexibility. Rendering materials more familiar may make the responses easier, but it may also lead to a more stereotyped response. On the other hand, unfamiliar materials may also, as our analysis of Cole et al.'s studies shows, cause difficulties.

We thus arrive at the problem of innovation of thought and cultural constraints thereon. There is, alas, no convincing evidence on the issue if one dismisses as of minor relevance, as the present author is inclined to do, studies concerned with innovation in which the innovation was a result of imitation or some other form of cultural contagion and not a result of the individual's reflection.

The reader may have noticed a gradual decrease in the quantity of evidence cited as we proceed from purely perceptual processes through memory processes to the higher processes of cognition. Although the evidence used is selected the presented selection reflects in some measure the status quo.

The topics of planning and of creative thinking are relatively neglected, although there are interesting descriptions of activities which *prima facie* involve such abilities. An outstanding activity of this type is the navigation of the inhabitants of Micronesia (Gladwin, 1970). The navigators set out from one tiny island to another equipped only with their knowledge of the ocean; in the sense, therefore, of having a distant aim in mind they do plan their journey. But Gladwin likens the task of navigation to that of a motorist driving through a town. Such planning is therefore judged to be a skill, which is probably relatively specific and not transferable to other planning.

The only large body of cross-cultural studies of planning is that of Porteus and his co-workers (Porteus, 1931; 1965; Porteus and Gregor, 1963). The planning involved in maze tasks is however of a rather specific nature since the goal and all the constraints are clearly apparent and no innovation in solutions is possible. It falls, therefore, short of planning in 'real life'. Nonetheless, cultural variations observed using maze tests are worth noting since they indicate yet another source of cognitive differences between cultures. Vernon (1966) compared samples of Canadian Indians and Eskimos on ability to plan. He found but small differences between sub-groups differing in acculturation but also obtained data suggesting that Porteus' maze scores relate to the ability. A recent and ingenious adaption of a maze test for use with Bushmen (Reuning, 1971; Reuning and Wortley, 1973) should be noted in this context.

Summary

The data show the presence of cultural influence at all levels of cognition extending from 'simple' perception to problem-solving. The mechanism whereby such influence is exerted is not well defined but both salience and familiarity appear to be important.

In problem-solving both the act to be performed and material are of consequence and consideration of these factors may prove more illuminating when unravelling the task than simple logical analyses.

In terms of our diagram therefore the data can be said to show cultural influence at all basic levels. In 'creativity' and planning activities, however, no sufficient data are available.

The suggestion which emerges from this brief review is that cultures may differ in the flexibility of their approach to problems, their responses being greatly influenced by cultural values. Such lack of ability to transfer from one plane of reasoning to another is not, however, confined to illiterate populations. Even a high degree of sophistication does not ensure flexibility. Thus Kochanowski (1584) wrote about a 'mathematician':

> He has surveyed the skies and the deep of the sea,
> He knows why the waves roll and the winds blow free,
> He proffers advice, boldly takes the floor,
> And yet knows not that his wife's a whore.

Notes

1 I am indebted to my colleague Dr N. E. Wetherick and to Professor G. Jahoda for their comments upon a draft of this paper.

2 Limitations of space are responsible for the omission of two important issues: (1) Relationship between language and thought (Whorf, 1940; Greenfield, 1966) and (2) Intelligence testing (Biesheuval, 1952; Vernon, 1969; Jensen, 1972; Ord, 1971; Irvine 1969; Grant, 1972).

Broad reviews of the cross-cultural studies are provided by Serpell (1976), Cole and Scribner (1974), Lloyd (1972) and Price-Williams (1976). More exhaustive reviews of specific topics can be found in Triandis et al. (1979). Entries of immediate relevance are contained in the second volume.

Apart from the specific approaches mentioned above the following are of relevance: Campbell (1964), Doob (1965), Dawson (1971) and Berry (1977).

The references given in the notes are intended as a mere guide and are not exhaustive.

3 A problem might, however, arise if different colours are regarded as focal in different settings. For example the *focal* yellow for grass may prove different from the *focal* yellow for birds. Will the focal yellow for triangles and squares be the same in all cultures?

4 For another application of this paradigm see Goodman's (1962) comparison of American and Japanese children; and Ross and Millsom's (1970) comparison of New York and Ghanaian children. It could be questioned whether the very precise but somewhat mechanical methods of scoring used in the latter study are sufficiently sensitive to cultural influences.

5 The 'perceptual' effects of Kendall's study are probably related to the 'predictive' responses of Ghanaian children investigated by Mundy-Castle (1967) and to Raven's Progressive Matrices (see Irvine, 1969).

References

Attneave, F. (1976) Multistability in perception. In R. Held and W. Ross (eds) *Recent Progress in Perception*. San Francisco: Freeman.

Bartlett, F. C. (1932) *Remembering: A Study in Experimental and Social Psychology*. Cambridge: Cambridge University Press.

Berry, J. W. (1966) Temne and Eskimo perceptual skills. *International Journal of Psychology 1*: 207–29.

Berry, J. W. (1977) Nomadic style and cognitive style. In H. McGurk (ed.) *Ecological Factors in Development*. Amsterdam: North-Holland Publishing Co.

Biesheuvel, S. (1952) The study of African ability, Parts I and II. *African Studies 11*: 45–8, 105–17.

Boas, F. (1938) *The Mind of Primitive Man*. London: Macmillan.

Bolton, N. (1972) *The Psychology of Thinking*. London: Methuen.

Brislin, R. (1974) The Ponzo illusion : additional cues, age, orientation and culture. *Journal of Cross-Cultural Psychology 5*: 139–61.

Bruner, J. S., Olver, R. R. and Greenfield, P. M. (1966) *Studies in Cognitive Growth*. New York: Wiley.

Bulmer, R. (1967) Why is the cassowary not a bird? A problem in zoological taxonomy among the Karam of the New Guinea Highlands. *Man 2:* 5–25.

Campbell, D. T. (1964) Distinguishing differences of perception from failures of communication in cross-cultural studies. In F. S. C. Northrop and H. H. Livingston (eds) *Cross-Cultural Understanding: Epistemology in Anthropology.* New York: Harper and Row.

Cole, M. (1975) An ethnographic psychology of cognition. In R. W. Brislin, S. Bochner and W. J. Lonner (eds) *Cross-Cultural Perspectives on Learning Behaviour.* New York: Halstead Press.

Cole, M. and Scribner, S. (1974) *Culture and Thought: A Psychological Introduction.* New York: Wiley.

Cole, M., Gay, J., Glick, J. A. and Sharp, D. W. (1971) *The Cultural Context of Learning and Thinking.* London: Methuen.

Dasen, P. (1972) Cross-Cultural Piagetian Research: a summary. *Journal of Cross-Cultural Psychology 3:* 23–39.

Dasen, P. (1974) The influence of ecology culture and European contact on cognitive development in Australian Aborigines. In J. W. Berry and P. R. Dasen (eds) *Culture and Cognition: Readings in Cross-Cultural Psychology.* London: Methuen.

Dawson, J. L. M. (1971) Theory and research in cross-cultural psychology. *Bulletin of the British Psychological Society 24:* 291–306.

Derȩgowski, J. B. (1970) Effect of cultural value of time upon recall. *British Journal of Social and Clinical Psychology 9:* 37–41.

Derȩgowski, J. B. (1972) Reproduction of orientation of Kohs-type figures: a cross-cultural study. *British Journal of Psychology 64:* 283–96.

Derȩgowski, J. B. (1976) Implicit-shape constancy: a cross-cultural comparison. *Perception 5:* 343–8.

Derȩgowski, J. B. (1977a) An aspect of perceptual organization: some cross-cultural studies. In Harry McGurk (ed.) *Ecological Factors in Human Development.* Amsterdam: North Holland Publishing Co.

Derȩgowski, J. B. (1977b) Some cross-cultural thoughts on perceptual continua. In Y. H. Poortinga (ed.) *Basic Problems in Cross-Cultural Psychology.* Amsterdam: Swets and Zeitlinger.

Derȩgowski, J. B. and Serpell, R. (1971) Performance on a sorting task: a cross-cultural experiment. *International Journal of Psychology 6:* 273–81.

Doob, L. W. (1965) Psychology. In R. A. Lystad (ed.) *The African World: A Survey of Social Research.* New York: Praeger.

Gladwin, T. (1970) *East is a Big Bird.* Cambridge, Mass.: Harvard University Press.

Goodman, M. E. (1962) Culture and conceptualization: A study of Japanese and American children. *Ethnology 2:* 374–86.

Grant, G. V. (1972) Conceptual reasoning: another dimension of African intellect. *Psychologia Africana 14:* 170–85.

Greenfield, P. M. (1966) On culture and conservation. In J. S. Bruner, R. R. Olver and P. M. Greenfield (eds) *Studies in Cognitive Growth.* New York: Wiley.

Greenfield, P. M. (1974) Comparing dimensional categorization in natural and artificial contexts: a developmental study among the Zincantecos of Mexico. *Journal of Social Psychology 93:* 157–71.

Guildford, J. P. (1959) The three faces of intellect. *American Psychologist 14:* 469–79.

Heron, A. and Dasen, P. (1979) Cross-cultural tests of Piaget's theory. In H. Triandis et al. (eds) *Handbook of Cross-cultural Psychology*, Vol. III. Boston: Allyn and Bacon.

Irvine, S. H. (1969) Figural test of reasoning in Africa. *International Journal of Psychology 4:* 217–28.

Irwin, M. H., Schafer, G. N. and Feiden, C. P. (1974) Emic and unfamiliarity sorting of Mano farmers and US undergraduates. *Journal of Cross-Cultural Psychology 5:* 407–23.

Jahoda, G. (1970) A cross-cultural perspective in psychology. *Advancement of Science 27:* 57–70.

Jensen, A. R. (1971) *Genetics and Education.* London: Methuen.

Kendall, I. M. (1977) Some observations concerning the reasoning styles of black South African workers: Perceptual versus conceptual considerations. *Psychologia Africana 17:* 1–29.

Kendler, T. S. and Kendler, H. H. (1967) Experimental analysis of inferential behaviour in children. In L. P. Lipsitt and C. C. Spiker (eds) *Advances in Child Development and Behaviour*, Vol. III. New York: Academic Press.

Kochanowski, J. (1584) Na matematyka, *Fraszki*, Kraków. Published recently in J. Krzyżanowski (ed.) *Dzieła Polskie*, Vol. I. Warszawa: Państwowy Instytut Wydawniczy.

Kroeber, A. L. and Kluckhohn, C. (1952) *Culture: A Critical Review of Concepts and Definitions.* Cambridge, Mass.: Peabody Museum.

Laroche, J. L. (1956) L'analyse des erreurs sur le matrix 38. *Bulletin du Centre d'Etudes et Recherche Psychotechnique 64:* 161–72.

Leibowitz, H., Brislin, R., Perlmutter, L. and Hennessy, R. (1969) Ponzo perspective as a manifestation of space perception. *Science 166:* 1174–6.

Lévi-Strauss, C. (1962) *The Savage Man.* London: Weidenfeld and Nicolson.

Lévy-Bruhl, L. (1966) *Primitive Mentality.* Boston: Beacon Press.

Lloyd, B. (1972) *Perception and Cognition.* Harmondsworth: Penguin.

Luria, A. R. (1976) *Cognitive Development: Its Cultural and Social Foundations.* Cambridge, Mass.: Harvard University Press.

Malinowski, B. (1937) *Sex and Repression in Savage Society.* London: Harcourt Brace.

Michael, D. N. (1953) A cross-cultural investigation of closure. *Journal of Abnormal and Social Psychology 48:* 225–30.

Mundy-Castle, A. C. (1967) An experimental study of prediction among Ghanaian children. *Journal of Social Psychology 73:* 161–8.

Nadel, S. F. (1937a) A field experiment in racial psychology. *British Journal of Psychology 28:* 195–211.

Nadel, S. F. (1937b) Experiments on culture psychology. *Africa 10:* 421–35.

Nadel, S. F. (1937c) The typological approach to culture. *Character and Personality 5:* 267–83.

Okonji, M. O. (1971) Cross-cultural study of the effects of familiarity on classificatory behaviour. *Journal of Cross-Cultural Psychology 2:* 39–50.

Ord, I. G. (1971) *Mental Tests for Pre-literates.* London: Ginn.

In search of a wider perspective 157

Porteus, S. D. (1931) *The Psychology of a Primitive People: A Study of the Australian Aborigine.* London: Edward Arnold.

Porteus, S. D. (1965) *Porteus Maze Tests: Fifty Years of Application.* Palo Alto: Pacific Books.

Porteus, S. D. and Gregor, J. (1963) Studies in intercultural testing. *Perception and Motor Skills 16:* 705–24.

Price, J. R. and Tare, W. (1975) A cross-cultural study of recall of time-related and non time-related verbal material. *International Journal of Psychology 10:* 247–54.

Price-Williams, P. R. (1962) Abstract and concrete modes of classification in a primitive society. *British Journal of Educational Psychology 32:* 50–61.

Price-Williams, P. R. (1976) Cross-cultural differences in cognitive development. In V. Hamilton and M. D. Vernon (eds) *The Development of Cognitive Processes.* London: Academic Press.

Price-Williams, P. R., Gordon, W. and Ramirez III, M. (1969) Skill and conservation: a study of pottery-making children. *Developmental Psychology 1:* 769.

Reuning, H. (1971) Experimentell-Psychologische Buschmann-Studien in der zentralen Kalahari. *S. W. A. Wissenschaftlich Gesellschaft Journal 26:* 17–43.

Reuning, H. and Wortley, W. (1973) Psychological Studies of the Bushmen. *Psychologia Africana Monograph Supplement No. 7.*

Rosch, E. (1975) Universals and cultural specifics in human categorization. In R. W. Brislin, S. Bochner and W. J. Lonner (eds) *Cross-Cultural Perspectives on Learning.* New York: Halstead press.

Ross, B. M. and Millsom, C. (1970) Repeated memory of oral prose in Ghana and New York. *International Journal of Psychology 5:* 175–81.

Segall, M. H., Campbell, D. T. and Herskovits, M. J. (1966) *Influence of Culture on Visual Perception.* Indianapolis: Bobbs-Merrill.

Serpell, R. (1971) Discrimination of orientation by Zambian children. *Journal of Comparative and Physiological Psychology 75:* 312–16.

Serpell, R.(1976) *Culture's Influence on Behaviour.* London: Methuen.

Tajfel, H. (1969) Social and cultural factors in perception. In G. Lindzey and E. Aronson (eds) *Handbook of Social Psychology,* Vol. III. Reading, Mass.: Addison-Wesley.

Thouless, R. H. (1959) Effect of prejudice on reasoning. *British Journal of Psychology 50:* 289–93.

Triandis, H. C. et al. (1979) *Handbook of Cross-Cultural Psychology.* New York: Boston, Allyn and Bacon.

Vernon, P. E. (1966) Educational and intellectual development among Canadian Indians and Eskimos. *Educational Review 18:* 79–91, 186–95.

Vernon, P. E. (1969) *Intelligence and Cultural Environment.* London: Methuen.

Werner, H. (1948) *Comparative Psychology of Mental Development.* New York: International Universities Press.

Whorf, B. L. (1940) Science and linguistics. *Technology Review 44:* 229–31, 247, 248.

Witkin, H. A. (1977) Cross-cultural perspectives on psychological differentiation in children and their implications for education. In Y. H. Poortinga
(ed.) *Basic Problems in Cross-Cultural Psychology*. Amsterdam: Swets and
Zeitlinger.

Witkin, H. A. and Berry, J. W. (1975) Psychological differentiation in cross-
cultural perspective. *Journal of Cross-Cultural Psychology 6*: 4–87.

8 Bits and spaces: Computer simulation

John Wilding

Introduction

In *The Mentality of Apes* Köhler (1925) described a problem which the chimpanzees managed to solve only after some abortive efforts. A banana was fixed high in the cage and a box was available which if placed beneath the fruit enabled an ape to reach it by climbing on the box. Attempts to program computers to solve such a problem force a careful analysis of the elements and processes involved. The theoretical approach of dissecting the task into elements and processes is known as information processing theory, and need not of course always have the goal of programming a computer to simulate the behaviour. The following analysis is a modified version of one given by Ernst and Newell (1969).

There are six relevant features of the situation: ape position on the ground, ape elevation, box position, fruit position, fruit elevation and hand contents. Using numbers to specify position on the ground and L for 'low' and H for 'high' position, the initial situation is given in Figure 8.1. The desired situation is 'hand contents: fruit' with all other features irrelevant. Other irrelevant features of the situation will be ignored; selection of the relevant features is discussed later.

Initial Situation: Ape position 1 (AP1), Ape elevation low (AEL)
            Box position 2 (BP2)
            Fruit position 3 (FP3), Fruit elevation high (FEH)
            Hand contents nil (HCO)

Step Goal

1 G1 Get fruit
       Match of initial and desired situations selects the most important
       difference: Hand contents.
2 G2 Change D1 (Hand contents)
3   G3 Apply REACH
           Pretest shows Box position ≠ Fruit position
4   G4 Change D2 (Box position)
5   G5 Apply MOVE BOX
                   Pretest shows Ape position ≠ Box position
6   G6 Change D3 (Ape position)
7   G7 Apply WALK
                           Pretest satisfactory
                           Move Ape position to Box position, giving:
                           AP2 AEL BP2 FP3 FEH HCO
8   G5 (reinstated) Apply MOVE BOX
               Pretest satisfactory
               Move Box position and Ape position to Fruit
               position, giving:
               AP3 AEL BP3 FP3 FEH HCO
9   G3 (reinstated) Apply REACH
       Pretest shows Ape elevation ≠ H
10   G8 Change D4 (Ape elevation)
11   G9 Apply CLIMB
               Pretest satisfactory
               Move ape to H, giving:
               AP3 AEH BP3 FP3 FEH HCO
12   G3 (reinstated) Apply REACH
       Pretest satisfactory
       Changes Hand contents, giving:
       AP3 AEH BP3 FP3 FEH HCF
13 G2 (reinstated) Change D1 (Hand contents)
       Report success

Fig. 8.1. Steps in solving the ape and banana problem

Four operations (operators) for changing the situation are postulated, each
with certain preconditions for its application and certain results:

Operator	Preconditions		Effect
CLIMB	Ape position	= box position	Alters ape elevation
	Ape position	= L	
WALK	Ape elevation	= L	Alters ape position

Operator	Preconditions		Effect
MOVE BOX	Ape position	= box position	Alters box and ape position
	Ape elevation	= L	
REACH	Box position	= fruit position	Alters hand contents
	Ape elevation	= H (i.e. on box)	

We also postulate a matching process to discover differences between the current and the desired situations and an ordering of these differences so that they can be eliminated in the correct order, from most to least important as follows: D_1 = hand contents, D_2 = box position, D_3 = ape position, D_4 = ape elevation.

Finally we need the concept of goals. In the problem-solving program from which the example is drawn, three main kinds of goal are distinguished: *transforming* the initial to the desired situation, *reducing* a difference between the current and desired situations, and *applying* an operator to the current situation. For *transform* goals the situation is examined for differences between it and the desired situation, which leads to a *reduce* goal and examination of the list of operators which can reduce the difference, which leads to an *apply* goal; the situation is tested to see whether the preconditions for applying the operator are fulfilled and if they are not a further reduce goal is set up, and so on. Figure 8.1 gives an outline of the steps such a system will take in solving the banana problem. This method of setting up a series of goals and subgoals to remove differences is known as means-ends analysis and has been observed in several investigations of human thinking.

Obviously real behavioural data to match this simulation have to come from natural observation of chimpanzees like that carried out by Köhler. Unfortunately he fails to provide many of the relevant details. However a similar analysis can be applied to problems in which more complex data can be collected from human subjects making a series of choices or thinking aloud. This simple example, however, will help to illustrate many of the main assumptions, characteristics, strengths and weaknesses of the approach.

Origins and History

The first description of a thinking task using a computer appeared in 1950, when Newell and Simon described the performance of the Logic Theorist program on theorems from Whitehead and Russell's *Principia Mathematica* (Newell et al., 1957). At this stage there was no intention to mimic human solution methods, but following comparisons of the program and humans, a new program was developed during 1957 and 1958 called the General Problem Solver (GPS) designed to match and therefore in some sense explain human performance (Newell and Simon, 1961). The program applied to the ape and banana problem was a direct descendant of the first GPS.

Psychological origins

Originally in the behaviourist tradition no events inside the organism were regarded as suitable for study; but Hull and others (for example Hull, 1952; Osgood, 1953; Mowrer, 1954; Kendler and Kendler, 1962) were forced to postulate intervening mediating responses to handle processes like transfer of learning, concept learning and meaning (see Chapter 3). The alternative tradition emphasized that simple associations are inadequate to explain productive thinking. The Würzburgers in the early 1900s found it necessary to include factors to explain direction in thinking which were not within the thinker's awareness. Selz (1927) shared the Gestalt view that elements do not act separately but combine into wholes. His main concern was with the process of thinking and he described in detail how this could be analysed as a cumulative or conditional sequence of operations (A + B + C, or B given that A failed) each of which 'is tied to a specific condition of elicitation'. Such a sequence either leads to a solution or, if it fails, to the start of a new sequence. A test determines if a solution is correct. When this process, which he regards as reproductive thinking, fails, productive thinking is required, by which new means are sought in methods derived from an analogous task. If this fails, 'means abstraction' is initiated, designed to discover new methods of solution. Selz's writings were hardly known in the United States until after the war. Newell and Simon got to know of them through De Groot's (1946) work on chess, and acknowledge them as a strong influence on their own ideas.

The Gestaltists attacked Selz, calling him the 'machine theorist', but shared with him the insistence that elements in a problem situation combine into new structures. The Gestaltists however did not believe these new structures were learned, as Selz did, but believed they depended on the way the nervous system works (see Chapter 2).

Duncker (1945) was dissatisfied with the refusal of earlier Gestaltists to investigate how the restructuring (insight) occurred. He asked subjects to think aloud and analysed the resulting protocols into what we would now call a 'flow diagram'.

In 1956 Bruner, Goodnow and Austin published *The Study of Thinking*, in which they investigated the discovery of classification rules for defining a class of stimuli or concept. The book represents an almost complete break with the American behaviourist tradition, and also fails to make a single reference to Selz, Duncker or any Gestalt writing. The subject was faced (in one task) with an array of cards differing in several ways and shown one card which was a positive exemplar of the rule to be discovered. By choosing cards and getting feedback on whether or not each was an exemplar, the subject attempted to deduce the rule. The major contribution of this study was to introduce the notion of strategies for performing the task. Possible ways of achieving the solution were identified and subjects' performance was then examined in relation to these. Thus in theory, though less easily in practice since subjects tended to vary their strategy, behaviour could be described in units much larger than single responses and it is assumed that behaviour is organized in a hierarchical manner, with single responses controlled by a higher process as well as by the preceding responses.

Two years later, in 1958, Bartlett published *Thinking* in which he drew analogies between skilled perceptual motor behaviour and thinking, arguing that both were hierarchically organized systems of elementary processes under the control of a higher executive. He also included some short verbal protocols from a cryptarithmetic task[1] which was later used extensively by Newell and Simon.

Origins in computer theory
The development of formal logic in the 1920's and 30s showed that ideas other than numerical ones could be symbolically represented and manipulated according to rules. Though human thinking is rarely based rigorously on logic (see Chapter 5), the idea of thought as a series of operations on symbols began to emerge and attempts were made to specify the type of system needed to carry out such operations, culminating in Turing's (1936) description of an all-purpose machine capable of doing them all.

In 1948 Wiener published *Cybernetics* and in 1949 Shannon and Weaver published *The Mathematical Theory of Communication*. This provided a method of measuring the information in an event in terms of the number of binary choices (bits) required to select that event from a set of equiprobable events. If the number of possibilities is two, one such choice is needed, if there are four possibilities, two choices are needed, one to divide the set of four into two sets of two and the second to choose the event from the pair in which it falls. This measure was quickly adopted by psychologists in a range of experiments. Though it was soon clear that its usefulness had been overrated, the concept of organisms as processors of information has survived and flourished.

The first digital electronic computer was completed in 1946 and more advanced machines were built in the next few years, the major changes being to a binary number system[2] and to built-in connections (the hardware) for different basic operations which can be switched on or off by instructions (the software) in the form of numbers. Thus a sequence of instructions can program the machine to carry out a sequence of the basic operations. A further advance is to store the sequence of instructions inside the machine as numbers and use a single instruction to start the machine carrying out the sequence.

There was originally a temptation to regard the switches and wires of the computer as analogous to neurons and axons, but this is not a helpful analogy (von Neumann, 1958). The more interesting comparison arises from the realization that the computer is a general purpose symbol manipulator not just a glorified calculator. Symbols can represent anything and be transformed, combined, deleted, moved; if thought consists of manipulating symbols representing the environment, then the computer can imitate thought, provided the organizing principles can be matched. The parallel is between steps in behaviour and steps in the program, but at a more minute level operations may be carried out quite differently in the computer and in the brain.

Since it is difficult to instruct the machine in numbers, 'higher order' programming languages adapted to the programmer's needs have been devised in which the instructions are in a form easily understood by the programmer (for example the arithmetic operations of addition, subtraction, multiplication and division can be symbolized by $+$, $-$, $*$, $/$). This requires a program inside the machine, called the compiler, which converts the higher order language instructions into the machine's language of numbers. With the development of interest in symbolic operations 'list processing' higher order languages were introduced which readily enabled operations on lists of symbols such as deletion, reordering, transformation and hierarchical organization. With a suitable set of basic operations available, a computer can be programmed to carry out any symbol manipulation task which can be precisely specified, though it may take a very long time, and could exhaust limitations of memory before finishing.

The above discussion has been concerned with digital computers, which are the most widely used. Analogue computers use continuously variable quantities such as voltages rather than on-off switches, but by making the steps sufficiently small a digital computer can match anything an analogue machine can do, though it may take a long time. The difference is thus not serious for present purposes, provided the ways in which a simulation differs from the reality are specified (such as time taken), and provided there is no assumption that underlying brain processes are being matched. Dreyfus (1972) has claimed that brains cannot be simulated by computers because the former are analogue and the latter usually digital, but his objections are well handled by Sutherland (1974) who points out that the brain clearly does operate on digital information at one level and Dreyfus offers no proof that analogue processes cannot be simulated on a digital machine.

Development

In July 1958 came the first publication directed at psychologists by Newell, Shaw and Simon. Also in this year Newell and Simon (1958) made optimistic and unfulfilled claims that within ten years a digital computer would be world chess champion, discover and prove an important mathematical theorem, and that most psychological theories would take the form of computer programs. In the same year a seminar was arranged to acquaint social scientists with simulation methods, out of which came Miller, Galanter and Pribram's *Plans and the Structure of Behaviour* (in 1960), which set out to demolish the reflex arc as a useful basic unit of behaviour and to replace it with the TOTE unit, standing for Test, Operate, Test, Exit. (Compare the means-end analysis of Figure 8.1.) In 1963 Feigenbaum and Feldman published *Computers and Thought* bringing together a selection of the best papers covering work on many topics.

In this there are examples both of *artificial intelligence* (getting computers to do tasks well) and *simulation* (getting them to do tasks in the same way as humans). Work on perception has tended to be confined to the first and has proved difficult, partly because it is difficult to get information about component processes and partly because these processes are not of a kind readily modelled on a digital computer, since a large amount of information enters the system in parallel, at least in the early stages, and the receiving systems interact continuously with each other and with memory systems. More than one theorist has suggested that perception involves analogue processes directly mirroring the input, continuously variable and simultaneously inter-active (e.g. Gregory, 1970). Though these can be modelled on a digital computer, the machine and the programming techniques are not conducive to this approach. In this essay I am considering principally what are usually considered more complex processes, in which by ignoring the 'small print' and confining the explanation to a level of behaviour where more information can be gained about the sequence of processes involved, rather more striking successes have been achieved than with the supposedly simpler processes.

In their 1958 paper Newell, Shaw and Simon identified the goals of a theory of problem-solving as follows: to predict performance on specified tasks, to postulate processes and mechanisms performing them, to predict incidental phenomena such as set and insight, to show how changes in the problem-solver and task will affect performance and to explain how specific and general problem-solving skills are learned and what exactly is learned. They 'mutually confuse' artificial intelligence and simulation techniques 'with advantage' because the best solutions throw light on human performance and vice versa. In the event the first two aims have received most of their attention, with some reference to the third; rather little has been done on variations in individuals and tasks and very little on learning. The later books (Ernst and Newell, 1969; Newell and Simon, 1972) are almost totally concerned with the first two issues and only briefly mention the others.

I shall now examine the main features of the approach, many of which are illustrated in Figure 8.1.

Main features of the approach

1. Computer simulation and psychological theories
Simulation is not the source of a theory; a theory must be derived from careful analysis of either the requirements of the task or behaviour while engaged on it or both. Ideas from programming strongly influence the task analysis and there is sometimes a danger that simulation rather than understanding becomes the goal. A simulation only aids understanding if its success depends on isolation of the mechanisms underlying behaviour; mere copying is not enough (building a radio by copying does not produce understanding of how it works). There is also a danger of assuming without justification that all behaviour is amenable to this type of analysis.

The language and concepts of programming provide a way of

describing processes of behaviour rigorously and qualitatively. Mathematical description is unsuitable for describing complex relations of psychological variables and words are imprecise and can lead to invalid conclusions. Information processing techniques combine 'the rigour and objectivity associated with Behaviourism with the wealth of data and complex behaviour associated with the Gestalt movement' (Newell and Simon, 1961; see also Anderson and Bower, 1973). Simulation requires precise specification of every detail and proves whether the suggested mechanism produces the predicted consequences; if it does not, precise modifications are required and their effect is testable.

2. Levels and units of description

Information processing theories describe behaviour at the level of symbol manipulation. The exact way in which the processes are realized neurophysiologically and biochemically (or in the compiler and machine language) is irrelevant. Explanation at such finer levels is impossible with our present neurophysiological knowledge and unlikely to be very informative for the behaviour we are interested in, and description in ordinary language concepts (phenomenological terms) is not sufficiently explicit to be explanatory.

The level of theoretical description has consequences for the description of behaviour. Usually it proves impossible to isolate elements of behaviour corresponding to the smallest elements of the theory (for example, the pretests in Figure 8.1) and matching is only possible at a grosser level, which may not be immediately available in the data. Newell and Simon (1972, p. 185 ff.) discuss the problem of choosing this grosser level in relation to dividing up a verbal protocol obtained from a subject while solving a problem, pointing out the need to find a level of description in which enough detail is left to show the main steps but not so much that these are obscured.

3. Communicating a theory

A computer program to carry out any reasonably complex task is very long and involved, especially if it is designed to handle several variations and not just one specific task. Consequently much of the detail is usually omitted in describing it. There is also a problem (Frijda, 1967) over specifying which aspects are essential to the theory, since programs use mechanisms built into the computer or available as standard routines in the programming language (for handling arrays or loops[3] for example), which could be carried out quite differently without affecting the end result. Nothing in the program shows which parts are relevant to the theory and which are not, and we have to accept the author's assurance that the results are due to 'his' part. In published descriptions not enough detail is given to decide the question. An adequate description would include all the relevant processes including input and output conditions, pre-conditions for activation and results (see the operations in the example), plus details of any extra operations needed to make the theory work, such as the comparison process in the example and the need to hold a stack of goals in memory.

4. Basic processes and structure of the mind

Thought processes are treated as sequences of manipulations of symbols representing elements in the external world. Computer science has shown that a certain set of these *elementary information processes* is needed for satisfactory performance (see Newell and Simon, 1972, p. 29). Thus the theories incorporate assumptions about basic cognitive abilities and also the necessary 'system architecture' (Hunt, 1971; Hunt and Poltrock, 1974) of short term memory, long term memory etc. which is needed to handle the processes. This fusing of ideas about perception, memory, language and thinking is a major gain of the information processing approach. Newell and Simon (1972, Ch. 14) suggest that strategies of problem solution derive from limitations such as those on short term memory capacity and speed of fixation in long term memory.

5. Knowledge structures

The elementary units and processes are organized into complex structures as in the example to provide a representation of the problem and a method for tackling it. These are given ready made to the program and successful performance depends on having only relevant information, all the relevant information and perfect retrieval, unlike an ape or human. Any change or loss of detail would change behaviour; if a JUMP operator were included or ape position were ranked above box position in the difference order, without other additions the program would fail. It is not clear how the correct order of differences could be available the first time the animal meets a new problem since other problems may have required a different order; it would have to be constructed during the solution in some way not specified in the program. A program in which the order is already available is thus a model of a skilled solver who has built the necessary structures during experience of similar problems or has devised strategies for achieving them in new tasks; in fact the program was originally designed to match performers who had the necessary skills available and only applied to the naive ape and banana problem during the attempt to extend its generality.

6. Problem space and heuristics

The representations of the initial and goal situations and the operators define the *problem space*, the set of possible situations which may occur. The number of these is one of the main determinants of task difficulty. In many cases the number is so large that the probability of success by random or orderly search through them is negligible. From a given position in a chess game some thirty moves are open to each player, giving about nine hundred possible sequences of a move by one player followed by a reply from the opponent. Methods guaranteed to find the best move or step (algorithms) are impractical and ways of reducing the problem space are needed. These are known as *heuristics*, a term coined by the mathematician Polya. They vary with the task and the solver, better solvers making use of better heuristics. Working backward is one heuristic, useful if there is one goal but several possible starting points (as in deriving a theorem from any one of a set of postulates or already proved theorems). Diagrams in geometry are another because they restrict what lines of attack are plausible (and were used by Gelernter et al. (1960) in a program to solve geometry theorems). In chess general rules like 'control the centre' and 'protect the king' act in the same way. We have met means-ends analysis in the example; another heuristic discussed by Newell and Simon (1972, p. 428) is planning, in which a simplified form of the problem is tackled first to work out an overall direction of attack. Wickelgren (1974) provides a collection of useful heuristics.

7. A general theory?

A general problem-solver could have a set of representations and methods, differing for different problems, and a way of selecting among them (the 'Big Switch' theory as Ernst and Newell, 1969, call it), or could deal with different problems in the same way. Such generality could be achieved through a common representation (such as the predicate calculus of logicians) or common methods. The first has been used but proved rather clumsy and restrictive, and Ernst and Newell opted for the second, using means-ends analysis as a general heuristic which had been observed in several tasks. Since their object was not simulation, but a case study of one possible way of achieving generality, they did not claim it had been demonstrated in all the eleven tasks they studied, or that this was the only way humans achieve generality. The different tasks had to be represented in different, but in many cases similar, ways and they discuss the difficulties and advantages of different forms of representation at length.

Though the goal of simulation imposed a need to be precise about the issue of generality, the important questions about how far different problems are represented in the same way and tackled by the same method and how far specific representations and methods are used remain to be answered from behavioural data. Some of the problems used by Ernst and Newell were not readily amenable to means-ends analysis, but can be solved by humans, so it seems likely that a range of heuristics is available to a good thinker, in which case the question arises of how suitable ones are selected for the problem presented. More recent research has abandoned the search for generality and, at least implicitly, moved toward the 'varied abilities' alternative.

8. Behavioural data

As Figure 8.1 shows, a good deal of qualitative information can be obtained from a simulation, and much more could have been given as the earlier discussion has indicated. However, most of the details in Figure 8.1 would not be available from observation of an ape solving the problem, and the tasks chosen for simulation have tended to be ones which could provide easily segregated units of behaviour at a fairly detailed level, such as concept learning tasks or games which yield a series of choices or problems where thinking aloud is possible, like logic, cryptarithmetic or choosing a chess move. These thinking aloud protocols present several problems. Newell and Simon (1972, p. 184) argue that they are sequences of behaviour to be explained, not introspective attempts at explanation, but clearly they can only be evoked in some sorts of thinking and constrain the possible level of explanation and tasks studied. Gaps may occur at critical points and the verbal behaviour need not be closely related to other aspects of thinking. Also thinking aloud may affect the whole thinking process in unknown ways (see Chapter 1).

9. Comparing simulated and behavioural data

Two qualitative sequences of behaviour have to be compared. The 'non-computed' data probably contain many events not present in the simulation like the ape scratching itself or kicking the box. The theory needs to specify exactly what it is intended to cover. Furthermore sequences of behaviour differ between individuals, especially on complex problems, and the usual averaging techniques are not appropriate. The simulator has the choice of trying to match common features occurring in most subjects or varying the program for different individuals.

Published comparisons of simulations and behavioural data are rather rare, brief and impressionistic. Often the same data seem to have been used in creating the program and in testing it; usually data from a single subject are offered without explanation of how they were chosen. The standard experimental method of making predictions from a simulation and then collecting the data seems to be ignored. To quote Hunt (1968): 'The reports of GPS and LT simulation simply do not meet reasonable criteria for supporting experimental evidence.' Extensive protocols from several subjects for cryptarithmetic tasks are given by Newell and Simon (1972) but no simulation with which to compare them. Some possible quantitative methods for making more reliable comparisons are outlined by Frijda (1967) and Reitman (1965).

One major difficulty is that an early difference between simulation and behaviour can set two sequences on quite different courses. Feldman (1961) in a careful comparison of data from a binary prediction task, set the program back on the same course as the human after each step to circumvent this problem; this solution is however less easy where the units of behaviour are not so readily identified.

10. Perception

No perceptual, selective or coding processes exist in the program; the situation is given ready made in all its details. The problem of selecting the relevant information and choosing a form of representation and method is pre-judged, though this may be critical to solution. If the ape failed to notice the box or represented it only as a container (as in the studies of functional fixity) or restricted the problem space inappropriately by regarding the box as immovable, the problem would be insoluble. Moreover different representations of a problem may contain the same information but alter its availability (see Newell and Simon, 1972, p. 59 ff.) or memorability (skilled chess players represent patterns of pieces as single units). The representation also affects difficulty by determining which operators can be applied;

calculating the distance travelled by a bird flying to and fro between two converging trains, given the speeds of all three and the initial distance between the trains, is difficult if we try to calculate the time the bird flies on each 'leg', but easy once we see the task as calculating the total time before the trains meet, because this allows simple operators relating time, speed and distance to be applied (Posner, 1973, p. 150). Amarel (1968) provides a theoretical discussion of this issue.

Newell and Simon (1972, p. 775 ff.) have made some attempt to investigate selection processes by studying eye movements of chess players and Newell (1972) has considered simulating perception for some tasks, but these efforts fall far short of adequate comprehension. As Lindsay argues (1973, p. 393), organisms can store information in the form of maps or images from which innumerable propositions can be derived, and no one has found out how to store information in this form in the computer, which usually stores propositional information (e.g. the ape is at position 1). Hunt and Poltrock (1974) on the other hand argue that humans abstract propositional information from pictorial inputs and quote Posner's (1969) experiments on the abstraction of prototypes from a series of variations of a pattern. Posner (1973, Ch. 3) himself, however, treats prototypes as iconic, and therefore non-propositional, concepts; both forms of representation are probably available as Lindsay's view implies.

Dreyfus (1972) argues that the information processing theories could only explain selection processes by exhaustive search, and the number of possibilities is too large; moreover serial search in verbal protocols is a slow process, and there is no reason to assume some other fast unconscious form of search which selects a subset of possibilities to be searched slowly and consciously. He argues that humans select by 'zeroing in' on the critical information, and that information on the fringe of consciousness, global perceptual organization, a sense of the situation and similarity to a 'paradigm' or typical case derived from experience all play a part. Hence any account of problem solving based on heuristics is inadequate because it cannot explain how the necessary preconditions for use of heuristics can be achieved. Dreyfus is correct in exposing this weakness, but his alternative to serial search is mere words and gives no indication of how he supposes the processes actually occur or proof that they are necessarily impossible to simulate (see Pylyshyn, 1974, for further discussion). The attempts which have been made to simulate perceptual processes suggest that the perceiver must possess complex rules and an internal model of the world to which the inputs can be matched (Hunt, 1974, Ch. 13), and thus incorporate at least some of Dreyfus's suggested processes.

11. Memory

As pointed out earlier, the program has exactly the information in memory needed for the task and perfect access to it. Every detail is important and loss of one brick would ruin the whole edifice. Human memory, on the other hand is messier, less reliable, but more flexible.

Due to the large amounts of information which have to be provided for solving even quite trivial problems, the memory capacity of the computer frequently limits the extension of a program to carry out a range of tasks. This is not just a technical problem to be solved by providing bigger memories because it requires a solution to the problem of how information is to be organized and retrieved. Existing programs for storing and retrieving information or for deducing new facts from stored information deal with very limited amounts of data (see Winograd, 1972). Quillian exhausted the capacity of a 32,000 'word' computer to handle just sixty English words and Winograd used a machine with an 80,000 'word' capacity to handle two hundred English words. As Dreyfus (1972) points out, a superficially simple concept like 'chair' involves a network of knowledge about human bodies, fatigue, furniture and so on. To prevent bizarre errors of deduction, such prosaic facts as that people who go out in the rain get wet must be given, and there is no definable set of primitive facts from which all knowledge can be deduced. Thus it is difficult to see a solution to this problem except by restricting programs to a limited data base (see Hunt, 1974, Ch. 14).

12. Learning

None of the existing simulation programs has any but very simple learning abilities, so the problem of determining the appropriate content for memory cannot at present be solved by allowing the program to accumulate its own information from appropriate experience. As Dreyfus (1972) points out, learning seems to need prior heuristics to guide it and this leads to an infinite regress. He concludes that computer simulation of human development in thinking is impossible, but we could equally validly conclude that human infants must start out with sufficient heuristics to pull themselves up by their own bootstraps, and much work on infant development would support this (see Chapter 4). There is no reason in principle why the initial abilities, if we could specify them, should not be incorporated in a learning program.

The only simple learning in Figure 8.1 is the ability to store the sequence of goals, in what is called a push-down stack, so that the program can 'back up' to them later (steps 7 to 8, 8 to 9, 11 to 12). The existing evidence on human memory suggests humans are bad at retaining such sequences. Another simple form of learning which might have occurred in a more complex example would be treating the same situation differently the second time it occurs because the first attempt had led to a dead end.

To incorporate learning which carries over to later problems some aspect of the program must be capable of changing, such as the heuristics or the method of representation. Neither of these has been explored, though one program has worked out the table of differences produced by each operator and another generated an ordering of differences after experiencing a series of problems. A chess program has been taught to improve its heuristics by cooperating with a skilled player (Zobrist and Carlson, 1973).

A third form of learning is to store and use past solutions. Uhr and Vossler (1961) devised a program for recognizing simple patterns which generated features, looked for them in patterns, and retained those which proved most useful in making the required discriminations; the Logic Theorist kept records of proved theorems as possible starting points for new proofs and rated them for usefulness to aid selection; Samuel's (1959) draughts program recorded earlier games and used them to select successful continuations from a position. However the problems of abstraction, coding and retrieval become very great with more complex tasks like chess. Even with the simpler Logic Theorist, the program was sometimes slowed down by having a list of proved theorems to consider, rather than being helped.

These flirtations with learning have highlighted the different possibilities, but have little to offer on how the whole complex structure required even for the simple example of Figure 8.1 evolved (see also section 5 above).

13. Single-mindedness

Neisser (1963a) has pointed out some major differences between programs and humans including the single-mindedness of the former. Some of the reasons for this have been mentioned in the discussion of the limited information provided to the program. Programs such as GPS are also single-minded in that only one thing occurs at a time. In an early protocol Newell and Simon (1961) noticed a human using two operators simultaneously but were not sure whether this was due to inadequate reporting or a real difference. Reitman (1965) has devised a system known as Argus to counter this criticism, in which several things can happen at once and compete with each other, resulting in sudden changes of direction. Even in this system there is no provision for two independent systems to function simultaneously, like driving a car and arguing politics.

The thought content of the single-minded thinker is assumed to be present in awareness, hence the possibility of tapping it through verbal protocols. No unconscious processes are assumed at the same level as the events reported (though it is accepted that events at a lower level and strategies at a higher level may be outside the thinker's awareness). However unconscious thought processes seem not uncommon in humans (Neisser, 1963b), as when a solution to a long-considered problem emerges suddenly while doing something else or symbolically in a dream.

14. Other sorts of thinking
It will already be clear that the problem-solving processes which have been discussed represent only a limited class of thinking activities, well-defined tasks with identifiable steps, a describable goal, initial situation, objects and operators. This picture needs some correction since a wider range of thinking processes has been considered than there has been space to deal with here; for example, Abelson (1973) simulated part of the belief system of a conservative politician, so that deductions were made consistent with the belief system when items of information were combined. There has, however, been little consideration of ill-defined tasks in which a major part of the solution is establishing limitations on the ill-defined aspects of the situation; in principle such tasks could be dealt with by establishing heuristics for fixing these limits.

Later development

As I have indicated, I have not attempted to survey all the relevant work. Though there are very many programs which carry out complex processes, there are in fact rather few which set out explicitly to match human performance. Most effort has been directed to artificial intelligence (see Minsky, 1968; Dreyfus, 1972; Hunt, 1974; Winograd, 1972, for a fuller picture). Several later efforts have used insights gained from GPS and more sophisticated versions of GPS have been developed. The main trend has been toward writing programs to cope with a limited task rather than extending the search for general principles. Where complex tasks have been attempted, the strategy has been to combine several independent subsystems in a 'heterarchy', which are called in turn by an executive. Significant examples are Anderson and Bower (1974) on human memory and Winograd (1972) on language comprehension. The former program does attempt to match many of the known phenomena and in some cases predict new ones. Winograd's program is an example of an approach to language comprehension which has developed directly from attempts to write language-comprehending programs and which differs sharply from approaches developed by psychologists on the basis of transformational grammar. Winograd's program matches human performance in the sense that it shows ability to act upon instructions and answer questions regarding a limited environment. It shows the strengths and weaknesses already noted for problem-solving programs (see Dresler and Hornstein, 1976, for a detailed discussion).

Conclusions

In conclusion, the main weakness of the simulation studies is the restriction of the possibilities to a limited set of situations, all of which must be precisely specified, without possibility of extension through learning. Problems of perception and coding are bypassed and decisions are made by the programmer about a large number of details of representation and operations. In theory the need to make these decisions should have produced a flurry of experimental effort to decide what humans actually do, or at least a detailed specification of the possibilities for experimental test; in practice the artificial intelligence theorist has made his decision on unspecified grounds and pressed on (probably knowing he will get no clear answers from psychologists anyhow!). There are however some areas where widespread experimentation has been stimulated by efforts to model performance on computers; the most striking example is probably the immense growth of research on semantic memory following Quillian's (1968) computer-influenced ideas about its structure.

There are several important gains from simulation. When theories are described in words it is often difficult to decide upon an adequate test because basic assumptions are not clear; computer simulation compels all details to be made explicit about complex processes, so a suitable test can be devised. Methods of testing, however, need improving. The necessity to undertake careful task analysis, and state the theory precisely and in every detail, plus the ability to describe processes and not just products are all clear benefits. From work with computers a number of concepts have emerged or been clarified which can usefully be applied to the analysis of behaviour, such as the hardware/software distinction, languages, levels of description, feedback loops, push-down stacks, specification of the basic processes needed to carry out different kinds of task, and so on. Finally there is the major gain that theories have to make assumptions about all the basic cognitive abilities in order to handle thought and are thus forced into a more unified view of the functioning of the organism

Notes

1 Cryptarithmetic problems are of the form

DONALD +

GERALD

ROBERT

and the task is to assign a digit to each letter consistently so that the addition is correct. Sometimes in the above problem the subject is also told that $D = 5$.

2 Binary numbers use only two symbols, 1 and ø (written thus to distinguish it from the letter O) which can also be represented by hole and no hole in a punched card or on and off positions of a switch; each symbol represents one bit of information. The seven decimal numbers ø to 7 are written in binary code; ø, 1, 1ø, 11, 1øø, 1ø1, 11ø, 111. Since long strings of 1's and ø's are hard to handle, they are usually summarized in groups of three using the eight numbers ø to 7. This is called octal coding. The binary sequence ø1ø 1øø 111 øø1 would be 2471 in octal code. The sequence is known as a 12 bit *word* because there are 12 binary symbols.

3 *Arrays* are used to represent elements with several features in a matrix; the ape in the example can be located in one of the six cells in a simple two-dimensional array with two dimensions of floor position (1, 2 or 3) and elevation (high or low). *Loops* provide a means of carrying out a sequence in the program several times before passing on to the next instruction.

References

Abelson, R. (1973) The structure of belief systems. In R. Schank and K. Colby (eds) *Computer Models of Thought and Language*. San Francisco: Freeman.

Amarel, S. (1968) On representation of problems of reasoning about actions. In D. Michie (ed.) *Machine Intelligence*, III. Edinburgh: Edinburgh University Press.

Anderson, J. A. and Bower, G. H. (1973) *Human Associative Memory*. Washington D.C.: Winston.

Bartlett, F. C. (1958) *Thinking: An Experimental and Social Study*. London: Allen and Unwin.

Bruner, J. S., Goodnow, J. J. and Austin, G. A. (1956) *A Study of Thinking*. New York: Wiley. (Science Edition, 1962).

De Groot, A. D. (1946) *Het Denken van den Schaker*. Amsterdam: North Holland Publishing Company.

Dresler, B. E. and Hornstein, N. (1976) On some supposed contributions of artificial intelligence to the scientific study of language. *Cognition 4* (4): 321–98.

Dreyfus, H. L. (1972) *What Computers Can't Do*. New York: Harper and Row.

Duncker, K. (1945) On problem solving. *Psychological Monographs 5* (5) Whole No. 270.

Ernst, G. W. and Newell, A. (1969) *GPS: A Case Study in Generality and Problem Solving*. New York: Academic Press.

Feigenbaum, E. A. and Feldman, J. (1963) *Computers and Thought*. New York: McGraw-Hill.

Feldman, J. (1961) Simulation of behaviour in the binary choice experiment. In E. A. Feigenbaum and J. Feldman (eds) *Computers and Thought*. New York: McGraw-Hill.

Frijda, N. H. (1967) Problems of computer simulation. *Behavioural Science 12*: 59–67.

Gelernter, H., Hansen, J. R. and Loveland, D. W. (1960) Empirical explorations of the Geometry-Theorem proving machine. In E. A. Feigenbaum and J. Feldman (eds) *Computers and Thought*. New York: McGraw-Hill.

Gregory, R. L. (1970) On how little information controls so much behaviour. *Ergonomics 13* (1): 25–35.

Hull, C. L. (1952) *A Behaviour System*. New Haven: Yale University Press.

Hunt, E. B. (1968) Computer simulation: Artificial intelligence studies and their relation to psychology. *Annual Review of Psychology 19*: 135–68.

Hunt, E. B. (1971) What kind of computer is man? *Cognitive Psychology 2*: 57–98.

Hunt, E. B. (1974) *Artificial Intelligence*. New York: Academic Press.

Hunt, E. B. and Poltrock, S. (1974) The mechanics of thought. In B. Kantowitz (ed) *Human Information Processing: Tutorials in Performance and Cognition*. Hillsdale, N. J.: Lawrence Erlbaum Associates.

Kendler, T. S. and Kendler, H. H. (1962) Vertical and horizontal processes in problem solving. *Psychological Review 69* (1): 1–16.

Köhler, W. (1925) *The Mentality of Apes*. London: Routledge and Kegan Paul. Pelican Books, 1957.

Lindsay, R. K. (1973) In defence of ad hoc systems. In R. Schank and K. Colby (eds) *Computer Models of Thought and Language*. San Francisco: Freeman.

Miller, G. A., Galanter, E. and Pribram, K. (1960) *Plans and the Structure of Behaviour*. New York: Holt, Rinehart and Winston.

Minsky, M. (ed.) (1968) *Semantic information processing*. Cambridge, Mass: M.I.T. Press.

Mowrer, O. H. (1954) The psychologist looks at language. *American Psychologist* 9 (11): 660–94.

Neisser, U. (1963a) The imitation of man by machine. *Science 139*: 193–7.

Neisser, U. (1963b) The multiplicity of thought. *British Journal of Psychology 54* (1): 1–14.

Newell, A. (1972) A theoretical exploration of mechanisms for coding the stimulus. In A. W. Metton and E. Martin (eds) *Coding Processes in Human Memory*. New York: Wiley.

Newell, A. and Simon, H. A. (1958) Heuristic problem solving: The next advance in operations research. *Journal of the Operations Research Society 6*: 6.

Newell, A. and Simon, H. A. (1961) GPS, a program that simulates human thought. In E. A. Feigenbaum and J. Feldman (eds) *Computers and Thought*. New York: McGraw-Hill.

Newell, A. and Simon, H. A. (1972) *Human Problem Solving*. Englewood Cliffs, N. J.: Prentice Hall.

Newell, A., Shaw, J. C. and Simon, H. A. (1957) Empirical explorations with the Logic Theory Machine: a case study in Heuristics. In E. A. Feigenbaum and J. Feldman (eds) *Computers and Thought*. New York: McGraw-Hill.

Newell, A., Shaw, J. C. and Simon, H. A. (1958) Elements of a theory of human problem-solving. *Psychological Review 65*: 151–66.

Osgood, C. E. (1953) *Method and Theory in Experimental Psychology*. New York: Oxford University Press.

Posner, M. I. (1969) Abstraction and the process of recognition. In G. H. Bower and J. T. Spence (eds) *The Psychology of Learning and Motivation*, Vol. 3. New York: Academic Press.

Posner, M. I. (1973) *Cognition: An Introduction*. Glenview, Illinois: Scott, Foresman.

Pylyshyn, Z. (1974) Minds, machines and phenomenology: some reflections on Dreyfus's *What Computers Can't Do*. *Cognition 3* (1): 57–77.

Quillian, M. R. (1968) Semantic memory. In M. Minsky (ed.) *Semantic Information Processing*. Cambridge, Mass.: M.I.T. Press.

Reitman, W. R. (1965) *Cognition and Thought: An Information-Processing Approach*. New York: Wiley.

Samuel, A. L. (1959) Some studies in machine learning using the game of checkers. In E. A. Feigenbaum and J. Feldman (eds) *Computers and Thought*. New York: McGraw-Hill.

Selz, O. (1927) The revision of the fundamental conceptions of intellectual processes. In J. M. Mandler and G. Mandler (eds) *Thinking: From Association to Gestalt*. New York: Wiley.

Shannon, C. E. and Weaver, W. (1949) *The Mathematical Theory of Communication*. Urbana, Ill.: University of Illinois Press.

Sutherland, N. S. (1974) Computer simulation of brain function. In S. C. Brown (ed.) *Philosophy of Psychology*. London: Macmillan.

Turing, A. M. (1936) On computable numbers, with an application to the Entscheidungs problem. *Proceedings of the London Mathematics Society (Series 2)*, 42: 230–65.

Uhr, L. and Vossler, C. (1961) A pattern recognition program that generates, evaluates and adjusts its own operators. In E. A. Feigenbaum and J. Feldman (eds) *Computers and Thought*. New York: McGraw-Hill.

Von Neumann, J. (1958) *The Computer and the Brain*. New Haven, Conn.: Yale University Press.

Wickelgren, W. A. (1974) *How to Solve Problems*. San Francisco: Freeman.

Wiener, N. (1948) *Cybernetics*. New York: Wiley.

Winograd, T. (1972) Understanding natural language. *Cognitive Psychology 3* (1): 1–191.

Zobrist, A. and Carlson, F. (1973) An advice-taking chess computer. *Scientific American 228* (6): 92–105.

9 Interpreting a dream: Psychoanalysis

John Radford

'The temptation to form premature theories upon insufficient evidence is the bane of our profession.'   **Sherlock Holmes**

Holmes, having as is generally thought been born in 1854, was almost exactly Freud's contemporary, and there are some resemblances between the consulting rooms in Baker Street and those in the Berggasse. To each came a succession of more or less distraught individuals, telling jumbled and fragmentary stories. From these and from selective observations of behaviour the world's first consulting detective, and the first analyst, would form a theory to account for the hitherto unaccountable

Apart from the many other comparisons that might be made (their liking for smoking, for cocaine, for ciphers, their dependence on companions who did not understand them) both leave us with many puzzles, not least what they were doing, how they did it, and why it was so influential. The answers are not made easier by the inadequacy of the evidence. The discrepancies of Watson's accounts are well known. Although Freud wrote voluminously, a count shows that his works include only twelve case studies that can be considered full-length, and references to some 130 more. Freud himself provided several revealing historical accounts of his work, and his correspondence with Fliess, published in 1950, reveals more. And there are researches such as those of Jones (1955) and Stewart (1969) on the development of Freud's thought, and of Bakan (1965), Reeves (1965) and Whyte (1960) on its background. Nevertheless the continued flow of publications suggest how much there is still to understand, and I cannot hope here to solve puzzles that fill major scholarly works.

At least part of what Freud thought he was doing is reasonably clear. One could say that his primary aim was therapy. (Freud continued to see patients to within a few months of his death.) R. S. Peters (1953) expressed this by saying that Freud was 'ostensibly a technologist': his purpose was, on the face of it, to find some means of removing troublesome symptoms.

The technology developed from suggestion by way of the talking cure hit on by Breuer to free association and interpretation. The classic method crystallized about 1900–5 (although there continue to be developments, minor within psychoanalysis proper, radical and bizarre outside it). From the start however Freud was a relentless theorist, endlessly sorting and recombining his knowledge, observations, and speculations in the effort to construct a workable model of the mental apparatus. What psychology textbooks call 'thinking' was only one aspect of this apparatus. It was a model in the sense that the gaps between observations had to be filled in by inference. Some parts of the apparatus, in any case, could never be observed directly. Or rather, perhaps, there is a continuum of degrees of accessibility. A possibly misleading analogy might be an architect trying to construct the plan of a house seen only from the street. A door and two windows suggest a passage and two rooms. What can be seen through the windows suggests a dining room and a drawing room. A general knowledge of houses, and an intimate knowledge of his own, suggest the existence of kitchen and bathroom, and where and how they might function. The architect's plan would be speculative, but intended as a true representation though both schematic and incomplete. There seems little doubt that Freud intended his account to be as true as he could make it, not just a way of looking at things (Skinner, 1954). In Boring's (1957) phrase, it was an 'as', not an 'as if'. The inexactness of this analogy may emerge as we go on.

However, Freud's practice of therapy and edifice of theory can also be seen, as he himself saw it (Freud, 1935) as a vast detour through the natural sciences, medicine and psychotherapy, returning in the last two decades of his life to general cultural problems that had fascinated him at the outset of his career.

These amounted to, in essence, the nature of man and his place in creation: and Freud believed he had found the essentials of the answer: 'I perceived ever more clearly that the events of human history, the interactions between human nature, cultural development and the precipitates of primeval experiences (the most prominent example of which is religion) are no more than a reflection of the dynamic conflicts between the ego, the id, and the superego, which psychoanalysis studies in the individual – are the very same processes repeated upon a wider stage.' (*An Autobiographical Study*, 1935.)

At least since the time of Thomas Hobbes (1588–1679) it has been apparent that for any account of human behaviour to be complete, it should be consistent at the physiological, individual, and social levels of analysis. Freud's attention in later years turned, or turned back, to the last of these. His first major psychological work (apart from the *Studies in Hysteria* (1895) written jointly with Breuer) was the ambitious, far-reaching, complex and uncompleted 'psychology for neurologists' now known as the *Project for a Scientific Psychology* (1895). Written in the form of correspondence to the semi-mystical scientist Wilhelm Fliess, it reappeared only in 1950. In it Freud attempted to devise an account of the mental apparatus based on, and consistent with, his extensive knowledge of the neurology of his time. The attempt was left, and Freud never returned to it. But as has become apparent since the *Project* was published, in many ways it foreshadows the main developments of Freud's psychological psychology.

The context

Some of the many difficulties in understanding what Freud actually did come, it seems to me, from the nature of the context in which his work arose and was continued. The influence of Freud has been so all-pervasive and diffuse, and so indissolubly linked with numerous other influences, that it is not yet possible to see his work in historical perspective. This is perhaps made more so by Freud's relative isolation from the rest of psychology. Freud's own knowledge of contemporary – that is, nineteenth century – psychology was minimal. Jones (1955) tells us that it seemed to derive only from hearsay. And as he points out, this is a cause of making Freud difficult for psychologists trained in particular ways of using language. Freud indeed largely invented his own terminology, and, besides, was by no means always consistent in his use of it (Jones, 1955). The possibilities and implications of an alternative language have been considered by later writers, e.g. Schafer (1976). Psychoanalysis as a profession has likewise tended to develop in relative isolation. Relatively few analysts have trained in academic, still less applied psychology: the classic road is that of Freud, through general medicine. And although perhaps a majority of psychiatrists derive at least something from Freud, psychoanalysts hold themselves apart from other psychiatric techniques.

Freud did have some first-hand knowledge of associationism (he translated into German some writings of J. S. Mill); and he attended lectures by Brentano, who was one of the chief influences in the 'act' psychology which was an alternative to the analysis of 'content' as propounded by Wundt and his followers. Mental phenomena, Brentano taught, are acts, and can be classified into three kinds, ideating, judging, and loving/hating. More important, however, are the general intellectual climate of the time and Freud's own specific training and inclinations.

Any detailed account of these is impossible here. But it is worth noting that, when Freud was first developing his techniques and theories, science, especially mental science, was by no means always rigidly separated from the mysterious and even the magical. The classical western systems of magic, indeed, enjoyed a revival at just this time. The atmosphere of Charcot's laboratory seems at times to have resembled that of the spiritualist séances that were so popular in the latter part of the nineteenth century. Phrenology, too, was at least a semi-respectable profession.

The advances of science seemed to some to constitute an attack on the bases of society itself. Perhaps the most relevant case is the furious religion/anti-religion debate that followed Darwin's *Origin of Species* in 1859.

On the other hand the growth of modern science not only disturbed traditional ways of thinking, but made it necessary to consider what distinguished scientific method from other approaches to natural phenomena. It is perhaps particularly instructive to single out the influential views of J. S. Mill. In *A System of Logic* (1843) Mill argued that the object of science was the discovery of causes: and that the method was that of induction, defined as: 'the process by which we conclude that what is true of certain individuals of a class is true of the whole class, or that what is true at certain times will be true in similar circumstances at all times.'

Freud was trained in medicine, with strong influences from various nineteenth century sciences. Many of these have been exactly documented. Freud himself states, for example, that '... it was hearing Goethe's beautiful essay on nature read aloud at a popular lecture by Professor Carl Bruhl just before I left school that decided me to become a medical student' (Freud, 1935); and that the theories of Darwin gave him the hope of a vastly increased understanding of the world.

The Darwinian view of evolution was one of the fundamentals of thought at the Brücke Institute where Freud spent six years; Ernst Brücke himself Freud acknowledged as having influenced him more than any other man. Brücke, too, championed the school of physiology of Helmholtz, like himself a pupil of Johannes Müller. Helmholtz stood by the principle of conservation of energy and the possibility of reducing all the forces in a system to two, attraction and repulsion. It was Brücke who with another of Müller's students, Emil du Bois Reymond, swore solemnly in 1842 to maintain the view that: 'No other forces than the common physical chemical ones are active within the organism . . .' Another influence, noted by Ramzy (1956), is that of Aristotle, which reached Freud through Brentano. Aristotle 'represents the realistic, rational, scientific, logical approach to the problems of the universe and of man'. Aristotle's emphasis on natural, biological development as movement from potentiality to actuality, and in the case of man the highest level of development as the exercise of reason, is clearly enough reflected in Freud.

During Freud's working life psychology grew and changed, sometimes influenced by psychoanalysis but on the whole giving little back. It was the time of the *schools*, and Woodworth (1931) treated psychoanalysis as one of them. The others were functional, structural, associationist, behaviourist, gestalt, purposive and holistic. Woodworth himself, as Boring (1957) says, did not want a school, but his *Experimental Psychology* (1938) summarized one of the main streams of psychological practice, the other being psychometrics. He mentions Freud once, to compare *transference* with *transfer*.

Our own contemporary psychology, one might say, starts at about this point. Freud died in 1939. The Second World War was one stimulus to quantities of new research and re-thinking. Recent years have seen the virtual disappearance of schools, but the emergence of new interests or revival of old ones: in subjective experience, in cognitive processes, in child development (with, at present, great emphasis on mother-infant interaction), in cultural factors. None of these was strange to Freud, and in one sense psychology proper is belatedly catching up with him. It is worth trying, once more, to see if we can see what he was up to.

The method

It is by no means easy. Let us tackle first the method. It is apparently straightforward. Normally an individual goes every working day to see the therapist, lies on a couch for fifty minutes, and says whatever comes into his head. The therapist responds variously. Were the procedure to be observed by an extra-terrestrial scientist he would also note certain other behaviour notably, I suppose, periodic signs of emotion on the part of the patient. It might be difficult to observe the significant feature of payment. The observer might also remark on resemblances to other situations. Observing more closely, he might group together other therapeutic practices (some of which are, of course, derived from psychoanalysis); some from an educational context, particularly the tutorial system; some from religious contexts, particularly the confessional, and the master-pupil interviews of eastern faiths of which the most refined examples, perhaps, are those of Zen Buddhism.

Reverting to a human standpoint, we note that comparisons have been specifically attempted between the last example and psycho-analysis (e.g. Fromm et al., 1960). A review of these however (Radford 1976) suggests that they are inconclusive and unsophisticated. The attempt to compare does direct attention to some significant features. One of these is the peculiar nature of the data. As far as I know, there is no complete record of an analysis in existence. (Although there are, of course, lengthy extracts.) Jones (1955) indeed states that it cannot be done: '... it would occupy many volumes and would be quite unreadable'. Apart from the fact that such considerations have not deterred other writers, Jones is of course thinking of it from the analyst's point of view: what as psychologists we wish to have are accounts by observers, such as we get for other dyads. With modern recording devices there is no reason why this cannot be done. And there is no reason why the analyst has to double as therapist and research scientist. There is an extensive, if somewhat inconclusive literature on the analysis of therapeutic interactions, e.g. Gottschalk and Auerbach (1966); Goldstein and Dean (1966); Kiesler (1973). And there are accounts by psychoanalysts, such as those of Glover (1955), Lorand (1948) and Reik (1948), as well as those of Freud himself. From these a very complex picture emerges. Taking first what the patient does, it is generally accepted that he must have some degree of motivation, and that he is to practice 'free association'. Actually as Freud himself pointed out, it is not free but determined, otherwise analysis would be impossible. Technically, it is the reverse of 'constrained association'; but the important freedom is rather an attempt not to hold material back for reasons of propriety, shame, etc. An analytic case study consists of the behaviour the analyst thinks important, and what he thinks it means. (Complicated further by the counter-transference – the emotional reactions the analyst develops towards his patient.) Even diagnosis and outcome, which might seem the most obvious facts, are seldom available in any controlled fashion, which is one of the causes of controversy over the efficacy of treatment. Even what *counts* as success is not generally agreed, still less whether it is achieved.

When it comes to what the analyst does things are still more complex. It seems from the investigations of Glover (1955) that there is practically no item of practice that commands universal assent. It is apparent at least, though, that what is being done requires discussion at several different levels. What these might be can only be hinted at here. There is first, perhaps, the attitude of the analyst. The famous phrase here is 'evenly suspended attention'. Immediately reminiscent of the attitude of a Zen master, this also suggests that analysis is much closer to some kind of skilled coaching than to a research technique. Two other well-known phrases are 'a dialogue between the unconscious of the patient and that of the analyst', and 'holding a mirror up to the patient'. The latter moves us to another level, for this mirror is an odd one. Actually, social skills are now often taught by a 'mirror' technique using video monitoring and recording. The analytic mirror has several characteristics. The analyst remains passive insofar as he offers no criticism of socially unacceptable material. But he selects some of the patient's behaviour for comment. Comment in itself may well be reinforcing, probably positively but perhaps negatively. Further, the comment is given from the analyst's particular stand-point, itself a complex matter. Perhaps the most elementary aspect is the transference. Although the phenomenon was noticed early – in Breuer's patient Anna O., in fact – its importance emerged only gradually. It has become fundamental to analytic practice that the patient's behaviour is interpreted as referring to the analyst.

It is less clear whether the transference is to be conceived of as, so to say, a hypothesis which is always supported, or a fact which is regularly revealed, or something which develops during, or because of, the analysis (see Davies and O'Farrell, 1976).

The analyst's comments constitute interpretation. But it is clear that interpreting in analysis means several different things. Let us take dreams, since Freud referred to their interpretation as a *via regia* to a knowledge of the unconscious. To begin with, obviously what is interpreted is not dreams as such, but what the patient recounts under the label 'dreams'. This is very different, since we know from experimental work that only a tiny fraction of dreams is recalled; since dreams do not come mainly in the form of words, which is normally the only medium the patient has for expressing them; and since we have no idea how the analytic situation itself may affect either recall or expression. In a sense 'dreams' are just a sub-sample of the highly selective sample of behaviour (largely verbal) that the analyst has to work on. As Reeves (1965) points out, there seems at first sight to be a puzzle in what that work consists of. What Freud says is:

> We have introduced a new class of psychical material between the manifest content of dreams and the conclusions of our enquiry: namely the latent content or (as we say) the 'dream-thoughts', arrived at by means of our procedure. It is from these dream-thoughts and not from a dream's manifest content that we disentangle its meaning ...
>
> The dream-thoughts and the dream-content are presented to us like two versions of the same subject matter in two different languages. Or, more properly, the dream-content seems like a transcript of the dream-thoughts into another mode of expression, whose characters and syntactic laws it is our business to discover by comparing the original and the translation. The dream-thoughts are immediately comprehensible, as soon as we have learnt them. The dream-content, on the other hand, is expressed as it were in a pictographic script, the characters of which have to be transposed individually into the language of the dream-thoughts. If we attempted to read these characters according to their pictorial value instead of according to their symbolic relation, we should clearly be led into error. (*Interpretation of Dreams, 1900*)

The puzzle might be that such immediate comprehensibility seems at variance with the irrational nature of the unconscious. But it seems clear that the dream thoughts are not themselves the unconscious, but only the expression of unconscious processes. It might be thought of like this. The dream is of a policeman. As such, it has no particular meaning; it is simply an image. This image can be translated into the idea 'father', which is immediately comprehensible. The policeman image is a suitable one for father because fathers are, like them, in authority; because a policeman has been encountered the previous day; and, perhaps, because the patient's actual father had some connection with the police. The symbol, although overdetermined, is also idiosyncratic; another patient would use a different one. But this idea, 'father', is not what exists in the unconscious. What exists there is, we suppose, a complex of reactions, and potential reactions, to 'father' and to father-like stimuli (such as a real policeman or, more particularly, an analyst). Just what determines likeness is not very clear. It seems to be a selection from physical characteristics, associations (which may be accidental), and situational features. Interpreting a dream is thus first of all translating the apparently random manifest content into the comprehensible latent content. It is then inferring from this what affective patterns lie behind it. It is also attempting to fit these inferences into an account of the patient which is based both on the general assumptions of psychoanalytic theory and on knowledge of the particular individual. Interpretation may also go further and add to theory, as is seen most substantially in Freud's own work.

However, interpreting to the patient is not any of these, though it is based on them. To pursue the hypothetical policeman, an interpretation of this to the patient might be (say): 'I think you are feeling very angry with me.' An identical interpretation might be given to a fantasy, a hestitation, or a late arrival. What is said depends on the analyst's intuitive, though theoretically-informed, judgement of what is appropriate, which in turn depends on knowledge of the patient's mental apparatus (to use Freud's phrase again) and on what is therapeutically useful.

This whole process is well worthy of continued investigation. However we can also consider the analyst as himself an investigator, as Freud, indeed, could be said primarily to have been.

The analyst has some advantages and some disadvantages. He has access to material which is almost certainly unique in amount (at any rate for individual subjects) and in content. No other situation would seem to allow such a detailed and uninhibited exploration of human thoughts and feelings.

Psychoanalysis has sometimes been criticized for depending on introspection. This is not really very pertinent. On the one hand, introspection is currently respectable again (see Chapter 1). On the other, the main difficulties of introspection do not apply strongly. One difficulty is that subjective reports cannot be directly compared: we can never tell with absolute certainty whether my experience of green is the same as yours. But analysis is not really interested in this, rather in the patient's use of and reaction to 'green'. Free association needs to be uncensored (at the conscious level) but it need not be skilful. It need not even be always truthful, since fabrications are equally mental phenomena.

There are however more serious disadvantages. An obvious one is that psychoanalysis deliberately excludes many sources of data, normally making no use of psychometrics or other sorts of psychological assessment, and very little of social or developmental information. Subjectivity and selectivity are handicaps in research, but they are not unique to psychoanalysis. Any scientist must make subjective judgements at every point, and total observation is logically impossible. What makes these points especially relevant is that psychoanalysis, as a method of investigation, is peculiarly resistant to replication and cross-checking. Each analysis is both unique and private; diagnosis, treatment, and criteria for cure are only partially agreed within the system itself, and certainly not outside it. It is not quite clear, however, whether these are matters of principle or only of practice.

Like Holmes, Freud noted those aspects of the case that seemed significant (both on occasion without seeing the client), and then with an intuitive leap, devised a hypothetical structure to account for them. It was not really deduction that amazed Watson, but a sort of induction. Whereas Holmes, however, would then take a cab (generally accompanied by at least one observer) to the scene of the investigation, Freud's theories were tested, as he once remarked, 'on the couch'. A couch can indeed be used for this purpose, as can any other place; but it has special difficulties. Freud was trained as, and considered himself to be, a scientist. But his route was through physiology and medicine: dissection of individual specimens and treatment of individual patients, with subsequent generalization. And it is worth noting that even the received psychology of the time set out to investigate the generalized 'mind', through the medium of good-class specimens in the shape of German professors. Individual differences, systematic experimentation, controls, and all the other accepted fundamentals of current psychology, were parallel developments, for ignoring which psychoanalysis can perhaps with hindsight be criticized.

We might note that large as Freud's claims were, and however insecure their basis, they hardly exceed those of Watson and Skinner, the apostles of hard-headed objectivity who, it may be thought, had little better evidence and a good deal less sophistication. And Spearman, the developer of factor-analysis, advanced his noegenetic principles not merely as a cognitive theory, but as the key to understanding the entire universe.

Be this as it may, we must now try to see briefly what was discovered.

The findings

It is of course impossible to condense Freud's many volumes into a few pages; and these volumes contain most intricate thinking, often at several different levels of analysis. And as has often been remarked, development is continuous throughout Freud's writing life which, like his analytic practice, continued almost to the end.

Freud's language has been mentioned. Let us illustrate this with three definitions of a basic term, anxiety, from accepted English, psychology, and psychoanalysis.

1. Uneasiness, concern; solicitous desire. *Concise Oxford English Dictionary*.
2. A chronic complex emotional state with apprehension or dread as its most prominent component. Drever: *Dictionary of Psychology*.
3. The response to some as yet unrecognized factor, either in the environment or in the self, (which) may be evolved either by changes in the environment or by the stirrings of unconscious, repressed forces in the self. Rycroft: *A Critical Dictionary of Psychoanalysis*.

Although the words are not Freud's own, this does suggest the idiosyncratic usage of psychoanalysis, to which definition, description, explanation and theoretical assumptions all contribute. For non-German speakers there is the added problem of translation: as Rycroft points out 'anxiety' is by no means the same as 'angst'.

Apart from deliberately formulated theories, Freud seems to have had predilections for casting his thoughts in certain moulds. Two very noticeable features are his preferences for dichotomies and for agencies. The instincts, for example, through their various versions, always come in pairs; primary processes are balanced by secondary.

The various mental systems that Freud distinguished often seem almost to have the status of living entities: they strive, they succeed or fail. The best known are the relative latecomers id, ego, and superego, but this feature is well developed in the *Project*.

Hilgard (1962) among others, has noted the persistence throughout Freud's thinking of certain guiding ideas. He selects three in particular, which likewise are found in the *Project*. They are: continuity of development; the persistence and influence of unconscious processes; and the view that current behaviour is often a resultant of conflict. Hilgard also commends an analysis by Rapaport and Gill (1959), who distinguished five metapsychological points of view in psycho-analytic theory. Freud himself had formulated three, which he named dynamic, topographic, and economic. Rapaport and Gill modified topographic to structural, and added two more, genetic and adaptive.

Briefly these are as follows. The *dynamic* point of view involves the assumption of 'psychological forces', deriving from inbuilt drives or instincts, which may act in conjunction or in opposition, in simple or complex ways (i.e. the effect of simultaneously acting forces may or may not be a mathematical product of the forces). The *economic* point of view assumes that all behaviour is regulated by psychological energy, which follows the laws of conservation and of entropy. The *structural* point of view assumes that the mental apparatus can be conceived of in terms of structures (notably id, ego, and superego), which are thought of as relatively permanent and as being in some hierarchical relationship to each other. The *genetic* point of view is really the developmental assumption that the present state of an organism is the outcome of the stages through which it has passed, each stage permanently modifying the course of development. Lastly the *adaptive* point of view, largely a post-Freudian development, stresses the mechanisms by which an organism is able to deal with, and become relatively independent of, the environment.

Hilgard, seeking consistency, wishes to reduce these five to two, grouping together the first two and the last three; however if they are thought of as ways of looking at the phenomena such reduction seems less necessary. It is, though, necessary to consider at least one other basic assumption, that of determinism. It is fundamental to Freud's thinking that psychological phenomena are caused, and that these causes can, in principle, be discovered – analysed, in fact – just as can those of any other natural phenomenon (though not by the same methods).

R. S. Peters (1958) has pointed out that this assumption led Freud into some confusion insofar as he failed to distinguish different sorts of cause. The most important distinction is between causes which can and those which cannot be affected by rational conscious deliberation. Thus given that psychoanalysis is able to provide a causal explanation for some hitherto unexplained act, say compulsive hand washing, in terms of unconscious forces over which the individual has no control, it sometimes seems that an identical type of explanation is to be given for, say, normal hand washing. It is true that it may be hard to distinguish two individual samples of behaviour; and also that a given act may have a mixed causality. But that there must be a logical distinction is clear. It is of course assumed in analytic therapy itself, the aim of which is to increase the sphere of rationality. And the psychological distinction appears in the non-adaptive, repetitive nature of compulsive acts, not logically related to supposed ends.

It is widely held (e.g. Jones, 1955) that Freud's greatest single achievement was to establish the existence of two sorts of mental process, primary and secondary. The achievement was not, of course, merely to remark that we often have bizarre and unaccountable thoughts, images, and wishes; nor that there are mental processes of which we are unaware. Freud referred to three blows to man's narcissism, delivered by Copernicus, Darwin, and himself: his is expressed most briefly, perhaps, in his retrospective remark of 1935: 'Psychoanalysis regarded everything mental as being in the first instance unconscious; the further quality of "consciousness" might also be present, or again it might be absent.'

This is not to equate primary/secondary with unconscious/conscious, but rather to stress the difficult and vulnerable emergence of the latter half of each pair.

The living organism comes into existence endowed with certain functions which involve interaction with the environment, and thus with drives to certain actions, directed towards certain kinds of objects: it must breathe, eat, and (less vitally) be warmed and touched. In some of these, the instant gratification for which the organism is, so to say, built is often not forthcoming. The result of this is excitation, and organisms are also so constructed that they tend to keep the level of excitation constant. Before seeing how Freud considered that this gives rise to thinking, we should note a point made by Reeves (1965): namely, that Freud 'took for granted a form of representative perception'. That is to say, the organism is not directly aware of the external world, but only of the effects of its own receptor organs discharging. The resulting product represents the external world more or less accurately.

Freud's most detailed account of the origins of thinking appears in *The Interpretation of Dreams*. It seems to involve the following steps:

1. the mental apparatus is originally so constructed that it tries to keep the level of excitation as low as possible;
2. accordingly it functions on a reflex system, with immediate discharge of external excitation;
3. this is disturbed by the demands of life, viz. physical needs;
4. these result in motility (expression of the emotions – crying etc.) which continues because it does not change the external situation;
5. external excitation can only be ended by satisfaction;
6. an essential component of satisfaction is a certain percept;
7. the memory-image of the percept is associated with the memory-trace of the excitation;
8. the next time the need arises, there is a psychic impulse (a wish) to revive the memory-image, and re-evoke the percept;
9. wish-fulfilment is equivalent to re-appearance of the percept, and the shortest path to this is the full cathexis (roughly, activation) of the percept by energy arising from the need;
10. in a primitive state of development, this occurs as an hallucination;
11. but this does not produce satisfaction, and the need continues;
12. the investment of energy in the percept has to be inhibited, and diverted into seeking a change in the external world;
13. this involves the introduction of a test of reality;
14. in turn this necessitates the creation of a second system which controls voluntary motility for a purpose remembered in advance;
15. this mental activity is thus 'a roundabout way to wish-fulfilment'; thinking 'is indeed nothing but a substitute for the hallucinatory wish'.

The phrase 'nothing but' is always a danger signal in psychology, and this exemplifies a tendency in Freudian theory to equate origins with explanations. It also raises the question as to whether thinking occurs in other species. I do not know that Freud said anything about thought processes in animals, but clearly the initial conditions must exist at least in primates, and some of the recent studies of these are relevant (see e.g. Wilson, 1977).

In discussing Freud's other contributions to the psychology of thinking, it becomes increasingly hard to maintain the artificial (though often convenient) distinction between thought and other processes. His most elaborate treatment is of mechanisms by which the contents of thinking may be transformed. These are seen in dreams, or more properly in the 'dream-work'; in jokes; and parapraxes (apparently accidental slips or mistakes) as well as in the production of pathologic symptoms.

Given that there are basic forms of mental activity which are characteristically impulses to action; and given that, when action is inhibited, new forms develop to find a 'roundabout way'; and given that the new quality of 'consciousness' may be present: given all that, why does consciousness develop further? The answer is repression. There is first of all primary repression of the emergence of an instinctual impulse. It seems that but for this, each impulse would fulfil itself instantly but falsely by hallucinating the desired object; and the organism would shortly die. Thoughts and wishes are here indistinguishable. In secondary repression derivatives and disguised expressions of instincts are kept from consciousness. In Freud's energy-system model, it is a matter of two forces (instinct and repression), one holding the other in check.

Repression is thus fundamental to the development of the ego, Freud's final term for grouping the emergent conscious/secondary/ rational aspects. The ego has to survive pressures not only from the instinctual id, but from the superego and from the outside world. In *The Ego and the Mechanisms of Defence* (1937) Anna Freud detailed, besides repression, regression, reaction-formation, isolation, undoing, projection, introjection, turning against the self, and reversal, as available options. These must involve elements of thought content, for example in making judgements; but in any case they must affect what one thinks *about*. (See, for example, Hudson, 1968; Hall, 1953; and Singer, 1966.)

Sublimation is often given as a defence mechanism, but is discriminable in that it is relevant more to normality than neurosis. It is the 'developmental process by which instinctual energies are discharged in non-instinctual forms of behaviour' (Rycroft, 1968). It is a crucial process for ego development and for the evolution of 'higher functions'; and thus for phenomena listed under the textbook heading 'thinking', both in general, and more specifically in respect of 'creativity'. In *Leonardo* (1910) Freud offered an account of how psychosexual development might relate to the output of one creative artist. This account hardly explains creative thought in general, but at least, it is one more approach to a puzzle that has baffled both psychometric, experimental, social and every other variety of psychological approach.

It is commonly accepted that novel ideas very often occur spontaneously rather than to order, although some individuals know of favourable predisposing circumstances. The processes that lead up to them are not available to introspection; nor can the thinker say why he prefers one to another. (See for example Ghiselin, 1952; de Groot, 1965). The notion that some 'unconscious' processes are at work has led to attempts to make these more available by drugs or meditation, or more explicit by such techniques as synectics (Gordon, 1961).

Here we should return to Freud's main work on how mental contents can be transformed, his account of the 'dream-work'. He described four main processes of the 'dream-work': condensation, displacement, 'making representable' and 'secondary elaboration'. Condensation, as Reeves remarks, owes a debt to associationism: 'The root processes of condensation appear to be (a) linking, (b) fusion, (c) complex interrelation on the basis of temporal contiguity, similarity, spatial contiguity and opposition – or all of these at once.'

However, it appears to me that condensation is often more like identification: two ideas are so to say collapsed into one, or become equivalent. In displacement, emotion attached to one object is transferred to another, usually having some connection or resemblance. 'Making representable' refers to casting the latent thoughts into dream forms, that is usually imagery (occasionally words); 'secondary elaboration' is a further stage, designed to make the dream more connected and rational.

Freud argued that similar processes can be seen in jokes. Humour seems to me at least partly a 'thinking' phenomenon; and despite a recent upsurge of interest (see Chapman and Foot, 1977) it is still far from understood. No general theory, including Freud's, seems adequate as yet; and Freud's general idea that jokes allow, like dreams, a partial and disguised expression to anxiety-related material seems plausible in some cases, less so in others. On the other hand it is very evident that a mechanism such as condensation is at least similar to punning. Further, many features of primary process thinking such as identity of wish and thought, confusion of identity, abandonment of laws of time and space and logical reasoning, are apparent in almost any sample of humour one takes.

One of the most elusive concepts in the psychology of thinking has been that of 'insight' (see Chapter 2). In psychoanalysis, it appeared that some conscious understanding was an integral part of treatment (one reason for abandoning hypnosis); but it also seemed that 'insight' must be emotional as well as intellectual.

At present, according to Brady (1962), it is generally agreed by analysts 'that the acquisition of insight is neither a necessary nor a sufficient condition for improvement' (i.e. in the patient). Whereas before both analyst and patient were, presumably, gaining knowledge of the real state of the latter's mental apparatus, insight now is 'essentially a conceptual framework by means of which a therapist establishes or attempts to establish, a logical relationship between events, feelings, or experiences that seem unrelated in the mind of the patient' (Marmor, 1962).

From the psychological point of view, we would wish to know just how such conceptual frameworks come to be accepted, and what are their objective criteria; as we would in such apparently comparable shifts as Zen awakening and 'thought reform'.

If there is some feature that is common to the phenomena we label 'thinking' it is perhaps the internal representation of objects and events, including those of our own bodies. We have to stretch it, I suppose, to include hypothetical representations of what might be. How this process started and developed, how it may be more or less realistic, and how it interacts with other aspects of the human organism, is what Freud tried to discover.

Some assessment

As Sherlock Holmes remarked: 'What you do in this world is of no consequence. The question is, what you can make people believe you have done.'

What people believe Freud did might be discovered by asking them. Judging from his apparent general influence, it must be a lot. As Jones (1955) points out, a major difficulty is the all-pervasive nature of concepts deriving (however loosely) from psychoanalysis. The whole of human society has besides changed so drastically in the last hundred years that it is almost impossible to distinguish the effects of one man.

Considered as a contribution to our understanding of human beings, however, rather than as a general cultural influence, Freud's work continues to be attacked and defended with equal vigour. One reason for this seems to be that the protagonists are arguing from numerous different standpoints. There is now a large body of experimental work aimed at testing hypotheses drawn from Freud's writings (see e.g. Fisher and Greenberg, 1977; Jahoda, 1977; Kline, 1972). Taken as a whole, it is inconclusive. This is partly because some of it is not very rigorous; partly because some of Freud's ideas were wrong; partly because some of his writings cannot be reduced to unequivocal hypotheses that can be experimentally tested. But it is fair to remark that it was not Freud's intention to provide such hypotheses; and also that experimentation, while perhaps the greatest single innovation in the study of human behaviour, is not as Jahoda remarks the only available approach or even *necessarily* the best. Freud, as Jahoda also points out, attempted to construct a framework within which to consider in effect all the most important aspects of behaviour and experience. Moreover it was a psychological framework, although Freud never perhaps fully abandoned the primacy of a physiological account which is manifest in the *Project*. The scientific status of the account is still hotly debated. There seems no doubt that Freud considered it to be a reality-matching description of events and their causal explanations: a scientific psychology, in fact. All sorts of alternatives to this view have been proposed. Rycroft (1968) for example argues that psychoanalysis is a semantic theory. The gist of this is that what Freud discovered was that: 'neurotic symptoms are meaningful disguised communications'. It can certainly be argued that this is one function they serve, but the whole question of status is then dodged.

More sophisticated accounts have been given of the conceptual status of psychoanalysis, for example Farrell (1963), MacIntyre (1958), but without any final conclusion. In this regard psychoanalysis might be considered as a special case of the general problem of what sort of thing a psychological theory is or could be. Likewise it exemplifies in a particular way the paradox of an objective theory which is itself part of its own subject matter: every psychological observation and theory is a piece of human behaviour.

Setting aside the large matter of empirical support, Freud's work is, as a minimum, still useful as an alternative perspective from which to view the phenomena of psychology and in the present case those of thinking. The actual use of ideas derived fairly directly from Freud is small in the investigation of thinking, apart from that by psychoanalysts themselves (e.g. de Monchaux, 1956; Palmer, 1973). These however are generally more interested in the ramifications of analytic theory than in developing a psychology of thinking.

Freud's name is not prominent in the indexes of textbooks on thinking. Even the older, and perhaps more eclectic, texts of Humphrey (1951) and Bartlett (1958) say very little of Freud. The present editors, possibly eccentrically, devoted half a chapter to him in 1974. Neisser (1976) refers seriously, if very briefly, to Freud, and remarks: 'It is surprising how contemporary Freud's theory is. *The Interpretation of Dreams* even includes flow charts on which the locations of Conscious, Unconscious, and Preconscious are clearly marked.'

It would be interesting if Neisser could find time to elaborate his view; or, perhaps, if those concerned with logic and reasoning, such as Wason, and Falmagne; or with development, such as Bruner; could systematically compare their work with Freud's. Such comparisons might interest only historians. On the other hand they might stimulate new ideas; they might show that there is more than one way of looking at things. Whether what Freud contributed to the psychology of thinking is right, or partly right, seems to depend not only on what he did, and what he thought he was doing, but on what kind of enterprise psychology itself is; and on this there is no general agreement.

Freud's psychology was in some respects a visionary one. There were the never-fulfilled ambitions of the *Project*; there was the continual attempt to embrace more and more phenomena; there was the circuitous route back to the widest questions of human existence. And an essential part of that was the notion of the growth of the reality principle, the emergence not only of individuals but of the human race from the thrall of primary processes. Such visions most psychologists perhaps find disturbing, or pointless; and as with psychology in general, there seems to be a massive gap between theoretical potential and actual achievement. Perhaps this must always be so; perhaps psychology and psychoanalysis are only relatively novel view points. Or one might argue that in thinking about ourselves, a new perspective is itself a new piece of knowledge. And perhaps one day, by means not yet entirely clear, we shall be able to eliminate the impossible; then, as we know, whatever remains, however improbable, must be the truth.

References

Arieti, S. (1962) The microgeny of thought and perception. *Archives of General Psychiatry 6* (6): 454–68.

Bakan, D. (1965) *Sigmund Freud and the Jewish Mystical Tradition*. New York: Schocken.

Bartlett, F. C. (1958) *Thinking: An Experimental and Social Study*. London: Allen and Unwin.

Boring, E. G. (1957) *A History of Experimental Psychology*. New York: Appleton-Century-Croft.

Brady, J. P. (1962) Psychotherapy, learning theory and insight. *Archives of General Psychiatry 16* (3): 304–11.

Chapman, A. J. and Foot, H. C. (1977) It's a Funny Thing Humour. International Conference on Humour and Laughter, Cardiff, 1976.

Davies, G. and O'Farrell, L. V. (1976) The logic of the transference interpretation. *International Review of Psychoanalysis 3*: 55, 64.

De Groot, A. D. (1965) *Thought and Choice in Chess*. The Hague: Mouton.

De Monchaux, C. (1956) The contribution of psychoanalysis to the psychology of thinking. *The Advancement of Science 12*: 558–62.

Drever, J. (1956) *A Dictionary of Psychology*. Harmondsworth: Penguin.

Falmagne, R. J. (ed) (1975) *Reasoning: Representation and Process*. New York: Wiley.

Farrell, B. A. (1963) Psychoanalysis – I. Psychoanalytic Theory, II. The Method. *New Society*, Nos. 38, 39 (20th, 29th June).

Fisher, S. and Greenberg, R. P. (1977) *The Scientific Credibility of Freud's Theory and Therapy*. Hassocks, Sussex: Harvester.

Frank, P. G. (ed.) (1961) *The Validation of Scientific Theories*. New York: Collier.

Freud, A. (1937) *The Ego and the Mechanisms of Defence*. London: Hogarth Press.

Freud, S. Standard Edition of the Works of Sigmund Freud. London: Hogarth Press. Original publication dates in text.

Fromm, E., Suzuki, D. T. and De Martino, R. (1960) *Psychoanalysis and Zen Buddhism*. Zen Studies Society Inc.

Ghiselin, B. (1952) *The Creative Process*. Berkeley: University of California Press.

Glover, E. (1965) *The Technique of Psychoanalysis*. London: Baillière, Tindall and Cox.

Goldstein, A. P and Dean, S. J., (1966) *The Investigation of Psychotherapy: Commentaries and Readings*. New York: Wiley.

Gordon, W. J. J. (1961) *Synectics: The Development of Creative Capacity*. New York: Harper and Row.

Gottschalk, L. A. and Averbach, A. H. (1966) *Methods of Research in Psychotherapy*. New York: Appleton-Century-Crofts.

Hall, C. S. (1953) *The Meaning of Dreams*. New York: Harper and Row.

Hilgard, E. (1962) The scientific status of psychoanalysis. In E. Nagel, P. Suppes and A. Tarski *Logic, Methodology & Philosophy of Science*. Stanford University Press.

Hook, S. (ed.) (1959) *Psychoanalysis: Scientific Method and Philosophy.* New York: Grove.

Hudson, L. (1968) *Frames of Mind.* London: Methuen.

Humphrey, G. (1951) *Thinking: An Introduction to its Experimental Psychology.* London: Methuen.

Jahoda, M. (1977) *Freud and the Dilemmas of Psychology.* London: Hogarth.

Jones, E. (1955) *The Life and Work of Sigmund Freud.* New York: Basic Books.

Kiesler, D. J. (ed.) (1973) *The Process of Psychotherapy.* Chicago: Aldine.

Kline, P. (1972) *Fact and Fantasy in Freudian Theory.* London: Methuen.

Lee, S. G. M. and Herbert, M. (1970) *Freud and Psychology.* Harmondsworth: Penguin.

Lorand, S. (ed.) (1948) *Psychoanalysis Today.* London: Allen and Unwin.

MacIntyre, A. C. (1958) *The Unconscious.* London: Routledge and Kegan Paul.

Marmor, J. (1962) Psychoanalytic therapy as an educational process. In J. H. Masserman (ed.) *Science & Psychoanalysis,* Vol. 5. New York: Grune and Stratton.

Munroe, R. L. (1955) *Schools of Psychoanalytic Thought.* New York · Holt, Rinehart and Winston.

Neisser, U. (1976) *Cognition and Reality.* San Francisco: Freeman.

Palmer, B. W. M. (1973) Thinking about thought. *Human Relations 26* (1): 127–41.

Peters, R. S. (1953) *Brett's History of Psychology.* London: Allen and Unwin.

Peters, R. S. (1958) *Motivation.* London: Routledge and Kegan Paul.

Radford, J. (1976) What can we learn from Zen? A review and some speculations. *Psychologia 19:* 57–66.

Radford, J. and Burton, A. (1974) *Thinking: Its Nature and Development.* London: Wiley.

Ramzy, I. (1956) From Aristotle to Freud: A few notes on the roots of psychoanalysis. *Bulletin of the Menninger Clinic 20:* 112–23.

Rappaport, D. (1951) *Organization and Pathology of Thought.* New York: Columbia University Press.

Rappaport, D. and Gill, D. M. (1959) The points of view and assumptions of metapsychology. *International Journal of Psychoanalysis 40:* 153–62.

Reeves, J. W. (1965) *Thinking about Thinking.* London: Methuen.

Reik, T. (1948) *Listening with the Third Ear.* New York: Farrar, Strauss and Cudahy.

Rycroft, C. (ed.) (1966) *Psychoanalysis Observed.* London: Constable.

Rycroft, C. (1968) *A Critical Dictionary of Psychoanalysis.* London: Nelson.

Sarason, I. G. (ed.) (1965) *Science and Theory in Psychoanalysis.* Princeton, N. J.: Van Nostrand.

Schafer, R. (1976) *A New Language for Psychoanalysis.* Newhaven: Yale University Press.

Singer, J. L. (1966) *Daydreaming.* New York: Random House.

Skinner, B. F. (1954) Critique of psychoanalytic concepts and theories. *The Scientific Monthly 79:* 300–5.

Stewart, W. A. (1969) *Psychoanalysis: The First Ten Years.* London: Allen and Unwin.

Whyte, L. L. (1960) *The Unconscious Before Freud.* New York: Basic Books.

Wilson, P. J. (1977) La Pensée alimentaire; the evolutionary context of rational objective thought. *Man 12* (2): 320–35.

Wollheim, R. (1971) *Freud.* London: Fontana/Collins.

Woodworth, R. S. (1931) *Contemporary Schools of Psychology.* New York: Ronald.

Woodworth, R. S. (1938) *Experimental Psychology.* New York: Holt.

10 Reflecting on the pre-reflective: Phenomenology

Neil Bolton

Phenomenology would not, at first glance, appear to be a very promising contributor to the psychology of thinking. It is not in any widely accepted sense a theory from which hypotheses may be deduced; indeed, it is a deliberate attempt to suspend both scientific and every day assumptions in order to describe phenomena themselves as they appear to consciousness: the phenomenologist's watchword is, 'To the things themselves'. The verification of phenomenological insights depends upon the investigator experiencing intuitions that are 'self-evident', in particular, intuitions of essences, or eidetic intuitions, rather than upon experimental assessment. And the movement arose as an attempt to answer philosophical questions to do with the nature of truth and knowledge rather than with psychological problems as such. In fact, a constant theme from the early work of Husserl (1900, 1901) to the work of Merleau-Ponty (1962) is a critique of 'psychologism', the reduction of knowing to purely psychological processes such that there are no objective grounds for distinguishing between true and false judgements.

In view of such profound divergences of approach between phenomenology and psychology it is not surprising that phenomenology has been either totally ignored by psychologists or has been at best accepted merely as lending support, but not developing, the standpoint of cognitive psychology: phenomenology's description of consciousness as actively directed towards its object, that is, as intentional, is seen as being compatible with the insistence of cognitive psychology that the subject actively processes information and constructs reality, but as adding nothing to it.

In the present chapter, however, I shall argue that phenomenology makes a most significant contribution to the psychology of thinking, that its approach is a justifiable one, leading to unique insights into the nature of thinking that allow one to place in perspective the major psychological theories of thinking, namely stimulus-response theory of concept formation, Piagetian theory, and cognitive theory in the form of information-processing approaches. Our first task, before embarking upon a critique of these perspectives, is to expand upon the phenomenological concepts which have been introduced so far, namely, the intentionality of consciousness, the critique of psychologism, the nature of eidetic intuition, and the attempt to suspend assumptions, which is known as the phenomenological reduction.

Intentionality

To reflect upon any act of consciousness is to become aware of the distinction between the act by which we are aware of the object and the object itself: the tree that I perceive remains the same tree despite the variations that occur in the way that I perceive it; the joke that I laughed at retains its identity although my appreciation of it is diminished by repetition; the rules of syllogistic reasoning are objects to which I can return again and again. Husserl (1901) saw that the traditional account of consciousness, deriving from Hume (1739), which recognizes only the diversity of mental acts and their dispersion over time, is incomplete since the sense of identity is just as fundamental a fact. The term, intentionality, refers to the function of consciousness in presenting meanings which retain their identity over time. These meanings – the objects of consciousness – are of a number of types: they include objects of perception, memory and thought. This doctrine sees consciousness and world as correlative, two aspects of a single whole. Thus phenomenology is opposed both to Humean empiricism.

which reduces consciousness to being a reflection of the world, and to idealism, which reduces the world to being a construction of the subject. For, although Husserl talked of intentional acts *constituting* the meaning of things, the term 'constitution' should not be taken to be synonymous with 'creation'. Merleau-Ponty (1962), in particular, has emphasized that 'it is a question of recognizing consciousness itself as a project of the world, meant for a world which it neither embraces nor possesses, but towards which it is perpetually directed – and the world as this pre-objective individual whose imperious unity decrees what knowledge shall take as its goal' (p. xvii–xviii). In understanding the contribution of phenomenology it is essential to realize that the intentionality of consciousness implies, not that reality is constructed in a series of interpretative acts, but that interpretations, that is, the fulfilment of intentions, take place within the context of a world that transcends them.

Consider Husserl's ideas concerning empty and fulfilled intentions (Husserl, 1901, 1929). To acquire knowledge of something is to fulfil an intention and to be aware, therefore, of the identity between the fulfilment and that which was intended. For example, in having a mere opinion about something, the meaning we possess is an 'empty' one and is fulfilled by means of confrontation with the things themselves; or, preparing to ride a bicycle is an empty intention which is fulfilled when one rides the bicycle; or again, trying to remember what someone looks like is fulfilled by successfully picturing him. The term intentionality should not be regarded as synonymous with empty intending for it encompasses both empty intending and the acts which fulfil those intentions. For Husserl, the fulfilment of an intention involves the intuition of the intentional object. Intuition is consciousness of an object in its direct presence, as opposed to intending the object absently. As Sokolowski (1974) points out, there is nothing mysterious about intuitions in the Husserlian sense. 'Intuiting a lake is swimming in it, seeing it, riding a boat on it, all as opposed to talking about the lake when we are nowhere near it ... A thing or a mathematical proposition is intuited by everybody in the same way, according to the style of presentation dictated by its kind of being. Some intuitions can be achieved only by several people working together; a complicated experiment requires several experts and many assistants to register the fact they are all looking for' (p. 27). The distinction between empty intention and direct intuition illustrates how phenomenology escapes the limitations of a naive empiricist view which has no place for the directing role of intentionality as well as that of traditional idealism which reduces the world to being a construction of the subject.

Merleau-Ponty (1962) states the matter succinctly when he affirms that perception is not primarily an act but the background against which all acts and interpretations stand out. If the world were constructed, he argues, it would be forever uncertain, the connection between its parts would be probabilistic and I should be engaged always in constructing new syntheses. But this does not correspond to how the world actually appears to us: 'the real is a closely woven fabric' (1962, p. x), the taken-for-granted setting for my thinking and for my explicit acts of perception. He distinguishes between the intentionality of actions, which refers to those occasions when we voluntarily take up a position, and operative intentionality, or that which produces the natural and pre-reflective unity of the world. Husserl (1948, p. 72) says that to talk of the activity of perception is to presuppose that something is already pregiven to us which we can turn toward in perception. Hence 'what excites us to perception is pregiven in our environing world and affects us on the basis of this world' (p. 72). Perception as an active process takes up meanings which are latent in a world which is experienced directly and prior to acts of interpretation.

Now it can be argued that such views may constitute a critique of those theories of perception that appear to be straightforwardly constructivist, namely, those that identify perception as a matter of processing information by selection and categorization (e.g. Neisser, 1967) or those which regard it as hypothesis-testing (e.g. Bruner, 1973; Gregory, 1970), but that this critique loses its force in relation to those views which accept that there is an interaction between the activity of the subject and the properties of the environment (Garner, 1974; Neisser, 1976). This latter view is known as critical realism (Riehl, 1876); it is the Kantian thesis that the development of knowledge comes about through the interaction of understanding (interpretation) and sense (confrontation with the things themselves). Thus, on Neisser's (1976) theory, anticipatory schemata direct the subject's exploration of the environment and the schemata are modified according to the information obtained. However, that this theory is quite different from phenomenology is readily apparent, since the former sees activity as directing perception, whilst the latter sees the active moments of perception as being directed by its passive or receptive moments. Interpretation occurs within a framework that exists for us prior to all acts of interpretation.

The critique of psychologism

In discussing intentionality, a distinction was made between the act and the object intended by the act. Husserl (1900) argued that one of the major errors of a psychological explanation of logical rules was a confusion of the act of judging and the judgement itself, for such an explanation asks us to believe that logical laws are nothing but mental operations, and that, accordingly, logic is reducible to psychology. But, if this thesis were true, we would also have to apply it to mathematical laws and conclude, absurdly, that mathematics depends upon psychology also. Moreover, if logic and mathematics were derived from experience, as psychologism presupposes, then they could only express their relationships as probabilities, but, again, this contradicts the nature of such laws where conclusions follow from the premises with absolute certainty. Thus psychologism fails to respect the objectivity of ideal relations (Husserl, 1929), assuming that what is not a 'real' object of the external world must therefore belong entirely to the realm of the mental. However, this view ignores the fact that ideal objects are transcendent to the mental activities in which they are formed, for they offer themselves to us, not as acts which are transient and simply repeatable, but as objects do, that is, as accessible to repeated observations.

Thus, Husserl maintained, whilst logical rules are formed within experience, they are not to be identified solely as phenomena of internal experience. The error of psychologism, and of psychology in general insofar as it models itself on the natural sciences, is to treat mental phenomena as having the same sense as physical objects and accordingly assuming that, if logical rules derive from experience, then they are reducible to experience as one set of objects to another. However, once the psychological is grasped in its essential nature as intentionality (i.e. as constituting the world of objective reality) then it becomes unthinkable to reduce it to being simply a part of that world. In this way we can see the complementarity of the two major themes of Husserl's philosophy – the critique of psychologism (Husserl, 1901, 929, 1954) and the attempt to understand how the logical rules which characterize reflective thinking have their roots in pre-reflective perience (Husserl, 1948). Psychologism accounts in large part for 'the tragic failure of psychology' (Husserl, 1954, p. 202) but there can be a non-psychologistic psychology which recognizes the unique being of consciousness. 'The only radical reform of psychology', Husserl (1960) wrote, 'is the pure development of an intentional psychology' (p. 49).

Husserl began the programme of an investigation of pre-reflective experience in *Experience and Judgment* (1948). The pre-reflective world is experienced passively, as pre-given, but it is nevertheless 'a field of determinative structure, one of prominence and articulated particularities' (p. 72). Against this background there are actual and potential intentions of anticipation, so that in the normal course of perception there is a continuous process of actualizing stimulation, and a progressive fulfilment of expectations which corresponds at the same time to a more precise determination of the object. Husserl argued that the development of logical concepts could be traced back to such experience. For instance, the logical concept of negation can be traced back to the disappointment of an anticipatory intention in perceptual experience: in observing a red sphere from one perspective, I anticipate that it will conform to the expectations of being red and spherical seen from another perspective, but this anticipation is not fulfilled and has to be replaced by another. That logical structures do not arise initially as a result of reflection but have their antecedents in pre-logical experience is also an assumption of contemporary developmental theory (e.g. Piaget, 1950; Bruner, Olver and Greenfield, 1966), witness the description of the logical structures of the sensori-motor period (see Chapter 6) or the search for the cognitive antecedents of language acquisition. Thus there is a parallelism between the method of phenomenology and developmental analysis.

Eidetic intuition

But we have now to characterize more precisely the phenomenological method and the way in which its insights are verified. It is not to be confused with introspection which aims to discover facts of consciousness, such as which colour the subject reports or whether he feels fatigued, for phenomenology aims to uncover the essences of conscious experience through intuition. We have seen that intuition is defined as that mode of experience in which the object intended is not only 'meant' but received as given. Husserl believed that every individu experience can be transformed into an essential insight by means of a special process called eidetic intuition or ideation. The object of such intuition is an essence or *eidos*. We can achieve an intuition of the ideal in the formal sphere (e.g. understanding a syllogism), in the material sphere (e.g. the essences of red, triangle, man, etc.), or in the realm of consciousness (e.g. memory, intentionality). It is this latter which is the province of phenomenology.

Husserl's most systematic treatment of the intuition of universals is in *Experience and Judgment* (1954), pp. 317–78. Chapter 3 of Sokolowski (1974) contains a most lucid exposition of Husserl's views.

A distinction is made between empirical universals and pure essences; the former are attained in three steps and must be attained before pure essences can be understood. At the most primitive level are judgements in which similar features are attributed to various individuals; but the objects only resemble one another: they do not share a common feature. Because individual features are meant in their concreteness and not as members of a class, such judgements do not transcend the situations in which they are used, although the form of such statements, 'This is that', represents the first stage of conceptual thinking. At the second level we form categories which subsume individuals according to a shared feature; each judgement takes the form: 'This is an instance of a category.' Here Husserl makes the same point as Inhelder and Piaget (1964), that it is only with the emergence of such universals that the individual is truly delineated, since the individual may now be determined against the universal. But, at a new level, we can focus on the universal and make judgements about it; our attention shifts from the individuals to that which remains the same in many individuals. The universal becomes an object of thought and we can now operate with full awareness of rules of negation and contradiction on instances which relate to such objects. Husserl calls them empirical universals; the concepts of empirical science occur at this level. Although such thinking aims at an exhaustive and coherent determination of parts and wholes, this ideal is never reached, for there are always further horizons to explore.

Eidetic intuition, however, does register the *a priori* structure of the object. Husserl at first believed that this form of intuition took place on the basis of the particular experience of an individual of a certain class, but later came to attach an increasingly important role to the imagination, until ultimately he saw the imagination as the decisive factor in revealing the essence of things. Eidetic intuition starts with an arbitrarily perceived or imagined sample of this or that kind of thing. This sample is then submitted to imaginative variation, which may totally disregard reality as it is, in order to investigate the characteristics that remain invariant: thus these characteristics arise as the essence of the object in question for they must be as they are for the object to be as it is. For example, a material thing must exist in time and space and must have extension if it is to be a material thing, that is, these characteristics form its essence; we cannot imagine a thing without these qualities. Husserl believed that eidetic intuition makes intuitively clear that which is sensed obscurely in an empirical universal.

The phenomenological reduction

Now phenomenology is concerned with the essential structures of consciousness, of memory, perception, thinking and so forth, and claims to be the *a priori* science for empirical psychology. Just as the exactitude of physics rests ultimately on an *a priori* system of forms characteristic of any possible nature, so the success of scientific psychology is in the last analysis dependent upon our bringing to clarity the essential structures of the psychological. In order to do this we must return to the pure phenomena themselves, setting aside all that is not essential to them. Above all, in attempting to make clear the nature of psychological phenomena, we must forsake the natural attitude, that which gives us the world as an object for our perception and thinking and the possibility of knowledge of that world as a self-evident fact, for in the natural attitude, in which consciousness is always directed to an object, it is impossible to escape reference to the non-psychological world. Thus in the phenomenological reduction we attend to the phenomena as they appear before consciousness, setting aside the world of objects which has arisen through conscious acts, in order to reveal the nature of those acts. Husserl (1954) talked of the 'life-world' as that which is pre-given to us quite naturally as a spatio-temporal world of things and as the taken-for-granted horizon in which we endeavour to achieve our goals. The life-world is character-ized by the natural attitude in which we pay no attention to those acts of consciousness which constitute a world for us. If we wish to attain an understanding of the precursors of the natural attitude, we must focus, not upon the products of intentionality, but upon the acts consciousness in which and through which we have an awareness of the world as always already there.

It is perhaps true to say that the aspirations that are evident in the reduction have been the least acceptable aspects of phenomenology both for those readers sympathetic to the movement and those reared in the tradition of British empiricism. The reduction is impossible, it is held, (a) because we cannot reflect upon the pre-reflective, (b) because there are no criteria for distinguishing valid from invalid eidetic intuitions, and (c) because we can never achieve knowledge which is presuppositionless.

One of the tasks of phenomenology is to describe that experience of the world which exists prior to acts of reflection and the emergence of the subject-object distinction. But, it is argued, it is only through reflection and its embodiment in language that this can be achieved and, if this is the case, the idea of the pre-reflective must remain forever an empty and therefore unnecessary concept (Kullman and Taylor, 1958). However, this criticism rests upon the mistaken assumption that language belongs to reflection alone so that the pre-reflective is fated to be a 'silent world'. Once, following Heidegger (1927) and Merleau-Ponty (1962, 1968), we distinguish between 'authentic speech', in which new meaning arises, and 'second-order' expression, we are no longer confronted with this problem, since it is authentic discourse which accomplishes the transition from the pre-reflective to the reflective world. In other words, once we restore to language its power to create a world, rather than simply expressing thoughts which are well-formed prior to language, then there is nothing impossible or mysterious about 'reflecting on the pre-reflective': it is simply to observe the mind at work in the constitution of reality. One is reminded of Merleau-Ponty's (1962) description of phenomenology as 'the study of the advent of being into consciousness'.

But how do we know when essential intuitions are valid? How can we assess competing claims? Sartre (1962), for example, claims that the essence of emotion is that consciousness becomes magical and says that 'a consciousness becoming emotional is like a consciousness falling asleep' (p. 78). However, one can contrast this point of view with that of Macmurray (1935) who argues for the positive role of emotion in understanding. In order to grasp the nature of verification in phenomenology we should begin by noting, following Sokolowski (1974), the distinction between verifying a judgement in the natural attitude and verifying one within phenomenology. Whilst in the former there is a recognizable distinction between framing a judgement ('the river is in flood') and verifying it (checking against observation), in the latter there is no interval between intention and verification. We do not say, 'I clearly and distinctly understand what Husserl means in his critique of psychologism but now I must attempt to see whether it is true.' For once we understand the meaning we do not have to go anywhere to find its truth: psychologism dissolves as soon as one recognizes its logical incoherence. That is to say, the method of verification of phenomenology is a critical one; it is an attempt to form judgements that are clear and distinct, i.e., coherent and non-contradictory. It is, of course, a difficult and continuing process, but, again, we are confronted with a refinement of a quite normal activity, not something essentially obscure and strange.

The criticism that the phenomenological reduction is an impossibility since our thinking can never be entirely free of assumptions must be met by an opposing question: are we entirely the prisoners of our own interpretations? If it is granted that the development of thinking allows us the possibility of overcoming the limitations of particular perspectives through reflection upon them (an ideal which this book itself is devoted to), the injunction of the reduction may be regarded both as an ideal we strive to attain and as a method of inquiry. On Merleau-Ponty's (1962) interpretation, 'The most important lesson which the reduction teaches us is the impossibility of a complete reduction' (p. xiv). This is why, he says, Husserl is constantly re-examining the possibility of the reduction. If we were simply victims of our own paradigms, the possibility of the reduction could not arise. On the other hand, we are in the world and our thinking occurs within the constraints imposed upon us at a particular time and place, and thus there can be no thought which embraces all our thought. We have, then, to bear both these facts in mind to recognize that the impossibility of the reduction does not undermine its force: its impossibility is revealed by the fact that we *need* to carry it out again and again.

To sum up, whereas psychologism, as we have seen, reduces thinking to being an activity of the subject, and therefore a psychological process that is fully describable without reference to criteria of truthfulness, phenomenology restores to thinking its inherent aim for objectivity. An examination of the structure of intentionality reveals its several aspects; by attending purely to our experience we can distinguish acts which merely posit reality from those whic confront us with actual existents and which therefore fulfil our empty intentions; moreover, the former demand their completion through the latter:

> Man's thinking, as far as it takes the form of the thought that is articulable in assertive statement, is an intending of entities that incorporates in its own structure a positing of the existence of entities in distinction from the mere intending itself, a positing of the possibility of the identity of intended and existent entities, and a requirement or demand that this intending *should* realize that identity. Thinking contains within itself the fundamental aim that gives rise to its ought and that makes it possible and necessary to seek for the means by which that ought is to be realized.
>
> This structure of thinking shows that man, as far as he is a thinking being, is a being in whose constitution there originates a truth-tension between ought and is that constitutes a demand for its resolution. Man *is* the aim at truth. (Hofstadter, 1965)

We can now see how phenomenology and the psychology of thinking should be closely related, for to think is to try to be truthful and to think about being truthful is to do phenomenology.

Phenomenology and the psychology of thinking

At the most general level it is possible to distinguish three major theoretical perspectives within the psychology of thinking. The first, of which S-R theory is an example, seeks to account for the organized nature of thinking by reference to the structure of the environment. The second, evident in certain information-processing points of view and in artificial intelligence, looks to the structures of the organism to account for intelligent behaviour. The third viewpoint, that of critical realism, argues for the interaction of the properties of the organism and the environment, and Piagetian theory may be taken as representative. Phenomenology, I shall argue, is not to be classed with any one of these; it offers important criticisms of all of them, and it represents a more coherent and comprehensive perspective by which the psychological theories of thinking may be judged.

Abstraction of resemblances and S-R theory

The similarities between the development of theories of concept formation in empiricist philosophy and in psychology lend strong support to Taylor's (1964) view that S-R theory can be regarded as a mechanistic transposition of traditional empiricist views on epistemology. Locke (1960) argued that to form a concept is to abstract from particular stimuli the element or elements identical throughout them; Berkeley (1708) denied the existence of abstract ideas in Locke's sense, asserting that if we form a concept we must have in mind a single, determinate set of qualities, not some universal idea: it was only necessary, he thought, for there to be resemblances between the particulars for the concept to be formed. But then there are concepts which subsume particulars between which there are not even resemblances. In Wittgenstein's (1953) well-known example of games, 'Don't say: "There *must* be something common, or they would not be called 'games'" – but *look and see* whether there is anything common to all. For if you look at them you will not see something that is common to *all*, but similarities, relationships, and a whole series of them at that' (p. 31). We see neither a common element nor the same resemblances running throughout but a 'complicated network of similarities overlapping and criss-crossing', a network which Wittgenstein called 'family resemblances'. A similar course of development of theories of concept formation is, as I have shown elsewhere (Bolton, 1972, 1977a) observable in experimental psychology with the doctrine of identical elements being supplemented by a theory of resemblances.

Now it is one thing to say that a concept can be defined by reference to the resemblances between its particulars, but quite another to say that concepts are formed by making a generalization from the perception of particulars. As Husserl (1901) pointed out, to be able to subsume certain particulars under a general category requires that the general concept has already been acquired, since, if this were not the case, we would not be able to generalize from the one to the other: we would not group together card games and wrestling unless there had already been an intuition in which we linked them as games. Husserl (1901) called this intuition 'ideational abstraction': it refers to the intuition of the general in the particular. The fundamental mistake of the empiricist is to assume that there are particular stimuli which need to be united by acts of abstraction. Phenomenology, on the other hand, asserts that the object of perception is experienced as typical or possibly typical.

To understand this position it is necessary to acknowledge the intentional nature of consciousness. As Mandelbaum (1965) has pointed out, the notion of family resemblances implies, as it would be used in everyday parlance, both physical resemblances and genetic ties. Members of a family are united through a common ancestry, although such a relationship is not itself one of the specific perceptual features of those who share a family resemblance. Similarly, with such concepts as 'games' or 'art' or 'tools' the analogue to genetic ties might be the purpose which tools embody or the motive behind the work of art. For example, it is only by reference to purpose that we are led not to link fighting with wrestling in spite of there being many points of resemblance. We are to look, then, not simply to the properties of the stimuli, but to the stimuli considered as intentional objects. The doctrine of family resemblances remains attractive so long as we fail to see this and the theory of abstraction is seen to be false as soon as we do.

For Merleau-Ponty (1962) the importance of the body's intentionality is convincingly demonstrated by cases in which it is absent. Schneider, a patient who had received a wound at the back of the head from a shell-splinter, is perplexed when asked simply to move his arm; he responds by moving his whole body until after a time his movements are confined to his arm which he thus eventually 'finds'. If he is asked to trace a circle in the air, he first 'finds' his arm, then lifts it up in front of him as a normal subject would do 'to find a wall in the dark' (p. 110); he makes a few rough movements, and if one of them happens to be circular, he promptly completes the circle. What Schneider lacks is not the capacity to think as such, since he proceeds in a deliberate fashion and can recognize the solution to the problem once found, nor bodily movement as such, since he is capable of the required movements, but what Merleau-Ponty calls 'motor intentionality', the power of the body to give the world sense before any acts of interpretation; this sense is not arbitrarily any sense, but rather a sense 'adherent in certain contents'. The active moments in perception and thinking thus rework a sense that is already latent in that which is given, because the body animates the world in its own way, but this animation is itself dependent upon the texture and field of the world in which it takes place.

What impairs thinking in Schneider's case is that he can relate things *only* by explicit interpretation. For instance, when asked to explain the analogy, 'the eye is to light and colour as ear is to sounds', he must have recourse to an explicit conceptual analysis before he understands it, saying, 'the eye and the ear are both sense organs, therefore they must give rise to something similar'. In contrast, the normal person understands the analogy first, then analyses it. Living thought does not consist of subsuming instance under some category, since the category imposes on the terms brought together a meaning external to them. The fact that the normal subject immediately grasps that the eye is to sight as the ear is to hearing shows that the eye and ear are immediately given to him as a means of access to one and the same *world*.

The viewpoint of cognitive psychology

Contemporary psychology is, however, more rationalist than empiricist, the dominant viewpoint being that man is active in the interpretation of reality. The belief that the world is constructed takes many forms; it is evident in the description of perception as hypothesis-testing (Gregory, 1976) or as involving deductive inferences (Bryant, 1974); it is evident in the field of artificial intelligence and in Simon's (1969) assertion that the behaviour of an organism is structurally quite simple since its apparent complexity is due to the contingencies of the environment in which it finds itself; but if we examine through work with computer programs the 'architecture of complexity' we shall discern common properties that are independent of specific content (see Chapter 8); it is, finally, the first principle of any cognitive theory of personality (e.g. Kelly, 1955) that the subject determines the world to which it shall adapt.

It is widely recognized (e.g. Newell and Simon, 1971; Fodor, 1977) that, whilst we have been relatively successful in producing computer programs that model intelligent human behaviour, such as chess playing or problem-solving, a difficulty which remains unresolved is how reality can be represented in intelligent machines in the powerful and flexible way in which human representations work. The assumption is made that once this is achieved computers will show all those characteristics of behaviour which are regarded as distinctively human; for example, they will be capable of creative thinking and the creative use of language. However, from the phenomenological perspective the assumption may be doubted. We have seen that perception is not, fundamentally, to be regarded as an act, for it is that which is given to us as the background of all our acts. Merleau-Ponty's (1962) remark that 'man is in the world, and only in the world does he know himself' (p. xi) must be taken quite literally as a denial of the view that man operates primarily or solely upon representations of reality. The pre-reflective world is not a world of representations, for it exists prior to the act of representation as that which is represented. Work on artificial intelligence may here be faced, then, with an insoluble problem, as Dreyfus (1972) and Still (1978) have argued. It is not a question, as Sutherland (1976) appears to believe, of this being only a limitation of digital computers on the grounds that computers which represent reality analogically might approximate more closely to the way in which humans represent reality. For what is at stake is the adequacy of *any* kind of representational model. Merleau-Ponty (1962) says that the purpose of the phenomenological reduction, of the return to the things themselves, is to return to the world which precedes knowledge; it is a world to which knowledge *refers* and from which knowledge derives; it is inexhaustible and transcends all formal representations. Thus, for phenomenology, there can be no computer model of thinking for the same reason that there can be no satisfactory theory of creative thinking. The mind's ability to outrun its own products is not a scientific problem; it is an essential part of human being.

Phenomenology may be regarded as defining the boundary lines of cognitive psychology. It is not doubted that behaviour is rule-guided and therefore open to representation. But to construe behaviour simply as rule-guided is to ignore, for the sake of a mistaken scientific ideal, that openness to the world which forms the background for all our rules.

Piaget's theory

However, such criticisms cannot be directed at Piaget's theory without qualification. Piaget, too, has attempted to avoid the pitfalls of empiricism and rationalism. However much his description of stages of development appears to imply an innately determined progress, the concepts of adaptation and equilibration suggest the significance of experience in intellectual development (e.g. Piaget, 1950). He has confessed that he remains 'very close to the spirit of Kantianism' (Piaget, 1972, p. 57) and his epistemological position appears to be that of critical realism: this is the Kantian view that knowledge is a result of the interaction between sense and understanding and it is paralleled by similar opposites: physical and logico-mathematical experience, figurative and operative knowledge, accommodation to the properties of things and assimilation of the things to the interpretive structures of the organism. Furthermore, it could be maintained, Piaget has provided us with a description of pre-reflective experience in his account of the sensori-motor stage of development. He would surely agree with Merleau-Ponty's (1962) view that the primary fact of consciousness is not 'I think', but 'I can'; yet he could claim that the structures of action are capable of being described (see Chapter 4). Finally, since Piaget has argued that different forms of explanation within psychology may be regarded as parallel or isomorphic (Piaget, Fraisse and Reuchlin, 1968), it could be that the explanations of the psychology of logical development, which trace logical and mathematical laws to psychological operations, will be entirely compatible with the programme of a genetic phenomenology (Husserl, 1948) which attempts to ground logical laws in pre-logical experience.

In spite of these important similarities between the two perspectives, however, there are equally or possibly more fundamental differences. Piaget (1972) is highly critical of the notion of pre-reflective experience, arguing that as soon as we take up a developmental position, the concept of 'the originary experiences of lived consciousness' is seen as mythical since all structures have a history, that is, they have to be related to a series of preceding structures. He believes that there is a contradiction between the idea that pre-reflective experience is the origin of our knowledge, the unchanging background for our acts of interpretation, and the idea that intentional consciousness is continually creating new meanings. How, he asks, if the latter is the case, can one avoid ascribing to pre-reflective awareness a capacity for development, in which case it loses its privileged status?

I have argued elsewhere (Bolton, 1977b) that Piaget pays too high a price for assimilating pre-reflective experience to the stages of intellectual development. Because he is unwilling to consider a form of consciousness which is in some sense not simply a part of the developmental process, he undervalues the spontaneous creativity of play, language and thinking. Play is seen as an imbalance of assimilatory over accommodatory activity; it is egocentric and non-adaptive (Piaget, 1951). Such a view entirely ignores the positive role of imagination in establishing possibilities for cognition and is inconsistent with experiments which demonstrate the usefulness of spontaneous play for problem-solving (Sylva et al., 1976; Zammarelli and Bolton, 1977). The development of language is dependent upon the development of thinking in the Piagetian perspective (Furth, 1969; Sinclair-de-Zwart, 1971). Granted that in more recent Piagetia

theory, it is acknowledged that verbal training can promote development in children who are 'operationally ready' to acquire a concept
(Inhelder, Sinclair and Bovet, 1974); nevertheless, the overriding
impression remains that language plays but a subsidiary role in
intellectual development. For Heidegger (1927) and Merleau-Ponty
(1962, 1968), on the other hand, 'Language accomplishes thinking'.
The distinction is drawn between the 'spoken word', that is, language
which is the depository of constituted meanings, and the 'speaking
word', which is the origin of the spoken word: it is the active and
creative power of speech to go beyond existing meanings. Such a view
makes language a part of the process by which new meanings occur,
rather than being the mere expression of an already constituted
meaning. Finally, although Piaget's theory has been criticized either
for underestimating the logical capacities of the child (Bryant, 1974) or
for overestimating them (Wason and Johnson-Laird, 1972), what is
perhaps more important is the assumed identification of thinking and
logical thinking and the total neglect of creative thinking. Phenomenology, on the other hand, places creativity at the very centre of thinking
without believing that it can be encompassed satisfactorily by any
theory: 'We must define thought in terms of that strange power which
it possesses of being ahead of itself, of launching itself and being at once
everywhere, in a word, in terms of its autonomy' (Merleau-Ponty,
1962, p. 371). The reduction of play to fantasy, of language to thinking,
of thinking to logical thinking all stem from the same source, from a
denial of the possibility that there could be a form of experience which,
whilst being compatible with a developmental process, yet remains
transcendent to it. The critical realism of Piaget, like that of Neisser
(1976), remains thoroughly constructivist: I have no knowledge of the
world, they tell me, which could both precede and transcend
interpretative knowledge.

The contribution of phenomenology

Phenomenology leads, then, to criticisms of all three approaches to
the psychology of thinking. From this perspective, whilst S-R theory
errs by ignoring the structures imposed by the organism upon its
environment, cognitive theory and Piagetian theory forget that the
world within which the subject's interpretations occur is given to him
as a world which is outside of all acts of interpretation and is, indeed,
their very framework. To be conscious is to have the world before one

as given and there is no need for explanations, whether empiricist or deductive, of this fact. There is no *problem* of creative thinking, that is, a problem which requires an explanation, for consciousness exists in the constitution of its objects, and, as Merleau-Ponty says, any explanation of this, whether reducing it to experience or to *a priori* forms, would amount to a denial of it. Phenomenology thus stands as a reminder to the psychologist of the limitations of formal explanation; if thinking is to be defined by reference to its capacity to go beyond existing points of view, there can be no theory of thinking which describes it exhaustively, no ultimate computer program, no set of logical rules, and no reduction to the contingencies of experience. If we understand the aim of the psychology of thinking to be the elaboration of such theories, the contribution of phenomenology to the psychology of thinking is to deny that the psychology of thinking can succeed in its task.

Phenomenology is not, therefore, primarily a psychological perspective and one would do it an injustice to regard it as such. Psychologism is the error of reducing experience to its subjective component and forgetting the objectivity of intentionality; it is in this sense that behaviourism should above all be criticized for its subjectivism, not its alleged objectivism. The interest of the phenomenologist, therefore, is in the way in which different realities present themselves to the subject. He is interested in, for example, delineating the essential nature of aesthetic experience (e.g. Dufrenne, 1974), not in terms of the different kinds of motives evident in aesthetic appreciations, but in relation to the question as to what constitutes the essential truth of aesthetic perception, that is, what is revealed in such perception. Husserl (1948) talked of the task of phenomenology as being the investigation of 'regional ontologies', that is, aspects of being in their essential nature. If it is possible to generalize from such a perspective to the psychology of thinking, it must be to conclude that the phenomenology of thinking would have quite a different direction and content from any purely psychological point of view: it will seek to discover the essences of cognitive realities, for only in this way will we learn about the essential nature of cognition.

The contribution of phenomenology is therefore twofold. On the one hand, it shows us that the power of the mind to present us with objectivities cannot ultimately be explained in a reductive manner and thus reminds us of the limits of formal psychological theories. On the other, it insists that the necessary first step in the study of thinking

Reflecting on the pre-reflective 221

is to determine the essential natures of the objectivities revealed through consciousness. For the phenomenologist, psychological approaches to problems of the explanation of thinking, such as the order of attainment of concepts, strategies in problem-solving, and so forth, worthwhile though they may be in themselves, will not simply summate to produce a comprehensive and coherent perspective: the essence of thinking will not be grasped from any number of empirical studies. Although it is commonly held that the explanation of the higher mental processes is one of the most challenging problems *within* psychology, we might conclude, in view of this brief review, that the most pressing need is to pass beyond the present limitations of psychology into phenomenology in order to determine what the fundamental problems in any account of thinking are and to equip ourselves with the means of dealing with them.

References

Berkeley, G. (1708) *Treatise Concerning the Principles of Human Knowledge.* London: Nelson (1945).
Bolton, N. (1972) *The Psychology of Thinking.* London: Methuen.
Bolton, N. (1977a) *Concept Formation.* Oxford: Pergamon Press.
Bolton, N. (1977b) Piaget and pre-reflective experience. In B. Curtis and W. Mays (eds) *Phenomenology and Education.* London: Methuen.
Bruner, J. S. (1973) *Beyond the Information Given: Studies in the Psychology of Knowing.* New York: W. W. Norton.
Bruner, J. S., Olver, R. R. and Greenfield, P. M. (1966) *Studies in Cognitive Growth.* New York: Wiley.
Bryant, P. (1974) *Perception and Understanding in Young Children.* London: Methuen.
Dreyfus, H. L. (1972) *What Computers Can't Do.* New York: Harper and Row.
Dufrenne, M. (1974) *The Phenomenology of Aesthetic Experience.* Evanston: Northwestern University Press.
Fodor, J. A. (1977) *The Language of Thought.* Sussex: Harvester Press.
Furth, H. G. (1969) *Piaget and Knowledge.* Englewood Cliffs, N.J.: Prentice-Hall.
Garner, W. R. (1974) *The Processing of Information and Structure.* Potomoc: Erlbaum.
Gregory, R. L. (1970) *The Intelligent Eye.* New York: McGraw-Hill.
Gregory, R. L. (1976) Perceptions as hypotheses. In S. C. Brown (ed.) *Philosophy of Psychology.* London: Macmillan.
Heidegger, M. (1927) *Being and Time.* New York: Harper (1962).
Hofstadter, A. (1965) *Truth and Art.* New York: Columbia University Press.
Hume, D. (1739) *A Treatise of Human Nature.* London: Oxford University Press (1888).

222 Thinking in perspective

Husserl, E. (1900) *Logische Untersuchungen*. Vol. 1. Halle: Niemeyer.
Husserl, E. (1901) *Logische Untersuchungen*. Vol. 2. Halle: Niemeyer.
Husserl, E. (1929) *Formal and Transcendental Logic*. The Hague: M. Nijhoff (1969).
Husserl, E. (1948) *Experience and Judgment*. London: Routledge and Kegan Paul (1973).
Husserl, E. (1954) *The Crisis of European Sciences and Transcendental Phenomenology*. Evanston: Northwestern University Press (1970).
Husserl, E. (1960) *Cartesian Meditations*. The Hague: M. Nijhoff.
Inhelder, B. and Piaget, J. (1964) *The Early Growth of Logic in the Child*. London: Routledge and Kegan Paul.
Inhelder, B., Sinclair, H. and Bovet, M. (1974) *Learning and the Development of Cognition*. London: Routledge and Kegan Paul.
Kelly, G. A. (1955) *The Psychology of Personal Constructs*. New York: Norton.
Kullman, M. and Taylor, C. (1958) The pre-objective world. *Review of Metaphysics 12*: 108–32.
Locke, J. (1690) *Essay on the Human Understanding*. Oxford: Clarendon Press (1924).
Macmurray, J. (1935) *Reason and Emotion*. London: Faber and Faber.
Mandelbaum, M. (1965) Family resemblances and generalization concerning the arts. *The American Philosophical Quarterly 2*: 519–34.
Merleau-Ponty, M. (1962) *The Phenomenology of Perception*. London: Routledge and Kegan Paul.
Merleau-Ponty, M. (1968) *The Visible and the Invisible*. Evanston: Northwestern University Press.
Neisser, U. (1967) *Cognitive Psychology*. New York: Appleton-Century-Crofts.
Neisser, U. (1976) *Cognition and Reality*. San Francisco: W. H. Freeman.
Newell, A. and Simon, H. A. (1971) *Human Problem Solving*. Englewood Cliffs, N. J.: Prentice-Hall.
Piaget, J. (1950) *The Psychology of Intelligence*. London: Routledge and Kegan Paul.
Piaget, J. (1951) *Play, Dreams and Imitation in Childhood*. New York: Norton.
Piaget, J. (1972) *Insights and Illusions of Philosophy*. London: Routledge and Kegan Paul.
Piaget, J. Fraisse, P. and Reuchlin, M. (1968) *Experimental Psychology: Its Scope and Method*, Vol. 1. London: Routledge and Kegan Paul.
Riehl, A. (1876) Der Philosophischen Kritizismus und Seine Bedeutung für die Positive Wissenschaft.
Sartre, J. P. (1962) *Sketch towards a Theory of the Emotions*. London: Methuen.
Simon, H. A. (1969) *The Sciences of the Artificial*. Cambridge, Mass.: M.I.T. Press.
Sinclair-de-Zwart, M. (1971) Sensori-motor action patterns as a condition for the acquisition of language. In R. Huxley and E. Ingram (eds) *Language Acquisition: Models and Methods*. New York: Academic Press.
Sokolowski, R. (1974) *Husserlian Meditations*. Evanston: Northwestern University Press.
Still, A. W. (1978) Perception and Representation. In N. Bolton (ed) *Philosophical Problems in Psychology*. London: Methuen (in press).

Sutherland, N. S. (1976) Computer simulation of brain function. In S. C. Brown (ed.) *Philosophy of Psychology*. London: Macmillan.

Sylva, K., Bruner, J. S. and Genova, P. (1976) The role of play in the problem-solving of children 3–5 years old. In J. S. Bruner et al. *Play*. Harmondsworth: Penguin.

Taylor, C. (1964) *The Explanation of Behaviour*. London: Routledge and Kegan Paul.

Wason, P. C. and Johnson-Laird, P. N. (1972) *The Psychology of Reasoning*. London: Batsford.

Wittgenstein, L. (1953) *Philosophical Investigations*. Oxford: Basil Blackwell.

Zammarelli, J. E. and Bolton, N. (1977) The effects of autonomy on mathematical concept formation. *British Journal of Educational Psychology 47*: 155–61.

Name index

Subject index

absent mindedness, 18
abstract materials in reasoning experiments, 99, 104, 106
act psychology, 4
algorithms, 169
analogue, *see* computers
arrays, 167, 177
artificial intelligence, 165, 166, 176, 216–17
assimilation and accommodation, xx, 66, 217, 218
association, 3; free, 1, 182; constrained, 3
Aufgabe, 3

behaviourism, 4, 5–6, 16, 167; *see also* Chapter 3
binary numbers, 164, 177
bit, 163, 177

carpentered world hypothesis, 137
categorization, 56ff.; *see also* concepts
chess, 13–14, 15–16, 165, 169, 170, 171, 174
circular reactions, 68, 69–70
competence and performance, 84, 85, 90, 107, 108
computer simulation, 16; *see also* Chapter 8

computers, 164; analogue, digital, 164, 165
concepts, concept learning, 51ff., 163, 173, 213, 214
concrete operations, 72, 83, 84
condensation, 196, 197
conscious experience, 5, 11, 12, 44, 45, 55, 56, 57; *see also* Chapters 9 and 10
construct validity, 116, 118, 122, 128
constructive deduction, 67
constructivist theories of cognition, 206, 216, 219
converging operations, 11
creative thinking, 17–18, 34, 37, 122, 123, 152, 196, 216, 217, 218, 219
critical realism, 206, 213, 219
crosscultural studies: of categorization, 140ff.; of Freud's theory, 133; of Gestalt theory, 133; of inferential thinking, 147–49; of memory, 145ff.; of perception, 136ff.; of Piaget's theory, 133, 149, 151; of thinking, 147ff.
cryptarithmetic, 163, 170, 171, 177
cultural amplifiers in Bruner's theory, 150–1
cultural salience and familiarity, 139
culture, definition of, 132
cognitive style, 122, 139, 140, 152

décalage, 71–2
demand characteristics, 7–8
determining tendencies, 3
directed thinking, 48
dreams, 188–89, 194, 196
dual process theory, 106, 107

ecological hypothesis, 137
egocentric space, 75–8, 80
eidetic intuition, 203, 204, 208–10, 211; see also insight
Einstellung, 3, 32, 36, 38
embedded figures test, 139
equilibration, 66, 217
expectancy, 47
experimental tests of Freud's theory, 198

facet analysis, 116
factor analysis, 112, 113, 116ff., 124
feedback loop, 177
focusing/scanning strategies, 57ff.
formal logic, defined, 90ff.
formal operations, 72
frames of reference: spatial, 81; conceptual, 84–5
Freud's theory of thinking, 191ff., 194, 199; see also condensation, repression etc.
functional fixation, 36, 42
functional relations, 25, 26

General Problem Solver, 162, 171, 175, 176
genetic epistemology, 65
genuine solutions, 34, 38
Gestalt psychology, 4–5, 16, 162, 167; cross-cultural studies of, 133; field, concept of, 26, 28; importance of structure, 33ff.; principles of organization, 26–8, 34, 41
grouping, logico-mathematical, 67

habit-family hierarchy, 48
hardware, 164, 177
heterarchy, 176
heuristics, 169, 173, 175

imagery, 3, 8, 9, 12–14
implication, 95ff.
information-processing theories, 159, 164, 167, 216
information theory, 163

insight, 105ff.; in Freud's theory, 197; in Gestalt psychology, 34ff., 42, 163, 166; see also eidetic intuition
instrumental activity in Piaget's theory, 66–71, 83
intelligence tests, 112ff.; and creativity tests, 122, 123; British Intelligence scale, 128; comparative studies, 125ff.; construction of, 112ff., 119; crosscultural studies, 126ff.; see also Chapter 7; Raven's Progressive Matrices, 115, 126, 127; Stanford-Binet, 115; Wechsler-Bellevue, 120, 127
intentionality, 4, 204–7, 214, 215, 220
interpretation, in Freud's theory, 182, 188, 189
introspection: ambiguity, 10; characterization, 5–6; classical, 2, 24; deception, 10; fallibility, 4, 6, 7; fractionation, 3; inaccessibility, 8–9; incompleteness, 9; individual differences, 10; interference, 6, 10; privacy, 6–7; rationalization, 10; relation to performance measures, 8, 11; retrospection, 6, 10; self-observation, 1, 2; self-reports, 1; subjectivity, 4, 6–7; thinking aloud, 1, 10, 15, 16, 170; unreliability, 4, 7–8, 11, 44; validity, 8, 11, 12–13
invisible displacements, 70
isomorphism, 26, 27

knowledge structures, 168

language and thought, 211, 219
language comprehension, 176
Logic Theorist, 161, 171, 174
logicism, 92
loops, 167, 177

matching bias, 11, 102, 105ff.
material equivalence, 96ff.
material implication, 92, 96ff.
means-end analysis, 161, 169; see also heuristics
mentalism, 4, 5
modus ponens, 97ff.
modus tollens, 97ff.
motor theory, 45

object concept, defined, 66, 67
object identity, 78
object permanence, 73–5